# COLERIDGE'S
# BLESSED MACHINE
# OF LANGUAGE

# COLERIDGE'S BLESSED MACHINE OF LANGUAGE

Jerome Christensen

CORNELL UNIVERSITY PRESS

Ithaca and London

Cornell University Press gratefully acknowledges a grant from
the Andrew W. Mellon Foundation that aided
in bringing this book to publication.

First published 1981 by Cornell University Press.
Published in the United Kingdom by Cornell University Press Ltd.,
Ely House, 37 Dover Street, London W1X 4HQ.

International Standard Book Number 0-8014-1405-9
Library of Congress Catalog Card Number 81-66644
Printed in the United States of America
*Librarians: Library of Congress cataloging information
appears on the last page of the book.*

For Carol

But what are my metaphysics? merely the referring of the mind to its own consciousness for truths indispensable to its own happiness! To what purposes do I, or am I about to employ them? To perplex our clearest notions and living moral instincts? To deaden the feelings of will and free power, to extinguish the light of love and of conscience, to make myself and others worthless, soul-less, God-less? No! to expose the folly and the legerdemain of those who have thus abused the blessed machine of language.

—Samuel Taylor Coleridge, *The Friend* (1818)

But how are we to guard against the herd of promiscuous Readers? Can we bid our *books* be silent in the presence of the unworthy? If we employ what are called the *dead* languages, our own genius, alas! becomes flat and dead: and if we embody our thoughts in the words native to them or in which they were conceived, we divulge the secrets of Minerva to the ridicule of blockheads, and expose our Diana to the Actæons of a sensual age. I reply: that in order to avoid inconveniences of this kind, we need write neither in Greek or in Latin. It will be enough, if we abstain from appealing to the bad passions and low appetites, and confine ourselves to a strictly consequent method of reasoning.

To have written innocently, and for wise purposes, is all that can be required of us: the event lies with the Reader. I purchased lately Cicero's work, de officiis, which I had always considered as almost worthy of a Christian. To my surprize it had become a most flagrant libel. Nay! but how? — Some one, I know not who, out of the fruitfulness of his own malignity had filled all the margins and other blank spaces with annotations—a true *superfœtation* of *examples,* that is, of false and slanderous tales! In like manner, the slave of impure desires will turn the pages of Cato, not to say, Scripture itself, into occasions and excitements of wanton imaginations. There is no wind but feeds a volcano, no work but feeds and fans a combustible mind.

—*The Friend*: attributed to Rudolphus Langius; perhaps written by Rudolph von Langen; perhaps written by Rudolph von Langen and amended by S. T. Coleridge; perhaps penned entirely by S. T. Coleridge

# Contents

# Acknowledgments

I thank M. H. Abrams for his steadfast and generous support. Alan McKenzie, Donald Seybold, and Dorothy Mermin have helped me with candid criticism of my strategy and style. I am grateful to Kenneth Johnston, who, acting on behalf of the Departments of English and Comparative Literature at Indiana University, provided me with a forum to test my ideas on a live and lively audience, and to Max F. Schulz for many remembered acts of kindness. The perceptive comments of my anonymous readers were of great help in revising the manuscript. I am in especial debt to Reeve Parker and Neil Hertz for their enthusiasm, their canniness, and, above all, their faith, not untested, that by a relatively necessary train of associations one could get from the Preface of *Observations on Man* to a conclusion on Coleridge's prose.

I am also grateful to Cornell University and the Purdue Research Foundation for financial support during the course of this project.

Chapter 3 appeared in an earlier version in *PMLA*, 92 (1977), 928–40, and is reprinted by permission of The Modern Language Association of America. A brief section of Chapter 4 appeared in *Studies in Romanticism*, 17 (1978). I thank the editors for permitting their appearance in revised form here.

Finally, grateful acknowledgment is extended to Princeton University Press and Routledge & Kegan Paul Ltd. for permission to reprint excerpts from the following publications: *The Notebooks of Samuel Taylor Coleridge*, ed. Kathleen Coburn, Bollingen Series L, Volume I, *1794-1804* (copyright © 1957 by

Princeton University Press), Volume II, *1804-1808* (copyright ©
1961 by Princeton University Press), Volume III, *1808-1819*
(copyright © 1973 by Princeton University Press); and *The Collected Works of Samuel Taylor Coleridge,* ed. Kathleen Coburn and
Bart Winer, Bollingen Series LXXV, Volume I, *Lectures 1795:
On Politics and Religion,* ed. Lewis Patton and Peter Mann (copyright © 1971 by Routledge & Kegan Paul Ltd.), Volume IV, 2
vols., *The Friend,* ed. Barbara E. Rooke (copyright © 1969 by
Routledge & Kegan Paul Ltd.).

J.C.

*West Lafayette, Indiana*

# Abbreviations

COLERIDGE'S WORKS FREQUENTLY CITED

BL    *Biographia Literaria*. Ed. with his aesthetical essays by John
      Shawcross. 2 vols. Oxford: Clarendon Press, 1907. 1973
      reprint. First published 1817.
CL    *Collected Letters of Samuel Taylor Coleridge*. Ed. Earl Leslie
      Griggs. 6 vols. Oxford: Clarendon Press, 1956-71.
CN    *The Notebooks of Samuel Taylor Coleridge*. Ed. Kathleen Coburn.
      Vols. I and II, New York: Pantheon, 1957, 1961. Vol. III,
      Princeton: Princeton University Press, 1973.
CCS   *On the Constitution of Church and State*. Ed. John Colmer. *The
      Collected Works of Samuel Taylor Coleridge*, X. Princeton:
      Princeton University Press, 1976. 1830 edition.
F     *The Friend*. Ed. Barbara E. Rooke. *The Collected Works of Samuel
      Taylor Coleridge*, IV. 2 vols. Princeton: Princeton University
      Press, 1969. All references to *The Friend* in the body of the
      text are to the first volume, the 1818 edition.
LRR   "Six Lectures on Revealed Religion, Its Corruptions, and
      Political Views," in *Lectures 1795: On Politics and Religion*.
      Ed. Lewis Patton and Peter Mann. *The Collected Works of
      Samuel Taylor Coleridge*, I. Princeton: Princeton University
      Press, 1971.
LS    *Lay Sermons*. Ed. R. J. White. *The Collected Works of Samuel
      Taylor Coleridge*, VI. Princeton: Princeton University Press,
      1972. First published 1817.


OTHER WORK ABBREVIATED

OM    Hartley, David. *Observations on Man, His Frame, His Duty, and
      His Expectations*. 2 vols. New York: Garland, 1971. First pub-
      lished 1749.

# COLERIDGE'S
# BLESSED MACHINE
# OF LANGUAGE

# Introduction

The publication of the massive *Collected Coleridge* has stimulated
and sustained the combined effort of numerous scholars and
critics to establish Coleridge as the central voice of the English
Romantic tradition. That enterprise proceeds warily, however,
at a time when not only the tradition but also the very concept of
a center are under steady and serious attack. Even with no tur-
moil in the contemporary critical climate, the conservative skills
of humanist scholarship would meet in Coleridge a severe test:
the formation of a canon and the certification of an authority
are very difficult endeavors in the case of a writer who produced
few books in the conventional sense but who instead thriftlessly
spent himself in marginalia, prefaces, aids, and manuals. An
even more delicate problem is the evident promiscuity of much
of that writing, which wantons with counterfeits and indulges in
plagiarism and other literary practices that violate humanist decorum. Committed to Coleridge's status, challenged by skeptics,
and sensitive to embarrassments, Anglo-American criticism has
sought to normalize Coleridge by executing several standard
interpretative tactics: by psychologizing him as neurotic or
addict, by idealizing him as prophet or thinker, or by partition-
ing him into part philosopher, part priest. Contrarily, continen-
tal influenced criticism has seized on the normal Coleridge as a
strategic opportunity to expose humanist paradoxes as contradictions and simultaneously to convict both Coleridge and Cole-
ridgeans of "bad faith" and "self-mystification." I aim not to
mediate those hostile extremes but to navigate them by present-
ing neither a normal nor an abnormal Coleridge. I do not seek
to reproduce what Coleridge thought; rather, my goal, both

more primordial and more attainable, is to produce the way Coleridge writes.

In my judgment Coleridge's importance for criticism is not that he is central but that he is eccentric, even peripheral, his texts a circle whose center is nowhere and whose circumference is everywhere. Although he endeavors to establish the philosophic critic as the curate of the word, as a civil man sagely cultivating his native land, Coleridge's prose does not do good, will not stay put, strays beyond the garden walls into the forest of error. Coleridge's script plots no romantic resolution, however; the prose never comes home; it returns instead the romantic myth as the writer's condition, figuring the writer as displaced person, wanderer in a language he can never fully possess nor entirely escape. With an ebullient vigor that baffles his best intentions, Coleridge's prose charts the daunting itinerary that awaits the post-enlightenment man of letters.

What follows is a portion of that map, limited to Coleridge's prose: his notebooks, letters, essays, and, especially, the two major works of the middle of his career, the *Biographia Literaria* and *The Friend*. Although the prose bulks enormous in the volume of Coleridge's literary output it has rarely received thorough critical attention. Criticism has been most often inclined to extract famously gnomic passages either to employ them as pretexts for independent meditation or to deploy them as blank counters juxtaposed hopefully in order to fashion yet another original reading of "The Rime of the Ancient Mariner," "Kubla Khan," or "Frost at Midnight." Whatever those techniques accomplish, such criticism has little to say about the prose. The rare direct engagement with the prose has usually served some nonliterary prejudice, often to demonstrate Coleridge's acuity or vacuity as philosopher, scientist, or mystic. Although such demonstrations do have historical value, I prefer to leave history to historians, and propose instead to reclaim Coleridge's prose for literature and literary criticism. Coleridge has always been his own best critic. His best criticism is not to be found, however, in isolated *aperçus* or tightly argued deductions. I am not sympathetic to the claims regularly advanced that Coleridge was a consistent literary theorist; but I do believe that the practice of Coleridge's prose is among the most theoretically interesting we have. Cole-

[16]

ridge's criticism is written into his readings of other philosophical, literary, journalistic, and autobiographical works—an ensemble that constitutes Coleridge's text. His miscellaneous writings, from prefaces to plagiarisms, themselves figure a method, however apparently immethodical, which eludes abstract, concise formulation but which can be practiced rigorously in a reading of the texts from which it is derived. The following reading of Coleridge works toward a prosaics that is fully Coleridgean.

My criticism of alternate perspectives has been the prelude to the admission of my own. I begin with David Hartley's *Observations on Man*—a work universally recognized as having had great influence on Coleridge, but which is little read. I use a thorough reading of Hartley as the basis for three claims, each of which counters previous scholarship, and all of which combine to form the initial perspective on the blessed machine of Coleridge's language. First, Hartley's influence on Coleridge persisted as a real force longer than is generally acknowledged. Second, that influence was, even on the superficial level of what "Hartley" meant to Coleridge, more complex than is widely supposed. Third, Coleridge never successfully completed the overthrow of association which he proclaimed in 1801.

Coleridge identifies the basis of his objections to the associationist model of the mind in a notebook entry: "I am much pleased with this Suggestion, as with every thing that overthrows or illustrates the overthrow of that all-annihilating system of explaining every thing by association/either *conjuring* millions out of o, o, o, o, o, oo—or into noughts." Because the associationist conceives of all knowledge and behavior as the consequence of the mechanical concatenation of discrete, valueless, cipherlike impressions, his explanation of "every thing" is tantamount to the annihilation of "all"—the irreducible unity of mind and world which for Coleridge is prior to and aloof from mere process. Hence Coleridge rejects associationism on its own terms. But equally important here are Coleridge's terms, which imply that the chain of impressions achieves the apparent comprehensiveness of "every thing" only in the way that a succession of zeroes can suddenly vault to millions, by means of the conjuror's light-handed addition of the one to head the series. It is not here and never will be the everything or nothing structure of associationism to which Coleridge objects; he endorses similar ontological presuppositions elsewhere, though in different language. He deplores the all too plausible sleight of hand that tricks everything and nothing out of *any* ontological status, that turns creation into sophistic play and sophistic play into a kind of creation. Coleridge would be the demystifier of that legerdemain.

Writing on Hartley, Coleridge endeavors to support the absolute integrity of creation by vindicating his belief in an authority in the free will that cannot be traduced by the associationist's philosophical machinery. Instead of vindication, however, we observe imitation. In the course of exposing Hartley's systematic inconsistencies, Coleridge inadvertently divulges the incapacity of discourse to turn those inconsistencies to the account of the will. In Chapter 2, I follow the Hartleian Coleridge in his letters and his notebooks through a maze of experiments, theories, meditations, and nightmares as, with desperate zeal, he attempts to locate an island of moral refuge amidst the stream of association, tormented all the while by the suspicion that any position he can assume is merely another interruption in an indefinite series of links and lapses. Counterpointing the resistance of discourse to prove the will is the tractability of language to reproduce the flight of error in all its eccentric variations. Lacking the words for the will, Coleridge attempts in the *Biographia,* as I show in Chapter 3, to anchor his self in the language of others and in the figures of rhetoric; but because his assertion of the will remains contingent on others' texts, his discourse tropes Hartley's inconsistency as Coleridge's caprice, philosophical error as rhetorical willfulness. By alerting his readers to the conjuration practiced by the associationist, Coleridge sensitizes us to the elaborate ways in which the philosopher figures in his writing and suggests not only a method for reading Hartley's prose but also for Coleridge's own—prose that finds the authority for its demystification in a stronger magic.

The particular importance of Hartley is the character that Coleridge gives him. I do not mean that Hartley would have been lost to the history either of philosophy or of literature without Coleridge's commentary. Wordsworth scholarship alone is studded with essays documenting Hartley's influence on the poet's conceptions. But Wordsworth, unlike Coleridge, gives us no way to *read* Hartley, and it is primarily as a speculative demonstration of a Coleridgean reading that I find Hartley rewarding. Yet the character that Coleridge gives Hartley is not solely speculative. One source of the enduring fascination of Hartley for Coleridge was that he could not dismiss him as mere sophist by impugning his character or motives as he did Hobbes and Hume. On the contrary, he explicitly described Hartley as the "master of *Christian* Philosophy"—a title of the highest esteem, which Coleridge would never have thought to give to Spinoza, Schelling, Fichte, or Kant and which he would have loved to have had conferred on himself. Coleridge's various engagements with Hartley's system show him trying to capture that title by attaining a mastery of the master and, in his mixed success, represent a critique of the dialectic of mastery only equalled in its suggestive complications by his similar contest with Wordsworth. The difference between Hartley's title "master of *Christian* Philosophy" and the lesser titles Coleridge did claim for himself, such as man of letters and philosophical critic, tells much of the story of Coleridge's career.

Consideration of *Observations on Man* furnishes an especially useful perspective on Coleridge because it requires an investigation of which perspective—human, divine, or other—makes possible observations on man. To advance his propositions Hartley needs a perspective, but any one he adopts must be, in terms of the necessitarian associationism it serves, figurative. Because of its singular, doctrinal literalmindedness the associationist's text illuminates its own figures in a hard, nervous glare, highlighting each as an instance of the proto-philosophical activity that Coleridge calls hypopoesis: "Hypothesis: the placing of one known fact under others as their *ground* or foundation. Not the fact itself but only its position in a certain relation is imagined. Where both the position and the fact are imagined, it is Hypopoesis not Hypothesis, subfiction not supposition." Hypopoesis is philosophy's rhetoric of the essential: the necessary artifice which installs an equivocation in necessity itself. Not simply a philosophical fiction, hypopoesis is the enabling figure that makes fiction as well as philosophy conceivable—subfiction of the fact and position of an original standpoint and of an author who must ultimately speak the truth or tell à lie. In Hartley, hypopoesis is the turn that makes associationism possible and the figure to which, constantly outwit by its own duplicitous origin, it always returns. Hartleian hypopoesis reflects both on the ontological disposition of the system that it underwrites and on the philosophical character of him who is doing the under-writing. As my reading of Hartley through Coleridge and Cole-ridge through Hartley will show, hypopoesis involves in roman-tic intimacy the figure of philosophy with the figure of the philos-opher—the fabrication of a substantive that acts, not in the world like the supposed will, but in the text as a subfictive trope.

 Coleridge identifies Hartley's hypopoesis in order to make a dialectical leap to clearer and sounder conceptions based on more solid and virtuous principles. One consequence of Cole-ridge's inability to master Hartley fully is that instead of adven-turous dialectic or patient deduction we get volatile diver-sions, displacements, and digressions. It might be said that once Coleridge fails the test of the will his will fails Coleridge. To its credit such an aphorism does justice to what has been called the existential character of Coleridge's thought: the sense that every problem he engages in his essays, no matter how abstract or derivative, is an authentic problem for his life. Nonetheless, the aphorism extracts a moral from a plot, which, if it has any sig-nificance, can have no moral at all, existential or transcendental. For on the certainty of the will, undone by Coleridge's own discourse, depends the possibility of *the* moral. I would account for the characteristic immediacy, even the sense of hazard, in Coleridge's prose as a result of the way philosophical issues, anchored by hypopoesis, all but bereft of their authority, are dispersed throughout every feature of Coleridge's text in a metamorphic display that in its motile indeterminateness begs the question of contrivance. To step beyond the bounds of the associationist dispute in the *Biographia* as I do in Chapter 4 is to see that those bounds are as hypopoetical in nature and tenden-tious in context as the propositions they contain. The incidents and opinions that Coleridge hopefully advances as stages in his intellectual or moral life read in the *Biographia* as nothing more or less than chapters in a *literary* life, which is neither a Shandean fiction nor an organic development but a writer's career. All aspects of the *Biographia* from the criticism of Wordsworth and the practice of plagiarism to the theory of the imagination remark on Coleridge's doubt of the ultimate propriety of the self, reflect his fear that in the course of his literary life he has become a mere man of letters, and replay the marvelous, uniquely Coleridgean ambit between self-loss and self-recovery. My final chapter on *The Friend* investigates Coleridge's intricate and occasionally obscure efforts to communicate the truth, which is morally meaningless unless communicated but is morally compromised by any vehicle of communication. In *The Friend* Coleridge explicitly joins the problem of truth with the problem of communication and discursively implicates both in the problem of an appropriate method.

A few words about my method. It will be evident to most readers that the work of Jacques Derrida—particularly *Of Grammatology*, "White Mythology," and "La Pharmacie de Platon"—has been an important influence on this book. His themes, such as the problem of writing, indefinite tropism, and the irresolution of origins, inform many of my own. I have found Derrida's writings instructive as a way to read prose that falls, as Coleridge's does, loosely under the rubric of the philosophical. Fundamentally, however, for me the seductiveness of Derrida's writings reflects the appeal that Coleridge has long had; and in my experience the affinity of the two makes the issues of priority and dominance merely irrelevant.

I am aware, however, that no critic who acknowledges Derridean influence can do so innocently within the ferment and friction of the contemporary critical scene, which seems to have divided between those newcomers who practice versions of critical methods recently disseminated by the French and those who adhere to the principles of criticism developed in great diversity by an antithetical Anglo-American tradition. Diffident theorist, I am wary of critical polemics and, out of a concern to be read rather than pegged, have persistently sought a discreet charm rather than an aggressive novelty in my critical language. What interests me about the dispute between humanists and deconstructionists is its relevance to Coleridge, or, to put it more precisely, Coleridge's relevance to it. If, in a strong sense, the

[21]

dominant critical methods in England and America in the last century and a half have been developments from a few of Coleridge's suggestions and examples, one would expect to find the model for the current antagonism there in the seed. And there it is. Coleridge's collection of essays *The Friend* could be, *mutatis mutandis,* successfully republished today as a polemical monograph entitled "The Dysfunction of Criticism at the Present Time" or, abbreviated, be delivered as a paper on a Modern Language Association panel called "What Hath Derrida Unwrought." By retaining in the 1818 version of *The Friend* the attacks on Napoleon and the Encyclopaedists that made up a large portion of the original periodical published during the Napoleonic Wars, Coleridge tropes the immediate, historical French threat into universal allegory. Because that fabulous aggrandizement of reality is also a critical reduction, it enables us to see that what binds together Coleridge's objections to French politics, philosophy, economics, and literature is a fundamental anxiety about an uncertain style—a style attributed to the French, but ultimately a style of which Frenchness is only a local and partial manifestation. Indeed, the more than radical hazard of this style, its blessedness, is such that the allegorical dualism that Coleridge concocts at the expense of genial amity cannot contain it by branding it as simply alien or evil. Coleridge's anxiety about French style, I argue, accurately reflects his anxiety about the incorrigible impropriety of his own. The threat of contamination by the other, which the Friend resolves to withstand, is always in Coleridge a defense against the knowledge of an infection within, a disease in the very heart of health. To risk an analogy, the published fears that deconstructionist criticism has set out to destroy literature by turning it against itself seem to defend against the realization that this has been the complicitous practice of criticism and literature all along and, moreover, to evade the difficult knowledge that the critical battle from the point of view of the humanist fiction of literature is really a battle between two masters.

What makes Coleridge's texts so invigorating and so important is that though they supply the paradigm in English of this pattern of defensive hostility, the mentor's version is not as mystified as the disciples'. For in staging the allegorical play of English organic virtue versus French mechanical vice Coleridge also dramatizes his craft. This is particularly true in the "Essays on Method," where he assembles together on the white heal-all of his page the characters of Plato, sophist, and writer. At the point in his text where Coleridge claims to have the most immediate, concrete things to say about method he retrieves from the distant past the age-old struggle between Plato, philosopher of the true word, and the itinerant wordmongers who could dress up anything for a quick sale. Coleridge repeats history's unequivocal verdict (first delivered by Plato himself) that the victory went wholly to the philosopher and that the sophists were entirely cast out. But the Coleridgean affirmation is its own denial. His reiteration of the conflict between Plato and sophist revives the marginal figure of the sophist within his own text as the shadow of his own method. When true method, Coleridge's method, returns to its origin it recognizes the sophist within. Although Coleridge tries to weave circles around that figure of capable language, his brilliant eccentricity reflects the charming displacement of the center that is the figure of the sophist. Coleridge's "Essays on Method," the exacting model for the matter and organization of my own essays, *is* a footnote to Plato and in that footnote a marginal comment on what escapes the platonic philosophical method. What escapes is the figure of the sophist, who neither lies like the poet nor tells the truth like the philosopher, but who traffics between the republic and its exiles—a correspondent for the writer of Coleridge's text. Coleridge, the author of modern literary criticism, is its best critic. His rhetoric is a new sophistic that keeps principled criticism alive as the opportunity for footnotes, for figures in the margin.

Reading Coleridge means questioning romanticism—a romantic project, for the most definite characteristic of romanticism is the obstinate questioning of its own ambiguous status: its lineage, inheritance, privileges, and powers. If, as Coleridge, Wordsworth, and Blake charge, the eighteenth century complacently wound down in the exhaustion of its understanding, romanticism first recognizes itself in its will to interpretation, its aspiration to a hermeneutics proper to a glory inexplicably forlorn. The precedent that guides that aspiration is the hermeneutical tradition of biblical criticism. It has become conventional to render romantic investment in the Bible as an ideal instance of protestant economy by interpreting it as the marvelously profitable transfiguration of religious myth into cognitive power. That argument, fundamentally an austere formalism, presumes the power it sets out to prove: the presumed power to interpret the Bible as coherent myth or paradigm is taken as evidence of the integral activity of the Romantic imagination, independent of any substantive affiliations between Romantic poems and Scripture. That apriorism accounts for the profit perceived in the Romantics' transactions with the sacred. But if one takes as perspective not a certain power but its precedent and condition the uncertain will, it becomes evident that the key to romantic concern lies in no particular interpretation of the Bible, in neither myth nor structure, but in the problem of interpretation and in its adjunct, the question of biblical authority. History happens. The Enlightenment *did* intervene between the suave patristic and medieval commentators and the nervy Romantics who lately sought to revive their example. Deistic and skeptical inquiries into the accuracy, coherence, and unity of the Bible, which resulted in charges of inconsistency, contradiction, forgery, and fiction, vitiated scriptural authority and boded the metamorphosis of the Bible into just another popular text circulating in the promiscuous relations of writers, publishers, and readers. Although the Romantics, and especially Coleridge, were familiar with the program of the Higher Criticism, none of them, least of all Coleridge, succeeded to the pacific sublime that was the habitual frame of reference for German hermeneutics. There are many reasons for this; most reflect the distinctiveness of the English Romantic man of letters, who at the end of the eighteenth century was the nexus of a historically novel kind of commerce: a rapid, volatile exchange among all the differing but not yet wholly distinct articulations of culture, society, and the self. What made this commerce new and disturbing was the deformation of the book which was its cause, occasion, and consequence, and of which the loss of authority in the Bible was the salient feature. The authority of the Bible, whether as inspired chronicle or myth, could not be economically appropriated as a new property of the self not only because authority had been disabled by inquiry but also because authority had become a matter for exchange. The Romantic will to interpretation, the will to restore the privileged order of author, word, and reader, emerged in the context of this historical deformation of the Book. Among the Romantics, Coleridge's work bears most eloquent witness to the translation of sacred book into problematic text; it reflects the lapse of authority in its marginal method.

The relations among will to interpretation, lapsed scriptural authority, and marginal method are most clearly adumbrated in Coleridge's wonderful essay in *The Friend* in which he recalls his encounter with the black spot of ink on the wall of Luther's room at Warteburg. There Luther, frustrated in his attempt to translate the tricky Hebrew into good Protestant German, supposedly engaged in aerial combat with the devil of language. The memorial of that struggle, an opaque, ineradicable mark on a white wall, taints the Lutheran pretext of faithful interpretation and becomes a text that diverts Coleridge's attention from the Bible that Luther had abandoned. Pregnant with demons of its own, the black spot taunts the reason and understanding of the pious tourist and tempts him into edgy, indefinite commentary. The spot of ink on Luther's wall is a concrete correspondent of the mark of the will on Coleridge's metaphysics. He strives to resolve system and self ethically by establishing the will as indubitable, moral origin, even at the considerable cost of infusing that psychic origin with the equivalent of the ambivalence proper to the sacred: the ineluctable (and, for Coleridge, debilitating) contrariety of pleasure and pain. But the will never settles anything for Coleridge—least of all its own recklessness. With him, as for the Romantics generally, the revival within of the primal sense of the antithetical is constantly preempted by an indeterminateness that cannot be subjected to understanding or reason before it is *read*. In order to write with the authority of his will the Romantic must first read; and that reading, whether of Milton, the Bible, Kant, Hartley, or himself, is an unauthorized, willful writing on the text he reads. Romanticism begins again and again because it always starts with an exegesis that is already there in studied anticipation of the book or theory of the book that would make such an exegesis meaningful. This applies whether the exegesis is sophistical like Coleridge's celebration of his friend's genius in Chapter IV of the *Biographia,* or diabolical like Blake's plates for the hermeneutical manifesto "Marriage of Heaven and Hell," or merely Wordsworthian like the vertiginously pronominal. "Was it for this" that begins the 1799 *Prelude*.

Romanticism has been the most congenial testing ground for contemporary theories of interpretation because of the lapse between Romantic exegesis and the hermeneutics that would make it possible. In Coleridge that lapse is the occasion of anxiety both less specific and more fundamental than what has been called the anxiety of influence. Influenza, as a case history of Coleridge would show, is just one disease that afflicts the man of letters, and the influential *Oedipus* just one play in the writer's repertoire. Coleridge's prose dazzles because it displays the ways in which the oedipal tragedy of precursor and ephebe can be simultaneously embraced and betrayed as the melodramatic resolution of a more marginal problem. In his treatise on the German *Trauerspiel*, Walter Benjamin sharply distinguishes the "extraordinary catastrophe of the tragic hero" from the "typical catastrophe" of Baroque drama, in which it is "not moral transgression but the very estate of man as creature which provides the reason for the catastrophe" (*The Origin of German Tragic Drama*). For Coleridge, as for the Romantics in general, it is neither moral transgression nor influence but the estate of man as writer which provides the reason for this typical catastrophe. Insofar as he is a latecomer, appearing among the ruins of a bookish tradition, Coleridge's writing is a mourning-play; but as he is also and always an *arriviste* in the margins of the text, his writing is also a morning-play. The play of mourning and morning, of a dawn that is a death, a play on words, is the hypopoesis that underwrites his writing, a fact and position that is, romantically, both his essential starting point and typical catastrophe; like a "limit of opacity," an "old grey stone," or a "glittering eye."

Though a Romantic, Coleridge is also a figure in his own right. And I will argue that a particular figure marks the oscillation of his optimistic advance from and anguished return to the catastrophe of his prose. That figure is the chiasmus, representative of true method and link between absolute principle and moral discourse. In Coleridge the chiasmus is where ex-

tremes meet. But that encounter is not, as the author would have
it, the methodical envoy of a dialectical empire. Instead the
chiasmus figures the promise of dialectic as merely the enabling
presupposition of a rhetorical practice; its elegant mechanics
render the concord of identity and opposite, proposition and
inverse, as a marginal yet indelible sophistication of metaphysical truth. Eddy rather than bridge, the chiasmus in Coleridge's
text tropes method as the indefinitely reproducible, always
liminal traverse between consciousness and unconsciousness,
will and willfulness, writer and text. Or, as in this notebook
entry, between desire and fulfillment: "the still rising Desire still
baffling the bitter Experience, the bitter Experience still following the gratified Desire." Whether it is regarded as the formal
feeling that follows great pain or as painful interruption itself,
the chiasmus is the blessed machine of Coleridge's language.

As the chiasmus figures rather than resolves Coleridge's will
to interpretation, so any interpretation of Coleridge which takes
this method as its starting point must inscribe within it the figurativeness of its own possibility and, thus, the anxiety of its own
undoing. This is a book that violates the conventional understanding of Coleridge. Indeed, this is a book that does not try to
understand Coleridge but attempts to read him. Spare in generalizations, my argument attempts to adhere as much as possible
to the text. The advantage of that practice lies in in its fidelity to
language that is at all times subtle, in most instances equivocal,
and that floats on figures resistant to reduction. It would be
disingenuous, however, to excuse my occasional recourse to figures by claiming that they are Coleridge's own; the writer's
possession of his language is precisely what Coleridge's prose
puts in question. Even fidelity, as it is one of my purposes to
show, can produce a mimesis of text and commentary that
verges on a more deeply disturbing infidelity: if not a rivalry at
least a duplicity, as figure echoes figure and digress counters
digress. I do not want either to belittle or to magnify that hazard.
I have sought clarity and consistency throughout. Yet the one
thing that Coleridge the critic surely teaches is that without the
risk of infidelity it would be impossible to read with any real
faithfulness at all.

Because I do subscribe to a methodological mistrust of the generalization, it may be of service here at the outset to summarize the main lines by which my argument advances in each chapter.

Chapter 1, "Observations on Hartley," is a reading of *Observations on Man* which addresses the tension in Hartley between his rationalistic aspirations for comprehensiveness and his fideistic commitment to an immaterial soul and a transcendent God. Though not the first or the most subtle philosopher who sought to navigate that contradiction, Hartley is remarkable for the scrupulous candor with which he engages the anomalies that his project encounters. The chapter begins with an examination of Hartley's preface from the perspective of Coleridge's later insight that the foremost difficulty confronting a rigorously necessitarian theory of association is to account for its own writing— a perspective that subjects to critical scrutiny both the figure of the philosopher and the philosopher's figures. The contorted conduct of the preface dramatizes Hartley's recognition of and initial reaction to the problem; the rest of the treatise shows both the resilience of the problem and Hartley's calculated endeavor to contain it within a broader metaphysical surview. The typical movement in Hartley's dialectic is from an apparent dualism toward a conceptual monism, which, however, he retreats from for religious reasons; the philosopher's next step is to attempt to preserve both difference and continuity by the invention of a third term which bridges the irreducible gaps between soul and body, God and man, and pleasure and pain. Faced with the need to justify philosophical invention, Hartley appeals to the principle of analogy. Because he exempts no principle from observation, he then turns to an investigation of the reliability of analogy itself, which he has presumed to be securely anchored in the authoritative voice of God. Under the observer's eye, however, God's voice, transcribed in Scripture, loses its privileged status and hence its unequivocal explanatory power; not the true key which explains once and for all analogical play, God's word appears as simply one more invention within a network of inventions. Hartley's earnest examination effaces both the pretext of dualism *and* monism as well as drastically destabilizing the vaunted stages of moral development. The implication is, as

Coleridge saw, the transformation of the mind into a place where indefinite, groundless inventions result from and reflect arbitrary configurations of ideas—an arbitrariness with no ultimate arbiter.

The subject of Chapter 2, "Coleridge and Hartley," is the curve of Coleridge's response to Hartley before the *Biographia Literaria*. From the first, Coleridge's stance toward associationism was complicated by the divergent views of Hartley available to him in the two editions of *Observations on Man* by Joseph Priestley and by Herman Andrew Pistorius. He could find authority for selecting aspects of Hartley's theory that he was comfortable with and for suppressing other, less attractive features by counterposing the two editions. Using the documentary evidence of the "Lectures on Revealed Religion," the letters, and the notebooks, I chart the vicissitudes of Coleridge's allegiance to Hartleian doctrine and examine in detail the evidence for his oft cited claim in 1801 to have overthrown association, which meant for Coleridge the positive establishment of the free will. I conclude that in this instance as in others Coleridge took the wish for the act. The refutation is stated neither in the letter nor elsewhere. Coleridge's pertinent fragmentary notations do record his contrivance of a variety of logical and experimental demonstrations to discredit the explanatory power of Hartleian mechanics, but although he is able to reveal the uncertainties that interrupt association, he is unable to subordinate those interruptions to a philosophical alternative at once certain and moral.

Chapter 3, "The Marginal Method of the *Biographia Literaria*," is an examination of the three chapters in the *Biographia* devoted to a confutation of Hartleian association. Although it is the final and fullest statement of his objections to Hartley's doctrine, Coleridge's argument here strangely bobs and weaves. As Coleridge had noted earlier, the only confutation of association is the will, but, fearful of subjecting its authoritative voice to the dislocations of discourse, in the *Biographia* he withholds the will from his prose. Instead he pursues a strategy of indirection by means of a tactic which I call a marginal method: a fragmentary, mobile, aggressively rhetorical mode of argument that reads like a series of marginalia on the texts of others. Coleridge skillfully overpowers Hartley's tentative inventions with striking figures of his own. But, though splendidly suited to exploit the inconsistencies of association, Coleridge's marginal criticism will not support a principled alternative. The policy of protectively withholding the will has the effect of exiling it; its decisive irrelevance to the conduct of Coleridge's argument is a disclaimer of the will's moral force and inalienable power. Coleridge's criticism of Hartley settles nothing; on the contrary, it unsettles the authority of the writer, who, dislodged from his will, must live in a borrowed home.

In "The Literary Life of a Man of Letters" I venture beyond the topic of Hartleian association and apply the method developed in the first three chapters to a comprehensive reading of Coleridge's "immethodical miscellany." My essay, in which I adopt the Coleridgean hypothesis of a symbolic relation between the unity of the work and the unity of the mind behind the work in order to investigate the unity of Coleridge's literary life, is structured by the question of structure. The second, third, and fourth sections of the chapter each explore the structural implications of a different aspect of Coleridge's initial statement of organizing intention. The second section advances from the topic of the "real *poetic* character of the poet" to the passage in Chapter IV where Coleridge witnesses to Wordsworth's original genius. That place has been closed to criticism like a chamber of maiden thought, but Coleridge himself ventilated it with enough cross currents of ambiguity and conjecture to feed, if not a volcano, at least the flickering film of doubt as to the absolute integrity of the origin he celebrates. The third section examines Coleridge's settlement of the long-continued controversy concerning the true nature of poetic diction." For Coleridge the fundamental error of Wordsworth's theory of diction is that it separates propriety from property and thus threatens the principle of self-possession on which meaning depends. In the course of contesting Wordsworth's theory and practice Coleridge illuminates the poet's radical subversiveness. In his dialectical maneuvers to discriminate the mistakes of the man from the inalienable integrity of the genius Coleridge trespasses on sacred ground; he exropriates Wordsworth's genius as the property of the critic and abrogates the "sacred distinction between things and

persons," which is the central tenet that the argument of the
*Biographia* endeavors to uphold. The last section considers the
*Biographia* as Coleridge's "exculpation" of himself from the
charges that have devolved on him as a "man of letters." I argue
that Coleridge's injunction, "be not *merely* a man of letters,"
should be taken literally in the *Biographia* as Coleridge's statement of his most literal fear. Once he has been lost to print the
man becomes a creature of the printing press, neither person
nor thing, and subject to endless, mechanical reproduction. The
promised redemption of such a loss—possible for any author
who publishes, suffered by Coleridge in the digressions and
plagiarisms of the *Biographia*—is the secondary imagination,
which is the principle and agent of return: the faculty to which
the *Biographia* returns and by which the *Biographia* is restored to
Coleridge. But that return is only made possible by the in-
ter(in)vention of the man of the letter, who returns Coleridge to
himself less than he was. The theory of the imagination unifies
neither the man who leads a literary life nor the book, which
graphs the chiasmic interplay of license/loss with censure/re-
demption. The writer can escape indefinite mutual implication
only by either the nervous piety of the "Conclusion" or the fantasy of the critical machine in Chapter XXI.

Coleridge thought of *The Friend* as a more important work
than the hastily composed *Biographia*. Its aim, to refer men's
opinions and behavior to their absolute principles, was the central project of Coleridge's career in prose and is the subject of
my fourth chapter, "The Method of *The Friend*." Coleridge begins by exemplifying the hazards that beset his project in the
complex "Fable of the Madning Rain." He elaborates on the
dangers of communicating the truth in a long introductory section wherein he contrasts an appropriately discreet communication with the irresponsible truthtelling of the French Encyclopaedists, who, by indiscriminately broadcasting right but inadequate notions, stripped truth of the reserve essential to its
moral force. The Friend justifies his deferral of the establishment of absolute principles as a precaution taken to protect that
reserve. That justification serves also as a defense of his obscure
style, which, he maintains, is the proper medium for the sublimity of the truth. By connecting truth to a particular style, howev-

er, the Friend arouses the suspicion that the sense of a profound truth in reserve may be solely a function of that style. Indeed, because it is fully adaptable to the fabrication of both the fact and position of truth, the Friend's periodic style may be a more serious hazard to the soul than the Jacobin rhetoric of the French. In his "Essays on Method" the Friend seeks to establish both his moral authority and a reliable channel for the communication of truth by first ritually casting out the sophists, archetypal enemies of all principle, and then describing a dialectical method, the discourse of reason. But the selections from Shakespeare that the Friend uses to illustrate method improvidently devour his thesis; and the chiasmus with which he figures method wantons with the antithetical division between philosophy and rhetoric by which he had hoped to establish its propriety. The truth that the Friend communicates is the figure of the Friend, of whom, as of Coleridge, it may be said that the philosopher is in the sophist, the sophist in the philosopher.

# [ 1 ]

# Observations on
# Hartley

When do we say that any one is observing? Roughly: when he
puts himself in a favorable position to receive certain impressions in order (for example) to describe what they tell him.
— Ludwig Wittgenstein, *Philosophical Investigations*

The fact that the philosopher claims to speak in the very name
of the naive evidence of the world, that he refrains from
adding anything to it, that he limits himself to drawing out all
its consequences, does not excuse him; on the contrary he
dispossesses humanity only the more completely, inviting it to
think of itself as an enigma.
— Maurice Merleau-Ponty, *The Visible and the Invisible*

I

Most expositors of *Observations on Man* either ignore Hartley's
preface or merely notice in passing its acknowledgment of influence. Such a practice seems especially careless when one considers that access to Hartley has been mediated for most readers by
Coleridge's criticism of the associationist. Not that the preface is
startlingly unconventional—it is largely just Hartley's account of
how he came to write his book and an apology for its imperfec-
tions. But with Coleridge in mind that very conventionality
should be provocative, since one of his major criticisms of the
associationist theory fastens on just this issue, how does an associationist come to write books? His most succinct version of that
criticism appears in "On the Principles of Genial Criticism":
"Association in philosophy is like the term stimulus in medicine;
explaining every thing, it explains nothing; and above all, leaves

[33]

itself unexplained."[1] Coleridge implies the Kantian criticism that associationist theories explain everything except for the prior presence of an invariable ordering process, but he also describes the contradiction in which associationists place themselves: they cannot explain either the originality of their own insights or the novelty of their philosophical writing about association. Even if we grant the probative force of Coleridge's comment, however, we are not absolved from confronting the active existence of the contradiction it marks: how could an associationist philosophy be written?[2]

Hartley's preface attempts to explain. It begins:

The Work here offered to the Public consists of Papers written at different Times, but taking their Rise from the following Occasion.

About Eighteen Years ago I was informed, that the Rev. Mr. Gay, then living, asserted the Possibility of deducing all our intellectual Pleasures and Pains from Association. This put me upon considering the Power of Association. Mr. Gay published his Sentiments on this Matter, about the same Time, in a Dissertation on the

---

[1]*Biographia Literaria*, ed. J. Shawcross (1907; rpt. Oxford: Oxford University Press, 1973), II, 222. Hereafter cited in text as *BL*.

[2]For discussions of Hartley's theory of the association of ideas, see Sir Leslie Stephen, *History of English Thought in the Eighteenth Century* (1876; rpt. New York: Harcourt, Brace and World, 1962), II, 53-59. George Spencer Bower, *David Hartley and James Mill* (New York: G. P. Putnam's Sons, 1881). Howard C. Warren, *A History of the Association Psychology* (New York: Scribner's, 1921), pp. 50-64; G. S. Brett, *History of Psychology*, ed. R. S. Peters (2d ed.; London: Allen C. Unwin, 1962), pp. 436-43; Walter Jackson Bate, *From Classic to Romantic* (1946; rpt. New York: Harper and Row, 1961), pp. 93-128; Richard Haven, "Coleridge, Hartley, and the Mystics," *Journal of the History of Ideas*, 20 (1959), pp. 477-94; G. R. Cragg, *Reason and Authority in the Eighteenth Century* (Cambridge: Cambridge University Press, 1964), pp. 216-29; Robert Marsh, *Four Dialectical Theories of Poetry* (Chicago: University of Chicago Press, 1965), pp. 87-128; Martin Kallich, *The Association of Ideas and Critical Theory in Eighteenth-Century England* (The Hague: Mouton, 1970; *Studies in English Literature*, 55), pp. 115-32; and Barbara Bowen Oberg, "David Hartley and the Association of Ideas," *Journal of the History of Ideas*, 37 (July-Sept. 1976), pp. 441-54. For discussions of the associationist context and its relevance to literature see Ralph Cohen, "Association of Ideas and Poetic Unity," *Philological Quarterly*, 36 (1957), 465, Walter J. Ong, "Psyche and the Geometers: Associationist Critical Theory" in *Rhetoric, Romance and Technology: Studies in the Interaction of Expression and Culture* (Ithaca, N.Y.: Cornell University Press, 1971), pp. 213-36, and Paul de Man, "The Epistemology of Metaphor" in *On Metaphor,* ed. Sheldon Sacks (Chicago: University of Chicago Press, 1979), pp. 11-28.

fundamental Principle of Virtue, prefixed to Mr. Archdeacon Law's Translation of Archibishop King's Origin of Evil.

From inquiring into the Power of Association I was led to examine both its Consequences, in respect of Morality and Religion, and its physical Cause. By degrees many Disquisitions foreign to the Doctrine of Association, or at least not immediately connected with it, intermixed themselves. I have here put together all my separate Papers on these Subjects, digesting them in such Order as they seemed naturally to suggest; and adding such Things as were necessary to make the Whole appear more complete and systematical.

I think, however, that I cannot be called a System-maker, since I did not first form a System, and then suit the Facts to it, but was carried on by a Train of Thoughts from one thing to another, frequently without any express Design, or even any previous Suspicion of the Consequences that might arise [original in italics].[3]

Hartley begins by telling his reader how his work literally began. The significance of that scrupulousness is evident in the citation of Dr. John Gay, whose theory of habit, a Lockean answer to Francis Hutcheson, was the antecedent of Hartley's doctrine of the association of ideas.[4] Rather than being a conventional acknowledgement by Hartley of influence on his thought, however, the citation testifies that what follows are not Hartley's ideas at all, nor did he seek after them: they came to him unpremeditated as the consequence of an external stimulus. Effacing himself before Gay's precedent, Hartley portrays himself as in effect what Coleridge calls a "mere quick-silver plating behind a looking-glass" (*BL* I, 82), a maneuver which enables him to give a rigorously associationist account of his role in promulgating the doctrine of association. For the associationist, biography must recapitulate epistemology.

---

[3]David Hartley, *Observations on Man, His Frame, His Duty, and His Expectations* (1749; rpt. New York: Garland, 1971), I, v. Hereafter cited in text as *OM*. A treatise outlining Hartley's theory was published anonymously in Latin in 1746. It has been translated by E. A. Palmer and published as *Various Conjectures on the Perception, Motion and Generation of Ideas*, ed. Martin Kallich (Los Angeles: University of California Press, Augustan Reprint Society, 1959), pp. 72-78.

[4]See John Gay, "Concerning the Fundamental Principle of Virtue or Morality," in *British Moralists*, ed. L. A. Selby-Bigge (Oxford: Clarendon Press, 1897), II, 282-83 for key passages.

According to Hartley his "Work" "consists of separate papers." Hartley did not write the papers any more than he now offers the collected result to the public: the papers were "written" and the work is "offered." The deliberate use of passive verbs to describe an analytically passive process continues: Hartley "was informed" of Gay's assertion, which "put [him] upon considering." From being put upon "inquiring" into the power of association, Hartley is "led to examine" its "Consequences." All of that seems both mechanical and necessary enough. But by "degrees" (which is the only way things can happen in Hartley's scheme) "many Disquisitions foreign to the Doctrine of Association . . . intermixed themselves." Plot begins in conflict; and suspicion attends the intrusion of these "foreign" elements. What can "foreign" mean? Ideas can have no kinship except as they are associated, and once they are associated, they are *ipso facto* not foreign to each other—unless, that is, we appeal to criteria independent of the associative process, and Hartley shrinks from that: his half qualification of the foreignness of the disquisitions, that they are "at least not immediately connected" tries, however unsatisfactorily, to quell just that implication. Perhaps, then, "intermixed" is the key to this strange predicament. Can intermixing be a different, inferior kind of association? Obviously not, since that conclusion would endanger the doctrine by opening it to an *ad hoc* profusion of mental operations in a parody of faculty psychology. Hence it is as much to extricate himself from the fatal implications of the mere notion of something foreign intermixing itself as it is to master those foreign elements that Hartley first *acts*, in introducing his first active construction: "I have here put together all my separate papers." That sentence represents not only the choice of a content and a form, but also the assumption of a historic, privileged, ordering "I." Hartley softens that *ordonnance*, however, by describing it as merely a putting together, so that his touch looks so light as to be mistaken for a mere homeostatic reaction. By calling that ordering a "digesting" Hartley adopts the perfect expression for his needs, one that tropes the activities of disposition and classification as physiological assimilation. His move cannot, however, quite eradicate the unsettling taint of foreign intermixture, nor can it cancel the quickened sense of a deficiency in the explanatory power of the doctrine of association. Hartley tries to defend against that sense by "adding such things as were necessary to make the Whole appear more complete and systematical." That addition is the crisis of Hartley's writing.

A crisis in a narrow space: the introduction of the active voice is allied to a putting together and followed immediately by the process which he aims to present and which in his own terms must be the mode of presentation. Certainly a pretext for the change can be located in the materials themselves, which "naturally . . . suggest" an order. But Hartley steps beyond the natural. He *adds* because he needs "to make the Whole *appear* more complete and systematical." Hence he modifies a foreign intermixture out of a fidelity to the complete truth and in spite of the risk that in its representation completeness will be only apparent. His preface tells the story of its hypopoesis.

Two questions follow from this analysis. Why, if Hartley's preface involves him in inconsistencies, does he bother to write a preface at all? Does not all this reduce to the simple contradiction that if it were actually true that everything proceeded necessarily by the association of ideas, there would be no need for Hartley to write his book? The latter question is next of kin to Basil Willey's charge that in Hartley's movement from an analytic, necessitarian model in his first volume to an ethically prescriptive, religious program in his second he stumbles over the contradiction of "is" and "ought."[5] Though telling, the charge fails to account for Hartley's real influence on astute readers like Coleridge who did, it seems, miss the barbed contradiction and unblinkingly swallowed Hartleian philosophy. The reason for that influence reflects the motive for taking the risk of both preface and book. Hartley's decision to represent the system of association in its completeness as well as his scrupulous resolve to note the consequent inconsistencies both stem from a moral commitment that determines *Observations on Man* throughout all its parts.[6] The reason for writing the book is to represent the truth in order that others may follow it. Both the morality *and*

[5]*Eighteenth-Century Background* (1940; rpt. Boston: Beacon Press, 1968), p. 152.
[6]See Robert Marsh, *Four Dialectical Theories of Poetry*, pp. 87-128, for a discussion of the analogues between Hartley's first and second volume. The biographical background for this approach can be found in "The Correspondence of Dr. David Hartley and Rev. John Lister," *Transactions of the Halifax Antiquarian Society* (Halifax, England, 1938), pp. 231-78; and in David Hartley, Jr.'s interesting preface to the 1791 edition of *Observations on Man*, pp. v-xix.

the text are added to the doctrine of association; both contradict it. For Hartley, as for Coleridge, writing and morality are primordially connected: all words are moral risks and must be written with care and candor. Hartley trusts that the marginal problems of communicating the truth—the problems of writing—will evaporate in his readers' lucid observation of the true system.

II

As befits a dialectical philosophy Hartley divides his single work into two reciprocal and provisional parts: Part I, "Containing Observations on the Frame of the Human Body and Mind, and on their Mutual Connexions and Influences," and Part II, "Containing Observations on the Duty and Expectations of Mankind." In Chapter I of Part I Hartley formulates the mechanism that propels his system.

The first section deals with the "*Doctrine of* Vibrations *and its Use for explaining the Sensations*" (*OM* I, 7). Hartley begins by rehearsing the familiar empiricist jargon of impressions, sensations, and ideas, but although he juggles the terms slightly differently than his predecessors, he is unable to derive a formula that would accommodate a distinction between external impressions and internal ideas as well as preserve a continuity between them. Undaunted, Hartley devises a physical model that would account for the continuous transmission of impressions through the nerves to the brain. He hypothesizes an infinitesimal vibration which is caused by sensation and passes through a "subtle and elastic" aether that permits the vibrations to be "*excited, propagated, and kept up*" (*OM* I, 13). Because the vibration eludes empirical observation, however, for corroboration of his hypothesis Hartley must rely on various examples of analogous vibratory activity which intimate "the general Tenor of Nature in this respect; *viz.* that many of its Phaenomena are carried on by Attractions and Repulsions." The evidences of that assortment of phenomena may, therefore, "serve as a Clue and Guide to the Invention, and afford a Presumption, that other reciprocal Motions or Vibrations have a great share in the Production of natural Phaenomena" (*OM* I, 28). That all these principles of attraction and repulsion "are dependent upon, and involved within each other . . . is agreeable to the Tenor of Nature," where "each Part, Faculty, Principle, &c. when considered and pursued sufficiently, seems to extend itself into the Boundaries of the others, and as it were, to inclose and comprehend them all" (*OM* I, 28-29). The evidence of *this* complex and continuous interinvolvement encourages Hartley to proclaim a synthesis. The brain, he concludes, is "in a common way of speaking, the Seat of the sensitive Soul, or the Sensorium, in Men," which, by means of the aether and vibrations, performs "Sensation, Thought, and Motion" (*OM* I, 31-32). The chain seems complete, with body and mind wedded in the sensitive (read *material*) soul.

But because the one metaphysical limit that Hartley places on his observations is his inalienable commitment to the existence of an immaterial soul, he must retreat from this resolution; he insists that he does not "in the least presume to assert, or intimate, that Matter can be endued with the Power of Sensation" (*OM* I, 33). As a stopgap Hartley ventures another hypothesis to preserve both his continuity between body and mine *and* the inviolate immateriality of the soul: "If we suppose an infinitesimal elementary Body to be intermediate between the Soul and gross Body, which appears to be no improbable Supposition, then the Changes in our Sensations, Ideas, and Motions, may correspond to the Changes made in the medullary Substance, only as far as these correspond to the changes made in the elementary Body" (*OM* I, 34). This invention marks the typical movement of Hartley's philosophizing: a dualism, such as the division between body and mind (impression and idea), is transformed into a monism (here materialism), the breakdown of which (in this case due to the privileging of the immaterial soul) occasions not a return to the original dualism but the generation of a third term (the "infinitesimal elementary Body") which seems to satisfy the monistic need while accounting for the differentiation the unity must undergo to preserve a cherished conviction.[7]

The same plot may be observed in Hartley's discussion of the

[7]The "infinitesimal elementary Body" has a medieval antecedent in the *tertium quid*. See C. S. Lewis, *The Discarded Image* (1964; rpt. Cambridge: Cambridge University Press, 1978), pp. 166-67.

relation of the doctrine of vibrations to the "sensible Pleasures and Pains." In order to establish an analytic boundary between what are in fact not kinds but degrees of feeling, Hartley proposes as analogue for the "infinitesimal elementary Body" a "minute and invisible Solution of Continuity," which is "that common Limit, and middle Point, which separates Pleasure from Pain" (*OM* I, 36, 37). An answerable hypopoesis, the solution of continuity, like the infinitesimal elementary body is the third term that articulates a romantic resolution: the satisfaction of monism sanctioned by the ethic of differentiation. Inevitably, however, the precariousness of the third term risks the whole systematic enterprise. The subfiction that is meant to reinforce continuity renders the need to do so suspect.

Compared to the complicated presentation of the doctrine of vibrations, the doctrine of the association of ideas unfolds like a well-oiled, mechanical flower. The argument is distilled in the propositions:

> Sensations, by being often repeated, leave certain Vestiges, Types, or Images, of themselves, which may be called, Simple Ideas of Sensation [Prop. 8, I, 56]. Any sensations A, B, C, &c. by being associated with one another a sufficient Number of Times, get such a Power over the corresponding Ideas a, b, c, &c. that any one of the Sensations A, when impressed alone, shall be able to excite in the Mind b, c, &c. the Ideas of the rest [Prop. 10, I, 65]. Simple Ideas will run into complex ones, by means of Association [Prop. 12, I, 74].

The clarity reflects Hartley's confidence in this aspect of his system, which as a process rather than a datum is immune to the effects of any prejudice regarding the breach or continuity between body and mind. Yet despite the clear superiority of association, Hartley does not abandon the doctrine of vibrations. On the contrary, he imports it directly into the discussion of the association of ideas as analogue. Thus for "simple Ideas of Sensation" there are "Vibratiuncles and Miniatures" (Prop. 9), for the association of "Sensations A, B, C, &c." we have an association of "Vibrations A, B, C" (Prop. 11), and so on. The deductive advance from one set of propositions to another is firmly bound up with the correspondence between the even and odd numbered propositions.

> Nor does there seem to be any precise limit which can be set to this mutual Dependence of the Powers of generating Miniatures, and of Association upon each other: However, they may both take place together, as the Heart and Brain are supposed to do, or both depend upon one simple Principle; for it seems impossible, that they should imply one another *ad infinitum*. There is no greater Difficulty here than in many other Cases of mutual indefinite Implication, known and allowed by all. Nay, one may almost deduce some Presumption in favour of the Hypothesis here produced, from this mutual indefinite Implication of its Parts, so agreeable to the Tenor of Nature in other Things. [*OM* I, 71]

This "mutual indefinite Implication" closely resembles earlier instances of correspondence, except that here Hartley ignores empirical procedures altogether and asserts that the existence of the two "Powers" is substantiated by mutual indefinite implication alone—a solution which escapes infinite regress only because it implies a "simple Principle," here provisionally identified as the "Tenor of Nature." Following the path of mutual implication, *Observations on Man* travels a dialectical spiral that starts with the brain and a mechanistic epistemology, that invokes the analogical principle of the tenor of nature, and that necessarily expands to ever larger ontological claims. Hartley's philosophy quests for the absolutely "simple Principle" that ultimately grounds and harmonizes all implications, for the third term that is not merely the name for continuity but continuity itself, for the bridge between the visible and the invisible—for the God who is, "according to the Scriptures, *All in All*" (*OM* I, 114).

### III

Hartley best describes the character of his philosophic activity in the note on his "Design" preceding Chapter I, where he prepares the way for his discussion of vibrations and associations by invoking Isaac Newton's "Method of Analysis and Synthesis." "I shall not," Hartley allows, "be able to execute with any Accuracy, what the reader might expect of this kind, in respect of the Doctrines of *Vibrations* and *Association*, and their general Laws, on account of the great Intricacy, Extensiveness, and Novelty of the Subject. However, I will attempt a Sketch in the best manner I can, for the Service of future Inquirers" (*OM* I, 6). To characterize his method Hartley adopts a humble but strategically astute metaphor from the visual arts. By promising a sketch he implies that he is only clarifying what he sees or, indeed, what anyone could see, a clarification undistorted by the mediation of his writing. He also relieves himself from responsibility for complete consistency or accuracy, though at the cost of burdening his work by an affiliation with the always unreliable arts.

The character of Hartley's sketching is evident in one of his early illustrations. Before he can establish the association of ideas Hartley must prove that there are ideas in the mind stable enough to be associated. He compares the continuance of all sensations to the "clear and precise Image" of a candle flame left in the "*Sensorium*, Fancy, or Mind." Although crucial as empirical corroboration of Hartley's theory, the problem with the evidence of the candle flame is that it can only be obtained in a severely limited manner: "At least this will happen frequently to Persons, who are attentive to these Things, in a gentle way: for as this Appearance escapes the Notice of those who are intirely inattentive, so too earnest a Desire and Attention prevents it, by introducing another State of Mind or Fancy" (*OM* I, 10). Neither the blind looking of inattention nor the violent looking of too earnest attention, Hartley's gentle way of looking is a middle mode of perception, which is directed toward a phenomenon, but which stops short of examining the phenomenon too closely—for when a person examines something too closely it is likely to vanish or, worse, change into something else, which, in turn, will change into more changes. Hartley's "gentle way," is the "infinitesimal, elementary Body" between dead apathy and dangerous desire. In order to ensure certainty Hartley retreats from understanding to the hypopoesis of a midpoint where he does not desire certainty; where he can save both the phenomena and the self's awareness of phenomena; save the necessary world and a moral, that is gentle, relation to it. He sketches.

Sketching may not be completely accurate, but accuracy, as we know from Plato, may harm rather than serve the truth. Hartley's Platonism inheres not in his philosophical system or in his formal method but in his ethos of unswerving fidelity to the truth without regard to the sacrifice of the ostensible. In these latter days, however, that ethos manifests itself as misgivings about the character of philosophical activity. On the bleached flatlands of the Enlightenment Hartley foregrounds the variable duplicity of any philosophical method, of all philosophical writing. Hartley's singularity in the Lockean tradition lies in his scrupulous tracing of the figure imbedded in the blank tablet supposed by eighteenth-century empiricism—a sketch that is the figure of the philosopher sketching. In spite of himself Hartley's observations show that the duplicity of philosophical writing is not to be subdued by cagey metaphor. For sketching is not a simple, unarticulated act: the artist must view the scene before he can sketch it as the natural philosopher must read nature before he can write about it. The vehicle of Hartley's metaphor catches complications from its tenor; and in order both to do justice to philosophical activity and to justify his philosophical inventions Hartley must supplement the metaphor of the sketch with a transitive figure of reading and writing:

> Let us suppose the Existence of the Aether, with these its Properties, to be destitute of all direct Evidence, still, if it serves to explain and account for a great Variety of Phaenomena, it will have an indirect Evidence in its favour by this means. Thus we admit the Key of a Cypher to be a true one, when it explains the Cypher completely; and the Decypherer judges himself to approach to the true Key, in proportion as he advances in the Explanation of the Cypher; and this without any direct Evidence at all. And as the false and imperfect Keys, which turn up to the Decypherer in his Researches, prepare the Way for the Discovery of the true and complete one, so any Hypothesis that has so much Plausibility, as to explain a considerable Number of Facts, helps us to digest these Facts in proper Order, to bring new ones to Light and to make *Experimenta Crucis* for the sake of future Inquirers. [*OM* I, 15-16]

The scientist invents aether because it explains things, and the invention in turn is justified by its simple explanatory power. Part metaphor, part method, the cipher analogue emblematizes

[43]

the analogical relation among all phenomena. To argue by analogy is to assume that nature is a cipher, just as to attempt to decipher nature requires reliance on analogy. That circular relationship assists the natural philosopher in his invention, since the "analogous Natures of all the Things about us, are a great Assistance in deciphering their Properties, Powers, Laws, &c. inasmuch as what is minute or obscure in one may be explained and illustrated by the analogous Particular in another, where it is large and clear. And thus all Things become Comments on each other in an endless Reciprocation" (*OM* I, 343). As scientific invention spans the tracing out and the forming of observations, so it connects the reading of a cipher and the drawing of an analogy. A solution of continuity, invention bridges reading and writing.

In his invocation of "endless Reciprocation," Hartley seems markedly more complacent about mutual indefinite implication than we have seen him elsewhere. His assurance stems from his confidence in the support that the properties of analogy supply the scientific imagination, properties themselves secured by the cipher emblem. The effectiveness of deciphering seems to furnish independent evidence of the value of analogy because it is analogical reasoning that discovers the mutual implication of parts in the cipher. The solution of the cipher determines the pattern, and with that solution mutual implication yields to simple explanation. In its success the method, appropriate to natural philosopher as well as decipherer, is justified.

Yet though Hartley can accept the possibility of proposition after proposition and key after key being invented, one suspects that he would be less happy about the possibility of complete explanation after complete explanation surfacing within a cipher. According to the model, a key is good only as long as it solves the cipher, but, on the other hand, *any* key is good as long as it solves the cipher. How can there be any assurance that the key discovered is the true key or that there *is* one true key? Hartley answers that objection in a later discussion of deciphering, where he also fastens philosophy and deciphering more tightly together.

It may be said with Justness and Propriety in general, that Philosophy is the Art of decyphering the Mysteries of Nature; that Criticism bears an obvious Relation to Decyphering; and that every Theory which can explain all the Phaenomena, has all the same Evidence in its favour, that it is possible the Key of a Cypher can have from explaining that Cypher. And if the Cause assigned by the Theory have also its real Existence proved, it may be compared to the Explanation of a Cypher; which may be verified by the Evidence of the Person who writes in that Cypher. [*OM* I, 350]

By answering one question, however, Hartley raises others. Suppose that we were to find something that looked something like a cipher. How could we know whether it was a code or just a random aggregate of incoherent characters? Hartley proposes as his aim "deciphering the Mysteries of Nature." Granting the appropriateness of the method of decoding to the particular properties of a cipher, what warrants the extension of that method to nature, which at first sight hardly looks like a code? That last question addresses a crux of Hartley's argument. It does not ask whether the particular hypotheses in *Observations on Man* are correct or not: Hartley would be perfectly willing to abandon any or all hypotheses were he presented either with better ones or with falsifying evidence; his emblem provides for any number of necessary revisions. No, what the question strikes at is Hartley's fundamental project of fully explaining all phenomena, for that project depends on the assumption that phenomena are unified and that a coherent world can be decoded. By stressing the analogy between world and code, Hartley impresses on his reader that the correspondence is *merely* analogical; he needs the cipher emblem as a support only because the codelike qualities of the world are not self-evident. Hartley can risk that inference because for him the analogy does not rest on the casual perception of a single scientific investigator—instead it bears on an essential connection between nature and a cipher, which, ultimately, signifies that *all analogies are essential*. Nature is a cipher, is encoded, because it has been made by God.[8]

Although Hartley reads the world like a book, he knows that

[8] In *Le Debat sur les ecritures et l'hieroglyphe aux XVII et XVIII siecles* (Paris: S.E.V. P.E.N., 1965), Madeline V. David distinguishes between the decipherer, who "has ventured to turn toward a dead writing" to exercise his skills "in the framework of historic research," and the cryptographer, for whom decoding is always a matter of "'modern to modern'" (p. 11). The passage from one to the other represents the figure of the philosopher in Hartley's text.

textuality can be a mixed blessing: words can harden into counters which merely reproduce the effect of mute circularity which
they are relied on to make intelligible. As with any code it is hard
to explain the cipher of nature unassisted, since "it is difficult to
explain Words to the Bottom by Words; perhaps impossible"
(*OM* I, 277). This is so because "Words refer to Words, and to
grammatical and logical Analogies in an endless Manner, in
these Things; and all the real Foundation which we have is in the
Words of Scripture" (*OM* II, 353). Beyond the formal assurance
of an author, then, Hartley's philosophical imagination, dedicated to certainty, needful of both guide and limit for its invention, requires substantive help from *the* Author, needs the kind
of testimony which, like that from a contriver of ciphers, verifies
the decipherer's key. The natural philosopher needs an "authoritative Voice," that will focus and justify his desire for certainty.[9]
The difference between the formal and the substantive reflects
the difference between *any* explanation of a cipher and the *true*
explanation of a cipher, which in turn parallels the difference
between an adequate organization of phenomena and a unifica-
tion of phenomena according to nature's essential meaning and
real purpose.

The need for an authoritative voice is the need for something
new to be added to the enclosed system of decoder and code,
which implies either one of two models. First, the decoder has a
key which seems to him true to the cipher, but he is uncertain
because the solution of the cipher should include a solution of
*him,* the decipherer, and he is uncertain. The addition of the
voice is, therefore, a triangulation meant to erase an otherwise
irreducible difference between decoder and code, to cancel the
figure of the philosopher. Second, the decoder has a key which
seems to explain the code accurately, but as it also explains him it

[9]Cf. Coleridge in a letter to Sir George Beaumont: "But my Track in 'THE
FRIEND' confines me to common Life and to Men acting as Individuals in the
daily Toils and Pleasures of common Life—And here I see before me an ample
Harvest of Facts—and I am well content, that such *is* the Direction of my Road:
for I listen with gladness and an obedient ear to Prudence while it remains
subordinate to, and in harmony with a loftier and more authoritative Voice—
that of PRINCIPLE" (*Collected Letters of Samuel Taylor Coleridge,* ed. Earl Leslie
Griggs [Oxford: Clarendon Press, 1956-71], III, 137. Hereafter cited in text as
*CL*).

includes him within the system. Thus he cannot determine whether he has the true solution without the reflective distance that a different voice and a different point of view supply. The Bible, the revealing word, is added to the hermeneutical situation of man in each of those ways. A necessary novelty, Scripture, the direct, authoritative voice of God, is the fountainhead of the pure Word from which we can draw a tonic to clear our understanding and nourish a judgment fit to deal with all the other words that require interpretation.

Though providential, the addition of the Bible involves the philosopher in a predicament. If nature is made by God and supplies us with the moral teaching necessary for our acquiescence in the Divine plan, why was it necessary for God to repeat Himself in Scripture? It is impossible to accept that such an event would be a mere superfluity: what God does must be necessary or nothing is necessary. On the other hand, it is impossible that the Scriptures have ontological priority, since that would cast strong doubt on the sufficiency of nature both for those who lived before the appearance of Revelation as well as for those who have not heard the Word since. Behind all this is Hartley's feeling that Scripture, which claims divine inspiration in an authoritative voice, must mean something special. God's text is here. It has been added to the world. But the addition of that text is as problematic for the certainty of divine truth as the addition of Hartley's text is for the certain system he intends to communicate. Scripture tests the possibility of communication; it is the trial of the Word.

What obtains for Scripture applies *a fortiori* to the New Testament and is especially urgent in consideration of "the Discourses, Actions, Sufferings, and Resurrection" of Christ (*OM* II, 169). The proof of the Bible's divine authority depends on the proof of Christ's divine mission, which in turn depends on the proofs of his historicity. There are three. First, "there seems to be a Necessity . . . for a suffering Saviour," so we can expect that there be one. Secondly, if we accept only the incontestable parts of the character of Christ, it will be difficult to believe "that God would permit a Person apparently so innocent and excellent, so qualified to impose upon Mankind, to make so impious and audacious a Claim without having some evident Mark of

Imposture set upon him. . . . Thirdly, the Manner in which the Evangelists speak of Christ, shews that they drew after a real Copy" (*OM* II, 167-69). Hartley directs his industry toward contesting the claim that the New Testament could be a forgery, the assertion that most directly challenges the singular authority of Scripture's voice. He tries to show both that the character of Christ, "manifestly superior to all other Characters, fictitious or real, whether drawn by Historians, Orators, or Poets" (*OM* II, 167), is so great that he must be imbued with divinity and that the character is so realistic that Christ must have been a man living among men. What begins as a defense of scriptural truth becomes an argument about narrative verisimilitude.

The shifting of the ground is more important than Hartley's success or failure in defending it, for once even the most gentle reader is arrested by the narrative complications of Scripture, the consequences of God being the author of this book are more unsettling than the proof of fraud. Why could not God write something unequivocal? Why this story with its inconsistencies, metaphors, and marvels? Why could not the world, God's "first Inscription" (*OM* II, 45-46), be sufficient? Why must the world be such an obscure text, filled with its own inconsistencies, its moral and natural evils? It seems that with only a few modifications things could be infinitely better. Hartley is prepared for such an objection: "If we alter any of the Circumstances of the Microcosm or Macrocosm, of the Frame of our own Natures, or of the external World that surrounds us, we shall have Question rise up after Question in an endless Series, and never shall be satisfied, unless God should be pleased to produce Happiness instantaneously" (*OM* II, 127). What Hartley is not prepared for is the conclusion, based on a close reading of his text, that any reading of any text is an altering of that text, just as any representation of the truth is its equivocation. When we look closely we see that God alters himself by taking on the form of man, as he alters himself by writing the Bible, as he alters himself by creating the world. God's addition to his self-sufficiency, perhaps "to make the Whole appear more complete and systematical," is a fall into language. When we look too closely in a desire for the truth, the truth vanishes; all that we have are

[48]

hypopoeses, which beget question after question in an endless series. In trying to imagine limits to the imagination the mind leaps over all limits. Invention can no longer be a simple pleasure.

The breakdown of the integrity of the Bible, the supposedly authoritative voice of God, reflects back through all the enterprises of the inquiring mind. Perhaps science is not deciphering at all; it may only be secular commentary—natural exegesis instead of natural philosophy. The desire for certainty leads the reader to an insensible yet radical difference which traces our all too utterable difference from God. Any action or desire or invention alters the self-sufficient unity of the Deity; even the most infinitesimal difference between self and God is sufficient for the imagination's unpremeditated and terrible flight. Only *in* God can we be justified in our belief that benevolence is the true key to the mechanics of association, for only there can our observation be clear: "With respect to Benevolence, or the Love of our Neighbour, it may be observed, that this can never be free from Partiality and Selfishness, till we take our Station in the Divine Nature, and view every thing from thence, and in the Relation which it bears to God. If the Relation to ourselves be made the Point of View, our Prospect must be narrow, and the Appearance of what we do see distorted" (*OM* II, 310). We can never be certain, "ought never to be satisfied with ourselves, till we arrive at perfect Self-Annihilation, and the pure Love of God" (*OM* II, 282). Since the self distorts our view of the world and prevents our philosophical sketch of the truth, only the loss of the self will permit true philosophy. Man must be where he wants to go in order to assure himself that where he wants to go must be.[10]

[10]Self-annihilation is the logical conclusion of men's instinctual "desire of knowing that what they appear themselves to know, has a correspondence in Reality." We can conclude with Coleridge that "it is not the desire of attaching *Outness,* an *externality* to our representations which is at the bottom of this Instinct; on the contrary this very attachment of Outness originates in this Instinct—But it is to possess *a ground* to know a fixed Cause generating a certain reason" ("On Certainty," *The Notebooks of Samuel Taylor Coleridge,* ed. Kathleen Coburn [Vols. I and II, New York: Pantheon, 1957, 1961; Vol. III, Princeton: Princeton University Press, 1973], III, 3592. Hereafter cited in text as *CN*).

IV

Regarded in terms of its spatial axis—that is, its investigation of the frame of man, the world, and the Bible for the true, necessary key that would permit a rule of life—Hartley's attempt to broaden his reader's surview leads to observations that suddenly narrow to a recognition of the text, and particularly Scripture, as the true problem and of exegesis as the true trial for the philosopher, who is always one step off the place he sketches for himself: reading when he would be observing, writing when he would be reading. Associationist philosophy broaches a nostalgia for the sacred book that is never quite there. But for Hartley, as for his critic Coleridge, the book one dreams is not tablets of stone; it is a narrative, a temporal as well as a spatial construct. And Hartley's work, like the texts of Coleridge that succeed to the associationist's precedent, is a narrative sketch—a temporal ordering of events that supposes an advance from beginning to end. Indeed, ordinarily when we think of necessitarian philosophy, we have in mind its temporal aspect, the ineluctable movement of phenomena on a certain track to an inevitable goal. On first sight the doctrine of the association of ideas, though it seems to nullify the effect of consciousness and will, does not seem well suited to sustain a strict necessitarianism, primarily because the association of ideas is consequent upon contingent impressions, the kind, force, and frequency of which cannot be predicted. Although Hartley does try to adapt his model to prediction and does claim that the moral development of the individual is necessary, he is not unaware of the logical problem. He does rather half-heartedly attempt to distinguish between accidental ideas and the core of ideas shared by everyone, but his energy flags because the logical objection which he tries to answer does not seriously bear on his argument. Instead his necessitarian projections derive from a consistent teleological orientation and depend on a radical reduction of impressions in kind and number.

We can speculate that one of the reasons why Hartley fixed on the concept of the vibration was to assure the dynamic and progressive character of association, which otherwise might be liable to drift into a theory of aimless accretion. It is, at least, by means of vibrations that Hartley first represents his necessitarian model, based on a difference in degree and kind:

> First, then, If we admit Vibrations of the medullary Particles at all, we must conceive, that some take place in the *Foetus in Utero*. . . . And these Vibrations are probably either uniform in Kind and Degree, if we consider short Spaces of Time; or, if long ones, increase in a slow uniform manner, and that in Degree only, as the *Foetus in Utero* increases in Bulk and Strength. They are also probably the same in all the different Regions of the medullary Substance. Let these Vibrations be called the *Natural Vibrations*.
> Secondly, As soon as the Child is born, external Objects act upon it violently, and excite Vibrations in the medullary Substance, which differ from the natural ones, and from each other, in Degree, Kind, Place, and Line of Direction. . . . Let these Vibrations be, for the present, called *preternatural* ones, in Contradistinction to those which we just now called *natural ones*. [*OM* I, 60]

Using vibration $A$ as an example of the preternatural vibration, $N$ the natural one, and $a$ as the sign of the continued, diminutive state of the preternatural, Hartley argues "that $A$ may overpower $N$, and $a$ become the natural State." The same process occurs to a greater degree with more vibrations, "$A, B, C, D, \&c.$" Although Hartley formally respects the different kinds of vibrations that $A, B, C, D, \&c.$ signify, he refers those kinds to a single composite *kind*, that is, preternatural, which he places in conflict with another kind of vibration, the natural (*OM* I, 62). The preternatural violently "overpower" the natural and become natural in turn.

That action imitates an unresolved plot: the two terms natural and preternatural imply a third, the supernatural. As the beginning and middle imply an end, so the plot of nature then overthrow implies a resolution: either a restoration or a reconciliation. That plot emerges most fully in Hartley's "general Analysis" (*OM* I, 41) of sensations under the rubric of pleasure and pain. From our observation of the way pleasure passes into pain and pain into pleasure "we may see, that the Pains are in general greater than the Pleasures; but then they are more rare for the same Reason, being such violent States as cannot rise from common Impressions" (*OM* I, 40). By applying an even more

[51]

general analysis, therefore, it can be shown that the necessary implication of pleasure and pain will tend, because of the greater number of pleasures, to necessarily diminish pain and produce a future state of pure pleasure like that at the origin, before the first pain of disruption:

> Thus Association would convert a State, in which Pleasure and Pain were both perceived by Turns, into one in which pure Pleasure alone would be perceived; at least, would cause the Beings who were under its Influence to an indefinite Degree, to approach to this last State nearer than by any definite Difference. Or, in other Words, Association . . . has a Tendency to reduce the State of those who have eaten of the Tree of Knowledge of Good and Evil, back again to a paradisiacal one. [*OM* I, 83]

Ultimately, then, association is mutual implication with a difference, the difference that ensures a necessary progressive movement toward an eventual restoration of a lost happiness.

Hartley is well aware that his cosmic optimism violates the convictions of many philosophers and believers:

> It may be said, That the Doctrine of Mechanism destroys the Notion of a particular Providence altering the Course of Nature so as to suit it to the Actions of Men. I answer, That laying down philosophical Free-will such an Alteration in the Course of Nature may perhaps be necessary. But if Man's Actions, and the Course of Nature, be both fixed, they may be suited to each other in the best possible Manner; which is all that can be required, in order to vindicate God's Attributes, as well as all that Man can desire. [*OM* I, 508]

The fundamental attributes of God are that He is the cause of everything and the end of everything. Thus, although Hartley directs many criticisms against the logical possibility of "philosophical Free-will," his basic grievance is that "to suppose that Man has a power independent of God, is to suppose, that God's Power does not extend to all Things, *i.e.* is not infinite" (*OM* II, 66). Free will, a breach in the frame of man, and a particular providence, a breach in the frame of history, fall under the same proscription. The existence of either would represent the single alteration that would mean the alteration of everything, for, as we have seen, "if we alter any of the Circumstances of the Microcosm or Macrocosm . . . we shall never be satisfied."

It is easier to determine what Hartley defends his mechanism against than to identify what it actually is. Perhaps it would be most accurate to call it "developmental." Instead of change, Hartley desires transition; instead of novelty, he values the new. Hence the movement from the original pleasure to the intermediate pain/pleasure to the new pleasure is actually no change but an unfolding, a discovering of what is necessarily there.[11] The transition from one stage to another, though violent and ostensibly qualitative, is not discontinuous: the vibrations persist through every stage, as does the necessary presence of God. Although a world was at one time created and a paradise was at one time lost, "those are not to be accounted for . . . being the Foundation upon which we go" (*OM* II, 128). Our first parents' sin was not the act of a free will but the disobedience of a child, as necessary a transition in the development of the world as the violent thrust of the foetus into the painful welter of infant sensations. We can isolate a qualitative transition, as we must to assure ourselves of the qualitative transition to heavenly peace; we can even discriminate stages of approach to that final transition through a careful calculation of the relative proportions of pain and pleasure; but we must not confuse transition with alteration, for with alteration supposed heavenly peace itself vanishes into a chasm that we shall desperately seek to fill with our fictions.

Our difficulties with biblical language, the impossibility of getting "to the bottom of Words by Words," can both be ascribed to our own deficiencies as readers and be taken hopefully as some indication, at least, that words *have* a bottom, accessible by better tools in some better time. We trust that linguistic ambiguities are, like the ambiguous mixture of pleasure and pain, only provisional:

Was human Life perfect, our Happiness in it would be properly represented by that accurate Knowledge of Things, which a truly

[11]See Thomas McFarland's discussion of Coleridge's development in *Coleridge and the Pantheist Tradition* (Oxford: Oxford University Press, 1969), pp. 161-63.

philosophical Language would give us. . . . But as human Life is, in fact, a Mixture of Happiness and Misery, so all our Languages must, from the Difference of our Associations, convey Falsehood as well as Truth. . . . And yet, since our imperfect Languages improve, purify, and correct themselves perpetually by themselves and by other Means, so that we may hope at last to obtain a Language, which shall be an adequate Representation of Ideas, and a pure Chanel [*sic*] of Conveyance for Truth alone, Analogy seems to suggest, that the Mixture of Pleasures and Pains, which we now experience, will gradually tend to a Collection of pure Pleasures only, and that Association may be the Means of effecting this. [*OM* I, 320-21]

Unlike moral behavior, which progresses through the combination of pain and pleasure, the development of an adequate language relates to that associative process only by analogy, for language possesses an associative dynamics of its own and requires its own stories.

Hartley offers two versions. One, biblical, supposes "that the Language, which *Adam* and *Eve* were possessed of in Paradise, was very narrow, and confined in a great measure to visible Things." If we assume that is true, then after "the Fall we may suppose, that *Adam* and *Eve* extended their Language to new Objects and Ideas, and especially to those which were attended with Pain; and this they might do sometimes by inventing new Words, sometimes by giving new Senses to old ones" (*OM* I, 298). That story is in accord with a more philosophical account: "If we suppose the most common visible Objects to be denoted both by short articulate Sounds, and by short Characters bearing some real, or fancied, imperfect Resemblance to them, it is evident, that the Sound and Mark, by being both associated with the visible Object, would be the Name of the Mark, and Mark the Picture of the Sound. And this last Circumstance seems to lead to the denoting all Sounds by Marks, and therefore *perhaps* to alphabetical Writing" (*OM* I, 290, emphasis added). That "perhaps" is likely the most crucial qualification in *Observations on Man*. It marks the recognition that the association of the mark with the object and the sound adequately explains only pictorial language. The problem of the origin and the necessary development of alphabetical writing persists:

As Persons, before they learn to read, must have very imperfect
Notions of the Distinction of Words, and can only understand
Language in a gross general Way, taking whole Clusters of Words
for one undivided Sound, so much less can they be supposed to
have any Conceptions concerning the Nature or Use of Letters.
Now all Mankind must have been in this State before the Invention
of Letters. Nay, they must have been further removed from all
Conceptions of Letters, than the most unlearned Persons amongst
us, since these have at least heard of Letters, and know that Words
may be written and read by means of them. And this makes it
difficult to trace out by what Steps alphabetical Writing was invented; or is even some Presumption, that it is not a human Invention. [*OM* I, 288]

Hartley's excursus has brought him, wary, to the gap that separates the pictorial mark and the linguistic sign, the natural image
from "mere arbitrary Representatives" (*OM* I, 289). Alphabetical writing seems an unnecessary and inexplicable novelty that
has no origin in association and that cannot be reconciled with
the grand mechanical march to perfect pleasure.

Hartley fills the gap, as he must, with the only solution of
continuity that he has, the suggestion that the alphabet "is not a
human Invention": "I come now to the Art of alphabetical Writing. This I conjecture to have been communicated miraculously
by God to *Moses* at *Sinai,* for the following Reasons, which,
however, I do not judge to be decisive ones" (*OM* I, 308). The
moment almost evaporates in its telling. Hartley's uncertainty
directs us toward his undecisive reasons, but even those are
reasons why the origin of writing could not have occurred earlier or elsewhere, not, as we would expect, reasons how it could
possibly occur here.[12] No reasons are offered because there *is* no
reason for or to this sudden, providential intervention of God.
That intervention fills the breach between hieroglyphs and the
alphabet with yet another breach, for the necessity of God's

---

[12]Although Hartley does not mention it by name, in his insistence on the divine
institution of alphabetical writing he seems to be controverting William Warburton's *Divine Legation of Moses.* By bringing down "the general history of writing,
by a gradual and easy descent, from a PICTURE to a LETTER," Warburton
tends to efface both the disjunctions between hieroglyph and alphabet and between speech and writing necessary to an essentialist theory of language and a
developmental history of language. Warburton, who finds that the "easiest, and

historical manifestation violates God's eternal necessity. This solution of continuity solves nothing; we only exchange one inconsistency for another. From the moment of this revelation language may progress by the same mechanistic dynamics as the economy of pleasure and pain, but with this difference: God's awful instauration has forever infused the alphabet with the ambivalence that belongs to the sacred; we can never be sure of our control over a blessed machine.

Hartley's deployment of divine providence as the solution to the problem of language and history is a recourse within the argument to a position toward which the argument as a whole courses. We shall be freed from a dangerous "Partiality" only if "we take our Station in the Divine Nature, and view every thing from thence, and in the Relation which it bears to God" (*OM* II, 310). Yet though we cannot help ourselves except by imagining what the world must look like from God's point of view, in Hartley we are continually surprising a suspicion that the very nobility of that prospect achieved by our mortal imagination may mark a betrayal of the idea of divinity that ostensibly justifies it. Although the divine perspective is endorsed as the preferred alternative of two possible points of view from which to observe association, it operates in the text as the dramatization of the philosopher's all too human incapacity to adhere to a single, steady point of view—an incapacity that is expressed as the doubling of all possible points of view and is represented by the contradictions that beset the Hartleian decoder.

If, during his observation of the world, the philosophical decoder cannot, because of his partial perspective, help but conceive of himself as just outside of an analogical system which to be fully and meaningfully deciphered must be presumed to include his figure within its message, the appeal to an authoritative voice invokes a key that is both inside and outside the code, a privileged solution of continuity, like the Bible, which connects

---

most natural expression of the abstract conceptions of the mind, was by arbitrary marks," continuously asserts then subverts the distinctions between natural and arbitrary, literal and figurative, useful and ornamental—subordinating those distinctions to the manipulative ingenuity of those in power who maintained their positions by exercising the power of pen and paper (*The Divine Legation of Moses Demonstrated*, [Vols. I and II, 1738-41; Vol. III, 1758; 10th ed., London: 1846], II, 183, 181, and *passim*).

the analogical system with its principle and explains the observer's place in the meaningful whole. But under closer inquiry that solution of continuity changes into another articulation of the system which it would explain. Bereft of its privilege the key is transformed into the pretext for a series of metonymic transactions (Bible to Christ to, say, the Eucharist) which reflect rather than satisfy the desire for that infinitesimal elementary body that will finally unify the whole by incorporating the philosopher in the philosophy. If, contrarily, the decoder conceives of himself and everything else as necessarily within the system of the code, to determine whether or not he is in possession of the try key requires him to appeal to an authoritative voice that comprehends the system of which he is a part. But because that voice, like the authoritative voice of God on Sinai, comes to him *ab extra*, its confirmation that he possesses the true key is simultaneously a denial that everything is within the code. Moreover, if that voice were truly from the outside, truly *the* key, the authoritative voice, perhaps engraved on tablets of stone, would itself appear encoded—a metaphor of the problematics it would cancel.[13]

Hartley projects a God that is the ideal version of the observer, an ultimate quicksilver plating that could frame and reflect the whole of man. But under his earnest examination the deity turns out to be just another foreign intermixture which repeats in a sublime scale the embarrassing figure of the philosopher, who, though he presumably means well, finally means effectively only as the trope which turns doctrine into desire, which ramifies rational inconsistencies as fanciful inventions. Although he sketches in the modest, moral hope that a future inquirer will someday complete the picture, the draft Hartley leaves, only too accurate a depiction of the futility of *ut pictura philosophia*, prefigures a reader who, despite his gentle inclinations, will, earnest apostate, eventually turn away from the associationist easel and adopt a discourse that wills to represent the truth without paint.

---

[13]Cf. Warburton: "GOD, they say taught him [Moses] the use of *alphabetic* letters, in the exemplar of the two tables written, as the text assures us, *with the finger of GOD.* . . . A common reader would be apt to infer from it, that letters were now well known to the Israelites, as GOD had thought fit to deliver the first elements of their religion in that kind of writing" (p. 207).

# [ 2 ]

# Hartley's Influence
# on Coleridge

Homer sailing from Thebes to the Island *Ion*; being landed
and set down on the shore certain Fishermen passed by him—
What have you taken? What they had taken they had left behind them—what they had not taken they had with them!—
Homer pines away & dies, unable to understand this Epi-
gram—his Ghost appears to the Fishermen because they each
take no fish, they had gone & hanged themselves—&c.—

—Coleridge, *Notebooks*

I

Coleridge first mentions Hartley in a letter to his brother
George in November of 1794, where he reports that he has
conducted "a diligent, I *may* say, an intense study of Locke,
Hartley and others who have written most wisely on the Nature
of Man" (*CL* I, 126). Although Coleridge does not tell how long
this study has been going on or why it was undertaken, it seems
likely that he first read Hartley sometime between mid-June and
mid-August of that year, probably on the advice of his new
republican friend Robert Southey. Coleridge had read Burke
and Paine before meeting Southey at Oxford in June of 1794,
but Southey's familiarity with and ardent espousal of William
Godwin's *Enquiry Concerning Political Justice* and of Joseph Priestley's political writings opened for Coleridge a new realm of
thought and, above all, action. Southey's influence emerges in
Coleridge's first letter to him, in which Coleridge's enthusiasm,
already evident in his behavior at Cambridge during the trial of
William Frend for sedition of the church, finds a new key. He
salutes his friend with "health and Republicanism" and for the
first time mentions the "pure system of Pantocracy" [*sic*] (*CL* I,
83, 84), the utopian scheme that was to be the subject of much

[58]

hopeful discussion and acrimonious argument in the future. On July 8, Southey borrowed a copy of the first volume of Hartley's ostensibly apolitical *Observations on Man* from the Bristol Library.[1] We might possibly suppose that Southey was reading the book on Coleridge's recommendation, were it not that the available evidence, slim though it is, supports the contrary hypothesis.[2] In response to a letter (now lost) from Southey, Coleridge writes on July 13, "Your Letter, Southey! made me melancholy. Man is a bundle of Habits: but of all Habits the Habit of Despondence is the most pernicious to Virtue and Happiness. . . . Consider the high advantages which you possess in so eminent a degree—Health, Strength of Mind, and con- firmed *Habits* of strict Morality" (*CL* I, 85). The emphasis in his "sermonizing" that Coleridge places on "Habits" seems to be a response to concern expressed by Southey. That he had been reading Part One of *Observations on Man* might account for a certain despondency in regard to the necessary mechanism of association; that Coleridge had not yet read the book would account for his translation of "associations" into the more famil- iar, though non-Hartleian "Habits." By the time Coleridge met Southey again in Bristol in early August, Southey had with- drawn the second volume of *Observations on Man* from the library,[3] and Coleridge almost certainly devoted some of the visit to gaining a first-hand knowledge of Hartley's work.

That knowledge was quickly assimilated and surely applied. In the November letter to his brother George, Coleridge uses Hartley, here hitched to the unexceptionable Locke, as a foil to deflect his brother's evident nervousness regarding his political beliefs:

Solemnly, my Brother! I tell you—I am *not* a Dǝmocrat. I see evidently, that the present is *not* the *highest* state of Society, of which

[1]George Whalley, "The Bristol Library Borrowings of Southey and Coleridge, 1793-8," *The Library, Transactions of the Bibliographic Society*, fifth series, 4 (Sep- tember 1949), 118.

[2]Walter Jackson Bate guesses that Coleridge read Hartley at Cambridge in 1793-94 (*Coleridge* [1968; rpt. New York: Collier Books, 1973], p. 12), but as Ben Ross Schneider has conceded, there is no conclusive evidence that Hartley was part of the Cambridge curriculum. See *Wordsworth's Cambridge Education* (Cam- bridge: Cambridge University Press, 1957), 109 n.

[3]Whalley, "Library Borrowings," p. 118.

we are *capable*—And after a diligent, I *may* say, an intense study of Locke, Hartley and others who have written most wisely on the Nature of Man—I appear to myself to see the point of *possible* perfection at which the World may perhaps be destined to arrive— But how to lead Mankind from one point to the other is a process of such infinite Complexity, that in deep-felt humility I resign it to that Being—'Who shaketh the Earth out of her place and the pillars thereof tremble'—[']Who purifieth with Whirlwinds and maketh the Pestilence his Besom'—Who hath said—that [']Violence shall no more be heard of'—'the people shall not build and another inhabit—they shall not plant and another eat[']—[']The Wolf and the Lamb shall feed together!'—

I have been asked what is the best conceivable mode of meliorating Society—My Answer has been uniformly this—'Slavery is an Abomination to every feeling of the Head and Heart—Did Jesus teach the *Abolition* of it? NO! he taught those principles, of which the necessary *effect* was to abolish all Slavery. He prepared the *mind* for the reception before he poured the Blessing—['] You ask me what the friend of universal Equality *should* do—I answer—[']Talk not of Politics—*Preach the Gospel!*"[1]

That those fairly pacific opinions are intended for the ears of Coleridge's solemnly clerical brother does not necessaily make them less than candid. Although this is not the bold rhetoric Coleridge lavished on Southey, it is a strain that he would repeat before various audiences, and one that is both truer to Hartley and to his own deepest concerns than a radical *praxis*. Nevertheless, this is a peculiarly timid necessitarianism. Coleridge has, for example, qualified his assertion of perfectibility almost out of significance: "I appear to myself to see the point of *possible* perfection to which the World may perhaps be destined to arrive—." By hedging a doctrine where emphasis is all, the qualifications give the determined resignation the sense not of a necessitarian optimism but of a pietistic quietism. A similar ambiguity marks the exhortation to preach the Gospel—a

[1]*CL* I, 126. Although I have followed Griggs's punctuation of this passage, I think that the interpolation of the last two bracketed quotation marks (after "Blessing" and before "Talk") is an error. It is doubtful that George has asked his younger brother what a friend of universal equality should do. More likely, the entire passage from "Slavery" to "Gospel" is Coleridge's representation of a repeated conversation.

charge to action that floats loose of both political and philosophical context. What can preaching the Gospel mean? Whether or not the unsteady equilibrium between activity and passivity, politics and religion, derives immediately from Coleridge's soothing rhetorical intentions, it is evidently based on a complicated, if unvoiced, set of discriminations. If this be Hartleian associationism, it is a special breed.

A genetic metaphor fits Coleridge's use of Hartley's work because the Hartley that Coleridge knew was not a single argument but a pair of divergent editions: Joseph Priestley's 1775 version, *Hartley's Theory of the Human Mind;*[5] and the 1791 edition of *Observations on Man*, which was edited by David Hartley, Jr., and included as a third volume the "Notes and Additions to Dr. Hartley's Observations on Man by Herman Andrew Pistorius, Rector of Poseritz in the Island of Tugen, Translated from the German Edition, Printed at Rostok and Leipsig, 1772." Their substantial difference reflects a tension in Hartley that became Coleridge's own. When Priestley, who had earlier praised Hartley's work as "without exception, the most valuable production of the mind of man,"[6] published *Hartley's Theory of the Mind* he reprinted *Observations on Man* without the second volume, excepting the sections "relating to the mechanism of the mind," and with almost all references to vibrations deleted—all for the sake of making the work "more intelligible."[7] The intelligibility to which Priestley guides Hartley is a thoroughgoing materialism, which makes the ethical aspects of Hartley's doctrine superfluous but which heightens the political implications of the system—implications that Priestley not surprisingly interprets as radical, even revolutionary.[8] Pistorius, on the other hand, respects the whole of *Observations* but devotes his exegetical attention to the second volume. He appreciates Hartley's system as a

---

[5]*Hartley's Theory of the Human Mind. With essays relating to the subject of it* (London, 1775).
[6]See Priestley, *An Examination of Dr. Reid's Inquiry into the human mind on the principles of common sense. . .* , 2d ed. (London: J. Johnson, 1775), pp. 161-162.
[7]Priestley, *Hartley's Theory*, p. v.
[8]See Priestley, "A Sermon, Preached at the Gravel Pit Meeting in Hackney, February 28, 1794, with a Preface Containing the Reasons for the Author's Leaving England," in *Forms of Prayer, and Other Offices for the Use of Unitarians* (London, 1794).

theodicy which frames a necessary progress of the individual toward a self-annihilation that eventually recuperates all evil, including the inconsistencies of the system in which the progress is formulated.[9] Whereas Priestley uses Hartley to urge a political activism, the conservative Pistorius finds justification only for quietism. For the former everything that is is good, if not right; the latter insists that everything that is is right, if not good. Coleridge, the reader of Hartley in both these editions as well as in the original, read a Hartley which, contrary to its reputation for bland simplification, enfranchised uncertainty, divergence, vacillation, and even apostasy.[10]

II

Although Coleridge's proclamation "I am a compleat Necessitarian" is often cited as evidence of his conversion to Hartleian associationism, the passage is seldom referred to its context. At the end of a long, energetic letter to Southey in the winter of 1794, Coleridge writes,

> I am a compleat Necessitarian—and understand the subject as well almost as Hartley himself—but I go farther than Hartley and believe the corporeality of *thought*—namely, that it is motion—. Boyer thrashed Favell most cruelly the day before yesterday—I sent him the following Note of consolation.
>
> 'I condole with you on the unpleasant motions, to which a certain Uncouth Automaton has been mechanized; and am anxious to know the motives, that impinged on it's [sic] optic or auditory

[9]See *Observations on Man*, ed. David Hartley, Jr., III, 482-83, 557-58, and *passim*.
[10]Part of Coleridge's interest in the German commentary on Hartley, it should be mentioned, can be attributed to the fact that it *was* German. The text of Pistorius is perhaps the earliest contact Coleridge had with contemporary German philosophy. Pistorius places Hartley in an international context. In the course of illustrating Hartley's argument Pistorius mentions the names of Leibniz, Wolfe, Mendelssohn, Rautenberg, Hume, Bonnet, Clark, Baumgarten, Voltaire, Aristotle, Jortin, St. Augustine, Blackburne, Tollner, Burnet, Reimarus, Semler, and Michaelis—many of whom Coleridge knew little or nothing about in 1794, most of whom were subsequently important in his intellectual development. A note from December 1803 is evidence that Hartley's intellectual guidance endured: "Hartley Books to be read in the following order—[ . . . ] Weishaupt, Reimarus" (*CN* I, 1724).

8

nerves, so as to be communicated in such rude vibrations through the medullary substance of It's Brain, thence rolling their stormy Surges into the capillaments of it's Tongue, and the muscles of it's arm. The diseased Violence of It's thinking corporealities will, depend upon it, cure itself by exhaustion—In the mean time, I trust, that you have not been assimilated in degradation by losing the ataraxy of your Temper, and that the Necessity which dignified you by a Sentience of the Pain, has not lowered you by the accession of Anger or Resentment.' [*CL* I, 137-38]

Coleridge's note is meant to be humorous, included here to amuse Southey with a virtuoso rendition of associationist doctrine, and applied to a distressing incident in a manner designed to produce a sense of the grotesque. The humor of the letter does not, of course, constitute proof that Coleridge is joking about being a complete necessitarian, no more than the previous paragraph proves his sincerity. It does show, however, that even in the first flush of his enthusiasm for Hartley, Coleridge preserved a distance from his conviction that neither Hartley nor Priestley ever exhibited.

One could hardly hope to be alone in making such an obvious point, and other commentators have preceded me.[11] But despite scholarly precautions, the passage has not yet been entirely restored to its proper context. If we move backward through the letter, we find a poem that Coleridge has tossed up for Southey's delectation:

> If, while my Passion I impart
>     You deem my words untrue,
> O place your Hand upon my Heart—
>     Feel, how it throbs for *You*.
>
> Ah no!—reject the thoughtless Chain
>     In pity to your Lover!
> That thrilling Touch would aid the flame
>     It wishes to discover!
>
>              [*CL* I, 137]

[11]See J. A. Appleyard, *Coleridge's Philosophy of Literature* (Cambridge, Mass.: Harvard University Press, 1965), pp. 35-36, and Robert Penn Warren, "A Poem of Pure Imagination," *The Rime of the Ancient Mariner* (New York: Reynal and Hitchcock, 1946), p. 79.

That, immediately preceding the profession of a belief in the "corporeality of thought"! Might not that high flown phrase be an hyperbolic gloss on the association of the heart's throb with the soul's passion? But we need not halt here. One paragraph earlier, just after the transcription of one of Lamb's sonnets, Coleridge criticizes his friend's style, which he then compares, unfavorably, with his own; he then switches to humble qualification and closes with an "exception." Here is what Coleridge says of himself: "And I cannot write without a *body* of *thought*—hence my *Poetry* is crowded and sweats beneath a heavy burthen of Ideas and Imagery. It has seldom Ease—the little Song ending with 'I heav'd the—sigh for thee'! is an exception—and accordingly I like it the best of all, I ever wrote" (*CL*, I 137). One need not be a Hartleian to see the resemblance between "body of thought" and "corporeality of thought," nor to agree that the transition from the former to the latter may owe as much to association of ideas as to any sudden wish to communicate a philosophical conversion.

To call this movement "associative" does not require us to abandon any reasonable motive or organizing principle, however. One aim immediately suggests itself: each brief performance—critical, poetic, philosophical—is directed toward Southey; all are pretexts for the rhetorical aim of moving him, whether to amusement or admiration; each performance fits into the context of amicable self-display that was a constant in their relationship from the beginning. The Hartleian element makes particular sense if we accept the reconstruction that Coleridge's first encounter with Hartley was inspired by Southey: Coleridge has appropriated the philosopher to whom the younger Southey had introduced him and has surpassed his friend with an offhand dexterity. This reconstruction does not prove that Coleridge did not completely believe what he was saying; it only admonishes us to keep our distance. When, two days before this letter, Coleridge defended to Southey his irregular behavior toward the matrimonial Sara Fricker, he remarked that in their previous relations he may have "mistaken the ebullience of *schematism* for affection" (*CL* I, 132). Perhaps it would be fair to say that in his early relationship with Southey, Coleridge was too liable to mistake the ebullience of affection for schematism.

As Southey continued to draw Coleridge closer to a match

with Sara, Coleridge countered by multiplying his efforts to engage his friend in a more abstract commitment. Later in December he writes, "I would ardently, that you were a Necessitarian—and (believing in an all-loving Omnipotence) an Optimist" (*CL* I, 145). It was probably in answer to a comment such as this that Southey forwarded the definition of an optimist that Coleridge penned in his notebook: "Optimist—by having no will but the will of Heaven, we call in Omnipotence to fight our battles!—" (*CN* I, 22).[12]

Early in 1795, Bristol became the new front in the continuing crusade of the young pantisocrats. There Coleridge and Southey delivered a series of lectures on political, religious, and historical topics, one aim of which was to raise money for the American venture.[13] Coleridge inaugurated the series with three political lectures, which were given in late January and early February.[14] Although the published texts of those lectures are equivocal enough to warrant almost any political interpretation of them (a potential that Coleridge himself later exploited), their delivery seems to have been quite another matter. At the time a writer for *The Observer* remarked admiringly of Coleridge's performance: "Undaunted by the storms of popular prejudice, unswayed by magisterial influence, he spoke in public what none had the courage in this City to do before,—he told Men that they have Rights."[15] Although not speaking extempore, Coleridge found that it is often of more immediate oratorical advantage to surrender to the inspiration of the moment than to rely on a prepared text or to await the more deliberate workings of omnipotence. His ebullience frequently overcame his prudence, and though, as he later claimed, he might never have been altogether a Jacobin, in the passion of his oratory it was, as he

---

[12]The attribution of this phrase to Southey is made by the editor, Kathleen Coburn, p. 22 n.

[13]The texts of Coleridge's "Lectures on Revealed Religion" (hereafter LRR) are in *Lectures 1795: On Politics and Religion*, ed. Lewis Patton and Peter Mann, Vol. I of the *Collected Works* (Princeton: Princeton University Press, 1971). My comments on the background, circumstances, and chronology of the lectures are derived from the introduction, pp. xxiii-lxxx.

[14]The first lecture was published at the end of February as *A Moral and Political Lecture*. The latter two compose *Conciones ad Populum, or Addresses to the People*, published in November of 1795. See *LRR*, 2 and 22-23.

[15]*The Observer. Part 1st. Being a Transient Glance at about Forty Youths of Bristol* (Summer 1795). Quoted in *LRR*, xxi.

[65]

admitted, possible to mistake him for one. In 1803 he recalls the passion in the course of once again correcting the mistake:

> What wonder then, if in the heat of grateful affection & the unguarded Desire of sympathizing with those who so kindly sympathized with me, I too often deviated from my own Principles? And tho' I detested Revolutions in my calmer moments, as attempts, that were necessarily baffled & made blood-horrible by the very causes, which could alone justify Revolutions (I mean, the ignorance, superstition, profligacy, & vindictive passions, which are natural effects of Despotism & false Religion)—and tho' even to extravagance I always supported the Doctrine of absolute unequivocal non-resistance—yet with an ebullient Fancy, a flowing Utterance, a light & dancing Heart, & a disposition to catch fire by the very rapidity of my own motion, & to speak vehemently from mere verbal associations, choosing sentences & sentiments for the very reason, that would have made me recoil with a dying away of the Heart & an unutterable Horror from the actions expressed in such sentences & sentiments—namely because they were wild, & original, & vehement & fantastic! I aided the Jacobins, by witty sarcasms & subtle reasonings & declamations full of genuine feeling against all Rulers & against all established Forms—.! [*CL* II, 1000-1001]

Coleridge evidently discovered that in public speaking as in public policy omnipotent Reason bowed before "blood-horrible" rhetoric, which dissolved all distinctions and subverted all principles in the revolutionary surge of "mere verbal associations." Coleridge would eventually "recoil with a dying away of the Heart & an utterable Horror" from his revolutionary excess, as he would eventually attempt to impose a sovereign control on the republican "ebullient Fancy" and "mere verbal association," but despite his efforts at repression, he was never able to preserve his principles from the tempting extravagance of a "Jacobin" rhetoric.

Coleridge's political lectures were prematurely terminated by what he later called "the persecutions of Darkness" (*CL* I, 155).[16] Southey followed with twelve or thirteen historical lectures in

---

[16]*LRR*, xxxii. The editors note that the deterrent was probably "the refusal of innkeepers and other owners of public rooms to lease them to anti-Government speakers."

March and April, lectures (never published) which were not immediately connected to contemporary political subjects. Coleridge himself returned to the lists in late May and early June, but his subject had changed. In the first series he had aggressively advanced his principles against all forms of unreasonable despotisms; in the second series he is primarily concerned with discriminating radicalisms. The major distinction he observes is between a pernicious atheistic (or deistic) radicalism and one founded on the benevolent principles of Unitarian Christianity; and his six lectures comprise both a defense of the authenticity of revealed religion and an application of it to the social issues of the day. Although there are many sources for Coleridge's argument, it seems clear that, as Peter Mann says, the Hartleian "doctrines of necessity and of the association of ideas together constituted the greatest single influence upon his thinking and had repercussions, as the Lectures on Revealed Religion make clear, upon many of his political as well as his religious attitudes."[17] The Hartleian influence is particularly strong in lectures one and three. In the first Coleridge adapts Hartley and Pistorius to argue that the direct intervention of God in human affairs was necessary, a proof of His very existence, and evidence that all things have been progressively ordered to man's greatest good. Employing Hartley's rebuttal of Humean skepticism, he conducts a defense of the possibility of biblical miracles, which is, ultimately, a defense of revelation itself.[18] Coleridge concludes the lecture with the Hartleian argument that the Bible must be the genuine record of God's divine intervention because it "is morally impossible, that so gross a forgery could have been received by a People [the Jews] whom we know from profane as well as sacred Historians to have been superstitiously jealous of their Traditions & Ceremonies."[19]

In lecture three, Coleridge adapts to the New Testament the

---

[17]*LRR*, lix.

[18]*LRR*, 112. It may seem that a defense of miracles is inconsistent with Hartley's denial of a particular providence, and that such a defense is a gross breach of logic for a necessitarian. On the contrary, the defense of miracles is part of the defense of the unity of the design of the Bible, which is a defense of the necessary unity of all phenomena: miracles are simply data that must be explained. The biblical miracles are part of a *general* providence, and they may only seem to be miraculous because of our ignorance of all the laws of matter. See *OM* II, 144.

[19]*LRR*, 118 and n. 1. Cf. *OM* II, proposition XX, 84ff.

argument he has already applied to the Mosaic dispensation, contending that the indubitable moral superiority of Christ as the Gospels represent him is miraculous proof that the messiah has arrived and a lesser miracle than the attribution of Christianity's spiritual triumph to the craft of forgers and liars. By means of the Hartleian precedent Coleridge endeavors to establish that Christian revelation is essential to the progressivist scheme avowed by all radicals, theists and atheists alike, since only the miracle of Christ indisputably instantiates the progress of the soul from a base sensuality to a love of neighbor and, through association, to a disinterested love of God.[20]

The evidence of the Lectures on Revealed Religion allows us to conclude that in 1795 Coleridge was a Hartleian. The assurance of a benevolent progress furnished him with the grounds for a fervent political optimism. That this progress begins, ends, and continually depends on the providence of the deity enables him to bind his ardent political convictions to an impeccable piety. The evidence also shows that Coleridge's Hartleianism in 1795 was a coherent balance of both Priestley's and Pistorius's versions. Coleridge has gone past Hartley to Unitarianism, but he does not profess materialism, nor is there any evidence of a belief in the "corporeality of thought." The blend can best be epitomized in the exhortation from the opening of lecture five, which echoes his remark to his brother six months before: "Go preach the Gospel to the Poor."[21] This New Testament phrase nicely balances the Christian radicalism of Priestley, who saw the universal preaching of the Gospel as a prelude to the Second Coming,[22] with the conservative quietism of Pistorius, who felt that the pious preaching of the Gospel was all that should be done to prepare man for his eternal (*not* temporal) estate. Such a balance could not be expected to last, however. Certainly the poor are always with us, but our notions of the Gospel and of ourselves as preachers are frail and all too changeable. We should be wary of taking too seriously Coleridge's ebullient optimism.

[20]*LRR*, 162.
[21]*LRR*, 195.
[22]Cf., for example, Priestley's remark in the Gravel Pit Sermon on the signs preceding the Second Coming: "Before this great event the gospel is to be preached to all the world" (pp. 20-21).

Southey took Coleridge seriously, or at least he pretended to
for his own purposes. And during the summer of 1795, it became obvious that Southey's purposes were increasingly divergent from those of his friend. The pattern of that divergence as
it is limned in Coleridge's mercurial letters shows that philosophical allegiances were not simply a matter of public posture
or disinterested argument for Coleridge but the pattern he used
to cut a figure which he then deployed in order to define himself
and determine his friends. By the summer the grand scheme of
pantisocracy had begun to unravel, largely because of Southey's
growing scruples and developing ambitions. By August Southey
had written that he was considering his prospects for a career in
the church. Coleridge wrote to him on the dereliction of principle such a career would mean, but concluded his sermon "disin-
terestedly" with the remark that "That Being, who is 'in will, in
deed, Impulse of all to all' whichever be your determination, will
make it ultimately the best—" (*CL* I, 159). This slapdash piety, a
benediction on the order of "your affectionate servant," became
a disputed text when Southey, having finally decided to abandon pantisocracy and embrace the bar, quoted it back to Coleridge as a blanket endorsement of whatever course he should
choose. We might anticipate Coleridge's response when to the
disappointment of discovering a bonded pantisocrat to be
pledged to the Temple is added the shock at finding his peri-
patetic friend become a sophist.

The two discoveries evoke different responses. When Coleridge wants to convince Southey that he knew all along his
comrade would stray, he moralizes along Hartleian lines: "We
commenced lecturing. Shortly after, you began to recede in your
conversation from those broad Principles, in which Pantisocracy
originated. I opposed you with vehemence: for I well knew that
no Notion on morality or its motives could be without consequences" (*CL* I, 164). To answer Southey's justification of himself,
which apparently exploited his friend's statement of necessitarian principles as a rationalization of his apostasy, Coleridge
veers into an entirely different tone:

> You quoted likewise the last sentence of my Letter to you, as a
> proof that I approved of your design—you *knew* that sentence to
> imply no more than the pious confidence of Optimism—However

wickedly you might act, God would make it ULTIMATELY the best—You *knew*, this was the meaning of it. I could find twenty Parallel passages in the Lectures—indeed such expressions applied to bad actions had become a habit of my Conversation—you had named, not unwittingly, Dr. Pangloss. And Heaven forbid, that I should not now have faith, that however foul your stream may run here, yet that it will filtrate & become pure in it's [*sic*] subterraneous Passage to the Ocean of Universal Redemption. [*CL* I, 168]

Coleridge accuses Southey of misprision, and he seems justified. But Southey has misread carefully, posing a necessitarian dilemma; and Coleridge's contortions reflect the subtle constraints placed on his intellectual movement. He recklessly separates a theoretical piety from a moral meaning. And his emphasis on "ultimately" nearly transcendentalizes it past human consequence: the ultimate referent of action has no bearing on the morality of motives and their immediate effects. As a result, the philosophical issues almost dissipate entirely: Coleridge's expressions are only a "habit of . . . Conversation"; he seems to embrace the disparaging charge of Panglossism. Characteristically, Coleridge's defense tends toward confession: he admits that his philosophical concern for ultimate consequences has always been subsidiary, secondary to the unstated bonds of immediate affection. But Coleridge snaps back to optimism with a rhetorical vengeance—truly calling omnipotence in to fight his battle. And in this flourish, the match for Southey's meanness, Coleridge, who has warped his principles to rhetorical advantage, becomes the mirror that reflects back on the sophist his own mottled image. Southey's misreading is like the well-placed chisel of a malicious stonecutter: Coleridge's solid position fissures erratically along the differences between sincere and mechanical language, intention and habit, immediate and ultimate, rhetorical and philosophical, meaning and implication, and so on. Those fissures spray out from the central split between Southey and Coleridge, an argument in which principles have become pretexts and the text has vanished. I have rendered the genesis of this split as a mistaking of the ebullience of affection for schematism, but there seems to be no such simple tradeoff between one thing and another. Southey's error lies in *taking* Coleridge's ebullience for any *thing* at all, be it republicanism, optimism, or pantisocratean aspheterism.

## III

The vicissitudes of Coleridge's relations with Southey baffle attempts to take Coleridge as a specific kind of Hartleian and epitomize the hazards awaiting generalizations regarding Hartley's influence on Coleridge's thought. The difficulty is partly textual. Most references to Hartley occur in Coleridge's letters, where his aims are mainly to amuse, to impress, to apologize, to educate, to supplicate—rarely to specify his philosophical premises and convictions. Hartley does serve a doctrinal purpose in "Religious Musings," however, where he appears in a footnote to the lines:

> Strong to believe whate'er of mystic good
> The Eternal dooms for His immortal sons
> From Hope and firmer Faith to perfect Love
> Attracted and absorbed: and centered there
> God only to behold, and know, and feel,
> Till by exclusive consciousness of God
> All self-annihilated it shall make
> God its identity: God all in all!
> We and our Father one!
>
> [37-45]

The mysticism apparently asserted in the verse is repudiated by the note, which urges the reader to see "this *demonstrated* by Hartley" and "likewise proved and freed from the charge of Mysticism, by Pistorius in his Notes and Additions to part second of Hartley on Man." It may be, as Richard Haven has argued, that the note represents Coleridge's attempt to substantiate mystical experience by the "empirical formulations of psychology,"[23] but what is at least as significant is the way the strain between text and note, poetic impulse and prosaic restraint, unsettles either a mystical or an empirical resolution of the lines, and

[23]"Coleridge, Hartley, and the Mystics," *Journal of the History of Ideas*, 20 (1959), 487.

[71]

foregrounds a reading process rather than a spiritual progress. The recent addition of the 1795 Lectures on Revealed Religion to the letters and notes, though it increases the evidence of Coleridge's early enthusiasm for association, does not justify generalizations regarding its depth. Coleridge appears strongly Hartleian in the lectures, but he also appears strongly republican and pantisocratean. The association of that associationism with politics, its highly rhetorical impulse, its echoes of the thoughts of a year before, its connection with a broken intimacy with Southey, suggest that this associationism is as likely the end of a "period" as the beginning of one. Even at the time Coleridge was preaching for pay; never again would he adopt the pretense of sermonizing to the poor. Surely, if Coleridge was ever seriously afflicted with a belief in Priestley's notion of the corporeality of thought, he was cured by the clarifying shock he describes in a letter to the Reverend John Edwards in March of 1796:

> Yesterday Mrs Coleridge miscarried—but without danger and with little pain. From the first fortnight of Pregnancy she has been so very ill with Fever, that she could afford no nourishment to the Thing which might have been a Newton or an Hartley—it had wasted & melted away.—I think the subject of Pregnancy the most obscure of all God's dispensations—it seems coercive against Immaterialism—it starts uneasy doubts respecting Immortality, & the pages which the Woman suffers, seem inexplicable in the system of optimism—Other pains are only friendly admonitions that we are not acting as Nature requires—but here are pains most horrible in consequences of having obeyed Nature. Quere—How is it that Dr Priestley is not an atheist?—He asserts in three different Places, that God not only *does*, but *is*, every thing.—But if God *be* every Thing, every Thing is God—: which is all, the Atheists assert—. An eating, drinking, lustful *God*—with no *unity* of *Consciousness*—these appear to me the unavoidable Inferences from his philosophy— Has Dr. Priestley [*sic*] forgotten that *Incomprehensibility* is as necessary an attribute of the First Cause, as Love, or Power, or Intelligence?—[*CL* I, 192-93][24]

---

[24]Coleridge was mistaken about the miscarriage. What Coleridge calls a "Thing" survived and was later christened "Hartley."

But this is an existential repudiation of Priestley's attempt to make Hartley and Hartley's God more intelligible, not a rejection or even a criticism of Hartley's *Observations*.

Part of the difficulty in determining Hartley's influence derives from the nature of the problem. First, as we have seen, there is the difficulty of deciding the text that Coleridge took as Hartley. Second, there is the problem of philosophical influence: do we say that Coleridge was a Hartleian if he says so candidly? sincerely? if he shows associationist elements in his poetry and prose? if he lived a Hartleian life? Answers to these questions depend on what philosophical prospect we choose from which to observe Coleridge—associationist or something else.

We might, with profit, consider the dispassionate summary of the evidence with which J. A. Appleyard closes his discussion of the relationship of Coleridge to Hartley:

> There is no difficulty gathering texts to show in a superficial way that Coleridge accepted the associationist doctrine in his early years. To Mary Evans he writes, explaining how completely she has become the object of his reveries: "My associations were irrevocably formed and your Image was blessed with every idea." To Thelwall, on the comparative sublimity of classical and Christian myths: "the difference in our tastes it would not be difficult to account for from the different feelings which we have associated with these ideas." In criticizing a poem of Southey's to him: "You, I doubt not, have associated feelings dear to you with the ideas . . . and therefore do right in retaining them." Again: "As to Harmony, it is all *associa-tion*—Milton is *harmonious* to me, and I absolutely nauseate Darwin's Poem." But this aspect of Hartley's system never interested him as much as its ethical and religious principles.[25]

Although Appleyard's opinion of the superficiality of the policy of extracting "association" from Coleridge's time-tempered

[25]Appleyard, *Coleridge's Philosophy*, pp. 36-37. The quotations are from *CL* I, 130, 281, 190, and 216. To this list ought to be added Coleridge's defense of "Religious Musings" against criticisms by John Thelwall in 1796: "*Some for each* is my Motto,—that Poetry pleases which interests—*my* religious poetry interests the *religious*, who read it with rapture—why? because it awakes in them all the associations connected with a love of future existence &c—" (*CL* I, 205). That rhetorical aim is a good way off from any mystical pretensions.

correspondence and his caution not to take too seriously (with a Southeian earnestness) Coleridge's acceptance of the doctrine of association are valuable, they do not necessarily disprove the importance of Hartley's influence.[26] One of Appleyard's aims is to distinguish the respectable tradition of responsible Aristotelian association from Hartley's parochial excess.[27] Although this corresponds to Coleridge's own tactic in the *Biographia Literaria,* there is no evidence that he had made that distinction in those terms before writing that book.[28] In fact, what evidence we have suggests the opposite: Coleridge firmly identified a mechanical, necessitarian associationism with Hartley and considered any earlier formulation of the doctrine as merely an anticipation. In one of his 1801 letters to Josiah Wedgwood on Locke, letters written only a few months before he will proclaim his "overthrow" of association, Coleridge states his conception of philosophical influence with vehement clarity:

> Ask what Locke did, & you will be told, if I mistake not, that he overthrew the Notion, generally held before his time, of innate Ideas, and deduced all our knowledge from experience. Were it generally known, that these Innate Ideas were Men of Straw, or scarcely so much as that—and that the whole of Mr. Locke's first Book is a jumble of Truisms, Calumnies, and Misrepresentations, I suspect, that we should give the name of Newton a more worthy associate—instead of Locke & Newton we should say, BACON & NEWTON, or still better perhaps, Newton and Hartley. Neither N. or H. discovered the *Law,* nor that it was a Law; but both taught & *first* taught, the way to *apply* it universally. Kepler (aye, and Des Cartes too) had done much more for Newton, than Hobbes had done for Hartley/even were it all true which it has been fashionable of late to believe of Hobbes. [*CL* II, 686]

[26] Appleyard was unaware of the contents of the Lectures on Revealed Religion when he wrote his book. His generalization is disputed in the introduction to *LRR* (lx).
[27] Cf. Appleyard, *Coleridge's Philosophy,* p. 36.
[28] Even in the *Biographia* Coleridge requires the words of J. G. E. Maass from *Versuch über die Einbildungskraft* to make the distinction. Although the differences between Aristotelian and Hartleian association are significant, Coleridge was not always sensitive to such differences except in the course of a polemic against a foe who ignored them. Otherwise, he tended to think synecdochically: one associationist standing for all.

We should also keep in mind that this is the same letter in which Coleridge describes Descartes as "the Predecessor of Hartley" (*CL* II, 689). In part, his extravagant evaluation of Hartley simply fuels Coleridge's vilification of Locke, but we must note that Hartley *is* lauded (he rises above Newton and Descartes) and that the praise includes both the recognition and rejection of claims of determinate Hobbesian influence. Aristotle is not mentioned. For Coleridge, to say association is to imply Hartley.

That dictum cannot be neatly reversed, however, for though association is Hartley, Hartley is not merely association but the law applied universally to all fields of human enterprise and aspiration. Coleridge retained Hartley high in his affections because he had dedicated himself to the candid demonstration that a single law could harmonize all phenomena. In this policy of reconciliation—outside with inside, philosophy with religion, head with heart—Hartley earned his title as the "great master of *Christian* Philosophy" (*CL* I, 236), and it is in this respect that Coleridge's relation to Hartley cannot be limited to a specific psychology.

Although hardly the sole influence on Coleridge's thought, Hartley is as important as any other intellectual influence in Coleridge's career—both as proponent of a particular philosophy and as the emblem of a way of philosophizing. Those who dismiss Hartley do so either out of allegiance to a highly problematic notion of progress in Coleridge's career or because of an interest in establishing the claims of a philosopher other than Hartley as *the* dominant influence on Coleridge.[29] Such motives

---

[29]Appleyard, who argues for Coleridge's progress toward Berkelianism, has both motives. His attribution to Berkeley of the source of Coleridge's "belief in the unity of man with the natural world and with God" (p. 46) is dismissed by G. N. G. Orsini, who regards the belief as an unphilosophical sentiment, "little more than a form of words" (*Coleridge and German Idealism* [Carbondale, Ill.: Southern Illinois University Press, 1969], p. 32). Although Orsini accepts Appleyard's claim that Coleridge derived his notion of nature as the "Divine Visual Language from Berkeley's *Alciphron*" (Orsini, p. 32; Appleyard, p. 49), the same analogy, implicit in Hartley, can be tracked back to Bonaventure's *Itenarium Mentis ad Deum* (Robert Marsh, *Four Dialectical Theories of Poetry*, p. 97 and n. 29). Cf. also *LRR*, 94-95 and n. 3. Further indirect evidence of the error in seeking an exclusive link with Berkeley on this point occurs in one of Coleridge's many polemical groupings of philosophers: "the three greatest, nay only three great Metaphysicians which this country *has* produced, B. B & H." A canceled sentence in the MS reveals that Coleridge meant Berkeley, Joseph Butler, and Hartley (*CL*

are understandable; they recapitulate the very reasons for which Coleridge tried again and again to dismiss Hartley and the doctrine of the association of ideas. He too was committed to a *mythos* of progress in philosophy and in his own philosophical career. That the overthrow of Hartley became vital to Coleridge's sense of progress does not, however, license the presumption that it occurred.

## IV

Coleridge's claim to have overthrown Hartleian association appears in a March 1801 letter to Thomas Poole:

> The interval since my last Letter has been filled up by me in the most intense Study. If I do not greatly delude myself, I have not only completely extricated the notions of Time, and Space; but have overthrown the doctrine of Association, as taught by Hartley, and with it all the irreligious metaphysics of modern Infidels— especially, the doctrine of Necessity.—This I have *done*; but I trust, that I am about to do more—namely, that I shall be able to evolve all the five senses, that is to deduce them from *one sense*, & to state their growth, & the causes of their difference—& in this evolvement to solve the process of Life & Consciousness.—I write this to you only; & I pray you, mention what I have written to no one.—At Wordsworth's advice I have intermitted the pursuit—the intensity of thought, & the multitude of minute experiments with Light & Figure, have made me so nervous & feverish, that I cannot sleep as long as I ought & have been used to do. . . . [*CL* II, 706-7]

---

II, 703 and n. 2). One ordering principle of that ostensibly eccentric cluster is that all saw nature as the divine language, analogous to the words of the Bible.

Thomas McFarland's *Coleridge and the Pantheist Tradition* contains an impressive criticism of the naive notion of philosophical progress (pp. 161-63), yet McFarland also overstates his version of influence. Fiercely committed to the paradigmatic importance of Spinoza and Spinozism for Coleridge, he presses too hard on too little evidence a claim for the empirical influence of Spinoza. McFarland strains to subdue the fact that Coleridge had practically nothing to say about Spinoza until 1801.

Most recently, in *Coleridge the Moralist* (Ithaca, N.Y.: Cornell University Press, 1977), Laurence Lockridge, intent on demonstrating Coleridge's "Romantic humanism," largely ignores Hartley, advancing instead the thesis that Joseph Butler is Coleridge's most direct influence in the liberal tradition—a claim based on "an unpublished and never delivered sermon of 1799" (p. 213).

These are large claims, though they are made in a manner at once both excited and oddly tentative. If the tentativeness directs attention to the coherence of the assertions, it becomes apparent that the passage lacks two important items: (1) the reasoning or evidence that overthrows association and (2) mention of Kant. Those omissions are almost certainly connected. Coleridge does mention Kant later in the letter, when he projects "a work on the originality & merits of Locke, Hobbes, & Hume," which will demonstrate his "attentive Perusal of the works of [his] Predecessors from Aristotle to Kant" (*CL* II, 707), and he had earlier referred to his study of Kant in a February letter to Poole announcing the letters on Locke, of which Poole received copies (*CL* II, 675-76). The arguments of those letters rely little on Kant, however; besides the insistent awarding of the philosopher's laurel to Hartley, they are so unKantian as to employ an associationist critique of Locke.[30] Yet here, he speaks of the instrumental extrication of the "notions of Time, and Space," a feat of unmistakably Kantian prowess,[31] though stated with baffling obscurity.

The first explanation of the obscurity regarding Kant is that Coleridge, just beginning his study of the German philosopher, was unsure of the full implications of Kant's critique. The second, and more important explanation is that Kantian metaphysics had not yet entirely been disengaged from British empirics. The announced overthrow was still underway.

That such is the case is demonstrated by the notation of a remarkable experiment that Coleridge performed with his son Hartley on the day following the letter to Poole:

> March 17, 1801. Tuesday—Hartley looking out of my study window fixed his eyes steadily & for some time on the opposite prospect, & then said—Will yon Mountains *always* be?—I shewed him the whole magnificent Prospect in a Looking Glass, and held it up, so that the whole was like a Canopy or Ceiling over his head, & he struggled to express himself concerning the Difference between the Thing & the Image almost with convulsive Effort.—I never before saw such an abstract of *Thinking* as a pure act & energy, of *Thinking* as distinguished from *Thoughts*. [*CN* I, 923]

[30]See *CL* II, 694-95.
[31]Orsini, *Coleridge and German Idealism*, p. 48.

Coleridge chooses a startling means of answering Hartley's question, which seems only to ask innocently, "Will what I see out there ever change?" Coleridge does not so much answer the question as overpower it, when, like a mute impresario of experience, he positions his mirror and, a distant deity, observes what father hath wrought. This at first sight. But look again. We have the tranquil setting: the child is looking steadily at the steady mountains. This is a stable epistemological symmetry: a fixed percipient joined to the fixed perceived. *"And then"* Hartley asks a question charged with instability: "Will yon Mountains *always* be?" Where does this question about unfixing, a question in itself an unfixing of the fixed symmetry, come from? It emerges from and marks the "and-thenness" of the boy's own mind, the temporal difference that articulates the steadiest gaze. That mental difference designates a difference between the changing inside and the changeless outside, which, in turn, emerges as the ambiguous question of a possible analogous difference (like the difference within, like the unfixing of the perceptual symmetry) occurring in the thing outside. The "and-thenness" of consciousness interrupts the apparently innocent moment of fixed perception as an intuition of temporality, which, projected, charges even the everlasting mountains with uncertainty. The "intuition" lacks any content; it does not *tell* the youth, "Remember Hartley, thou art mortal"—rather it is the interruption (formal, structural) itself that gestures toward temporality. The interruption, the unfixedness, is before words, before an intuition can be made. In the same way the temporal difference is not really *inside* the child's mind because the temporal difference occurs only as the *inside* of the mind discovers its interiority in the difference from exteriority. We can claim to be following Coleridge here, for his answer to his son's question retraces that projection, compels the child to introject the difference he has naively supposed, and makes innocence know its own, altogether human duplicity. The "magnificent prospect" in the looking glass doubles the scene. The action makes a difference in the mountains, but because it is a difference without a change, it cannot be ascribed to an alteration in the *being* of the mountains. As with the emergence of Hartley's "and then" the difference must be attributed to the percipient, not the perceived. But, as Hartley's struggles show, there is no difference in perception of the thing or the image: otherwise there would be words to express the difference. There *is*, however, something that makes the perceiving mind different from its perception, that is, some mental activity besides a perceiving, which merely stands in a fixed and passive relation to perceptions. The determinant difference, then, is within the percipient, between something that can be expressed because perceived and something that cannot be expressed because it is prior to perceiving. Note that it cannot be *expressed*. The difference is represented by Hartley, the philosopher, as the vital difference that God's appearance on Mt. Sinai makes, which is indicated but not expressed (communicated, told) by those sublime ambiguities, the Ten Commandments. Here that inexpressible, decertaintizing something is called *"Thinking,"* which is the prior, essentially human activity that differentiates man from object and, insofar as it unfixes perception by introducing a dislocating "and then," differentiates the mind itself. This thinking may be, we may want to call it, we may wish it were, a "pure act & energy," but that metaphorical label is only an "abstract" image of the imageless; it might as well be called "struggle" or "convulsion" because it can only be isolated as an unfixing that occurs between the mind and something else, and within the mind "itself" as always "something else."[32] The mountains will not always be because nothing *is* except a thinking that can only be traced in its conceptual difference from all other acts of mind and in its temporal difference from itself. We know it only as an equivocal interruption of associative perception; we hypopoeticize it as the ego.

Suppose, however, that thinking *has* been established as "pure act & energy." The next move would be to reconstitute all knowledge and perception from this autonomous foundation. That move, connecting the pure world of thinking to the world of causation, is projected by Coleridge in the letter to Poole: "I shall

---

[32]The pure act, which manifests itself in an almost convulsive paralysis of action may be compared to the pure will, which manifests itself in sin. As A. O. Lovejoy observes in "Coleridge and Kant's Two Worlds," "All the noumenal egos . . . are *bad* egos" (*Essays in the History of Ideas* [Baltimore: The Johns Hopkins University Press, 1948], p. 279.

[79]

be able to evolve all the five senses, that is, to deduce them from *one sense*, & to state their growth, & the causes of their difference—& in this evolvement to solve the process of Life & Consciousness." Once again Coleridge supplies the commentary for his text, in a notebook entry that follows the experiment with Hartley: "Babies touch *by taste* at first—then about 5 months old they go from the Palate to the hand—& are fond of feeling what they have taste [*sic*]— / Association of the Hand with the Taste—till the latter by itself recalls the former—& of course, with volition. March 24, 1801" (*CN* I, 924). In her note to this entry, Kathleen Coburn alludes to a similar opinion of Erasmus Darwin's, expressed in the chapter "Of Instinct" in *Zoonomia*, and she appropriately connects this entry with one from November 1800, where Coleridge observes that "Hart. seemed to learn to talk by touching his mother" (*CN* I, 838). To those entries may be added another: "A Babe who had never known greater cruelty than that of being snatched away by its mother for a half a moment from the nipple in order to be kissed" (*CN* I, 888). We should not be misled by the tone of this: no greater cruelty is still cruelty and constitutive of the infant's development. The conjunction of taste and touch in the oral grasp of the nipple is broken by the mother; and that differentiation precipitates the others: the discrimination of hand and mouth at five months, the touch/talking of the older child. That this necessary process of constructive development begins with a cruel pain (inflicted from outside) agrees with Hartley's model of an aboriginal pain that overcomes the natural vibrations, differentiates the foetal rhythm of the child, and leads to the development of the human faculties. Although Coleridge's observation registers an advance in his professed aim of deducing the five senses from the one, the continuity he derives owes as much to the operation by which the senses are differentiated as to any discovered property of the senses themselves—and that operation, completely independent of any "thinking," is Hartleian association, predetermined right down to the generation of volition as a consequence of the "sufficient Repetition of the proper Associations" (*OM* I, 105). To read this back into the letter to Poole is to realize that, despite the vague implication that the deduction of the five senses from one has something to do with the extrication of

[80]

space and time, Coleridge not only fails to connect his two worlds, his theory of evolvement undermines the overthrow of association in the very assertion of it.

It has puzzled some hard-line adherents of the overthrow-of-association reading of Coleridge that he would, even after (considerably after) his supposed triumph, advise Godwin in 1803 of a project baldly inconsistent with the implications of that usurpation: "A friend of mine [William Hazlitt], every way calculated by his Taste & prior Studies for such a work is willing to abridge & systematize that work [Abraham Tucker's *The Light of Nature Pursued*] from 8 to 2 Vol. . . . I would prefix to it an Essay containing the whole substance of the first Volume of Hartley, entirely defecated from all corpuscular hypotheses—with new illustrations—& give my name to the Essay" (*CL* II, 949). The to-be-defecated "corpuscular hypothesis" is "all the nonsense of vibrations," which Coleridge had already dismissed in an 1800 letter to Godwin (*CL* I, 626). The planned essay would be a duplication of Priestley's edition of Hartley, unless the "illustrations" were meant to distinguish Coleridge's contribution. If we consider the entries regarding the deduction of five senses from one as plausible illustrations, we can see that they make Coleridge's plan coherent. Hartley's model of the development of the senses depended on the vibrations following a steady line of direction in the brain and automatically activating the correspondent motor nerves. "After a sufficient Repetition of the motory Vibrations which concur in this Action, their Vibratiuncles are generated, and associated strongly with other Vibrations or Vibratiuncles" (*OM* I, 104-5). After that, association takes over. By postulating a single original sense (like Freud's later postulate of the aboriginal monad of primary narcissism) capable of being differentiated through association, Coleridge could efficiently defecate the corpuscular hypothesis and maintain the substance of Hartley's theory.

Doubtless in the famous letter to Poole, Coleridge reveals a will to overthrow Hartleian associationism and necessitarianism, just as he asserts a determination to "immediately publish by CHRISTABEL, with two essays annexed to it, on the Praeternatural—and on Metre" (*CL* I, 707). But, as Coleridge himself observed, "a strong wish often imposes itself on the mind for an

[81]

actual power."³³ Neither the refutation nor the publication was executed until much later; neither project was ever completed. Coleridge could safely profess his powers to Poole because he was consistently Coleridge's good conscience, sympathetic to both aspirations and failures.³⁴ That this project was even less certain than most can be ascertained by Coleridge's nervous request that Poole should not publicize the news of his breakthrough.

Both Coleridge's wish for an overthrow of association and his failure to effect it are attested to by the series of refutations which he undertook at various times between 1801 and the writing of the epochal chapters in the *Biographia*. In 1803 he begins a long letter to Southey with this rebuttal of Hartley:

> I hold, that association depends in a much greater degree on the recurrence of resembling states of Feeling, than on Trains of Ideas/ that the recollection of early childhood in latest old age depends on, & is explicable by this—& if this be true, Hartley's System totters—If I were asked, how it is that very old People remember *visually* only the events of early childhood—& remember the intervening Spaces either not at all, or only verbally—I should think it a perfectly philosophical answer / that old age remembers childhood by becoming 'a second childhood.' This explanation will derive some additional value if you would look into Hartley's solution of the phaenomena / how flat, how wretched!—Believe me, Southey! a metaphysical Solution that does not instantly *tell* for something in the Heart, is grievously to be suspected as apocry[p]hal. I almost think, that Ideas *never* recall Ideas, as far as they are Ideas—any more than Leaves in a forest create each other's motion—the Breeze it is that runs thro' them / , it is the Soul, the state of Feeling—. If I said, no *one* Idea ever recalls another, I am confident that I could support the assertion. [*CL* II, 961]

³³*The Friend*, p. 31.
³⁴Elsewhere Coleridge blessed Poole for his steadfast refusal to succumb to the seduction of Coleridge's necessitarian arguments: "I love and honour you, Poole! for many things—scarcely for anything more than that, trusting firmly in the Rectitude & simplicity of your own Heart, and listening with faith to its revealing Voice, you never suffered my Subtlety or any Eloquence to proselyte you to the pernicious Doctrine of Necessity / all praise to the Great Being who has graciously enabled me to find my way out of that labyrinth—Den of Sophistry, &, I would fain believe, to bring a better clue than has hitherto been known to enable others to do the same" (*CL* II, 1037).

That this is "the mature expression of the rejection of the association mechanism and the substitution for it of a ground of feeling"[35] is an opinion hard to credit. There is no positive substitution here, only a change of emphasis from ideas to feeling. The mechanism remains the same whatever the shift in the supposed ground. As for this being a mature statement, one finds the closest analogy to it in the "immature" imagery of the "Aeolian Harp," which is contemporary with the Hartleian *Religious Musings*:

> And what if all of animated nature
> Be but organic Harps diversely fram'd
> That tremble into thought, as o'er them sweeps
> Plastic and vast, one intellectual breeze,
> At once the Soul of each, and God of all?
>
> [44–48]

The difference between the two views parallels the distinction that Coleridge is explaining to Southey. In the "Aeolian Harp" passage, the stimulus to thought is an external cause, uniform for all minds. The "Breeze" or "state of Feeling" of which Coleridge writes to Southey is an individual state that stimulates and harmonizes the movement of the "Leaves" or the association of ideas. Similarly, the substance of the argument that Coleridge directs against Hartley in the letter above is a distinction between causes. That may be adequate as a preliminary criticism of a *single* law of association, but it does not endanger the doctrine of a *necessitarian* association.

Coleridge's quarrel with Hartley seems to depend on his increasing aversion to "the Little-ists" (*CL* II, 709)—a stance which involves a Kantian criticism of Hume's notion of sensation.[36] Yet Hartley does not seem mindful of Hume's argument and, despite some shared presuppositions regarding perception, is far from the Scot's skepticism. Hartley's analytic

---

[35]Appleyard, *Coleridge's Philosophy*, p. 58. He also helpfully cites (pp. 57-58) evidence of the transition from images to feelings as units of perception in Coleridge's thought. See *CL* I, 558, 511, and *CL* II, 709.

[36]"How opposite to nature & the fact to talk of the one *moment* of Hume; of our whole being an aggregate of successive sensations. Who ever *felt* a *single* sensation?" (*CN* II, 2370).

reduction of perceptions to letters ("*A, B, C, D, &c.*"), though it does designate discrete sensations, also suggests aggregates of like sensations and composite ideas of feelings. The major aim of his division of the necessary progress of man into thematic groupings, such as imagination and ambition, is to provide grounds for feeling; in the same way his struggle to establish the benevolence of God is an attempt to locate the ground of *all* feeling. One way to summarize Hartley's position in eighteenth-century English philosophy is to note that he sought to bring an epistemological elementarism into systematic balance with a moral and theological holism. Because Hartley subordinated his elementarism to a divinely ordained unity, Coleridge was at first able to admire him. Because Coleridge came to feel that Hartley's attempt at a balance not only failed but also endangered the moral and theological whole, he later denies Hartley. Coleridge's objection to Hartley's elementarism is, then, an important aspect of his response but only a partial one, both because of Hartley's aspiration to a higher unity and because a similar elementarism is characteristic of most British empiricists of the eighteenth century.[37]

Coleridge's rejections and refutations are repeated again and again. In a letter to Poole in 1804, in which he congratulates his friend on his staunch resistance to necessitarianism, Coleridge mentions his discovery of the "central Sophism" appearing in all the arguments on the subject, "viz. that all have hitherto, both the Necessitarians & their Antagonists, confounded two essentially different Things under one name—& in consequence of this Mistake the Victory has been always hollow in favor of the Necessitarians" (*CL* II, 1037). Although Coleridge once again

---

[37]The most trenchant account of elementarism and Coleridge's response to it remains that of M. H. Abrams in *The Mirror and the Lamp* (1953; rpt. New York: Norton Library, 1958), pp. 160 ff and 171 ff. As Abrams notes, the empiricists' (Hobbes, Locke, Hume, et al.) concern for discrete ideas led to the convenient abbreviation of all perceptions into what were "primarily, if not exclusively, visual images, replicas of the objects of sight. Coleridge," Abrams goes on to observe, "remarked acutely that the 'mechanical philosophy' insists on a world of mutually impenetrable objects because it suffers from a 'despotism of the eye'" (p. 160). Coleridge's remark regarding the "despotism of the eye" (*BL* I, 74) works well as a criticism of a tendency of all elementarist epistemology but less well as a refutation of the salient characteristic of Hartley's necessitarian psychology: the systematic implication of part and whole.

fails to specify what that sophism is, our speculation can be more assured in this than in other instances: by "two essentially different things," he must mean a caused volition and a free will. That is a Kantian distinction, however, and one which Coleridge had discovered some time before. Why the excitement? Because the crucial piece of evidence that Coleridge felt he needed with which to explode the sophism was not rational or even intuitive, but experimental. Eager to refute Hartley, anxious under the influence of the German philosophers, Coleridge seeks to enfranchise his own philosophical insight by observations that will empirically validate, or at least justify, his hypothesis of the autonomous, morally effective will.

A few days before his enigmatic remarks to Poole, Coleridge jotted this entry in his notebook:

> Of the intimate connection of Volition, and of the Feeling & Consciousness of Volition, on the state of the Skin, I have noticed long ago in a former Pocket-book. . . . My Speculations thence on double Touch, &c &c &c, and thence my Hope of making out a radical distinction between this Volition & Free Will or Arbitrement, & the detection of the Sophistry of the Necessitarians / as having arisen from confounding the two.—Sea sickness, the Eye on the Stomach, the Stomach on the Eye / Eye + Stomach + Skin—Scratching & ever after in certain affections of the Skin, milder than those which provoke Scratching a restlessness for double Touch/Dalliance, & at its height, necessity of Fruition.—Fruition the intensest single Touch, &c &c &c; but I am bound to trace the Ministery of the Lowest to the Highest, of all things to Good / and the presence of a certain Abstract or Generical Idea, in the Top, Bottom, & Middle of each Genus. [CN I, 1827]

The distinction between double and single touch, although evidently important, is very obscure. Coburn's note to the passage helpfully directs us to the perceptual experiments of Thomas Wedgwood,[38] one of Coleridge's benefactors, and an active scientific researcher, who shared with Coleridge a keen interest

[38]CN I, 1827 n. Wedgwood's notes were published as "An Enquiry into the Origin of our Notion of Distance" in the *Quarterly Journal of Science and Arts*, vol. 3. They are reproduced in Eliza Meteyard, *A Group of Englishmen* (London: Longmans, Green, 1872), pp. 395-406, from which I quote.

in the problems of perception, and whose notes on the origin of
the notion of distance give us a perspective on the concept of
double touch and suggest how it could be of use to Coleridge.[39]

Wedgwood disputes Berkeley's contention that "the eye per-
ceives only length and breadth, not depth or distance, from
itself." Depth, Berkeley thought, is acquired only by the addition
of the sense of touch.[40] Wedgwood's own experiments prove,
however, that touch is incompetent for the ends to which Berkeley wants to assign it: touch can readily be deceived as to distance; certainty depends on the eye.

On the same principle depends the common experiment of a body
seeming double when felt in the angle of the tips of the first and
second finger crossed. A person is blindfolded and desired to
attend to the impression of touch from a body so placed: the bandage being removed, he is directed to look at his fingers while the
object is placed as before. He will say, that the first time he felt two
bodies at a distance from each other, and that now he feels only
one: in his prior experience, if similar sensations occurred on the
remote sides of those two fingers, they had always been occasioned
by the contact of two bodies; when the bandage was removed, and
he saw that there was but one, he immediately perceived that he
felt but one. As the sensations of touch from the same impressing
body must have been the same in both cases, the supposed difference in them must have been owing to some circumstance of vision:

[39]In his *Coleridge's Poetic Intelligence* (London: Macmillan, 1977), John Beer
theorizes that Coleridge's distinction between double and single touch was owed
to his reading Euler's *Letters to a German Princess* and his speculations on animal
magnetism (pp. 82-86). I find Beer's ingenious argument interesting but uncon-
vincing. He supplies too little evidence for Euler's influence and completely
ignores the precedent in Wedgwood. Beer's theorizing nonetheless leads him
into some fascinating comments on Coleridge's response to romance. Our divergence is on one of the most elusive areas of Coleridge's intellectual concern,
about which one can only be tentative, although, without doubt, recent use of the
phenomenon of touching-touched has been used as evidence for the impossibility of the perfect auto-affection on which transcendental self-reflection rests. See
Jacques Derrida, *Speech and Phenomena* (Evanston: Northwestern University
Press, 1973), pp. 78-79, and, esp., Maurice Merleau-Ponty, *The Visible and the
Invisible* (Evanston: Northwestern University Press, 1968), pp. 9, 254-57. Merleau-Ponty employs the phenomenon as evidence for the elemental chiasmic
activity of "mediation through reversal" (pp. 214-15; see also, pp. 130-55).
Rudolph Gasche cites Derrida and Merleau-Ponty in "Deconstruction as Criti-
cism," *GLYPH* 6 (Baltimore: The Johns Hopkins University Press, 1979), p. 185.

[40]Meteyard, *Group of Englishmen*, p. 395.

in the first case the experimenter was deceived by a visual idea; in the second he was rightly informed by a visual impression.[11]

This helps with Coleridge's note. Volition seems to be organically connected with the state of the skin and with the tactual, *outside* sense. It is, like touch, a mechanical and, on the whole, efficient way of dealing with the world. But the phenomenon of double touch shows that touch-volition by itself is liable to be deceived in its mechanical association and to fail to organize perceptions properly. The knowledge of that failure comes through the corrective supervention of the eye, which parallels the inner organization of the will. There is, then, a "radical distinction" between the associationist touch-volition and the organization of the eye-will.

The explanatory power of this scheme is inadequate for two reasons. First, the supervention of the free will occurs in everyday association as a break in that association: it is first a disorientation that subsequently reorients the mind in a new train of association. Here the supervention of the will (the eye) disturbs a deceit: interruption comes first; correction follows. When the blindfolded man recovers his sight, the associative train of double touch is instantaneously interrupted, and he is thrown into uncertainty; but when he says, "I now know my error," he actually means, "I now *see* my error"—a sign that the perceptual train of touch has already been replaced by that of the eye (subject to its own deceits? its own interruptions?). The Wedgwood structure corresponds to that which Coleridge discovered in his experiment with his son—with the substitution of will-volition for thinking-thought and touch-double touch for sight-double sight—except that the touch-double touch experiment includes a positive reorientation absent in the earlier experiment. We should not be deceived by that reorientation, however: it is finally only a shift in the organs of perception, the relocation of associative activity on another, as yet undisturbed level.

Second, the entire physical process of touch-double touch is merely an analogue for the will-volition relation. As it remains

[11]Ibid., pp. 397-98.

[87]

on the level of perceptions and physical response, the process can be no more than a metaphor for a relationship that extends beyond perception to the nonphysical conditions of perception. The difference between Wedgwood's and Coleridge's use of the experiments, then, is that Coleridge treats the results symbolically, as devices to endow metaphysical problems with "extraneity." For Coleridge, "Language & all *symbols* give *outness* to Thoughts/ & this the philosophical essence & purpose of Language/" (*CN* I, 1387); the perceptual observations and experiments compose a language that gives the metaphysical problem an "outness" instrumental in *forming* a solution. The problem, nevertheless, remains a metaphysical one: some thoughts, such as the notion of an autonomous will, have more *inness* than others. The embodiment of the problem, which is instrumental in forming a solution, prohibits the taking of a solution from the body. Symbolizing the problem in language, therefore, charges it with all the properties of language, particularly the flattening effect of linguistic circularity. The will can indeed be *worded,* but as Hartley's observations show, "it is difficult to explain Words to the Bottom by Words; perhaps impossible," and the "will" is one name for that which, one supposes, is at the bottom of words. At the moment of its concrete manifestation in symbols, the will is at its nearest approach (like the God who manifests himself in a supervention on the text of history), but also at its farthest remove.

The crux can be rescued from mere paradox by tracking Coleridge a little farther through the labyrinthine elaborations of his attempt to apply Wedgwood's distinction to "The Ministry of the Lowest to the Highest." In a later notebook entry he writes:

Touch—double touch/[1]Touch with the sense of immediate power [2]with retentive power—[3]retentive power extinguishing the sense of touch, or making it mere feeling—& the gradations preceding this extinction/[4]retentive power simply, as when I hold a thing with my Teeth/[5]with feeling not Touch in one part of the machinery, both in the other, as when I press a bit of sugar with my Tongue against my Palate/[6]with feeling & even touch but not specific stim*ulari* (esse sub stimulo) as when I hold a quill or bit of fruit by my lips—1. mem. vi/Riley. inacts of Es*sex.* 2. The Lips, or the thumb and forefinger in a silent pressure. 3. The Hand grasping firmly an inanimate Body—that is the one extreme of this third Class—the other would be a Lover's hand grasping the soft white hand of his mistress / Here the retentive power and nisus modify but not extinguish the Touch—it tells the story still & the mind listens to it.—[CN II, 2399]

This seems to be a tentative ranking of the organic faculties in an analogue to the categories of the understanding. As Coburn notes, the numerals (1) match with each other; she interprets mem. vi./Riley. inacts of Es*sex* to be a code for the *membrum virile*, the phallus. The ranking is from the highest to the lowest. The phallus is, for Coleridge, the erect penis in its figurative mode. It stands for (stands forth as) the union of the vital or personal with the organic or impersonal; it is the "mutually assimilant Junction" of "*Love* & Lust" (*CN* I, 1822). Hence the importance of the hierarchy and the analogy: the phallus unites the outside and the inside, free will *in* volition. Coleridge does not develop this argument, however. Of course, there are complex psychological reasons for his failure to do so, one symptom of which is his avoidance of naming the male organ except in code. But perhaps the difficulty can be more simply stated as a predicament in terms of the problem. Once the penis is figured as the phallus, it takes on a necessary life of its own; the reification is out of the figurer's control: he is impotent before his figure of potency. As an objectification of a philosophical problem, the supposed "mutually assimilant junction" is situated outside of the philosopher. The figurative phallus is different from the actual penis. Thus the paradox of an impotent potency. To show that this is Coleridge's fantasy and not my own, let me quote from the conclusion to the entry preceding 2399 a coded sentence that follows a Coleridgean revery on impotence: "Important metaphysical Hint the influence of bodily vigor and strong Grasp of Touch in facilitating the passion of Hope: 5, 21, 14, 21, 3, 8, 19—in all degrees even to the full 5, 14, 19, 8, 5, 1, 20, 8 ment and the 2, 15, 20, 8 at once." The coder as Coburn decodes him: "eunuchs—in all degrees even to the full ensheathement and the both at once" (*CN* II, 2398 and note; the code is a simple transposition of a numeral for each letter of the alphabet: 1 = A, 2 = B, etc.). Because Coleridge knew that it is possible to be a eunuch even to the full ensheathement, to be impotent in poten-

[89]

cy, the wishful symbolism of the phallus could only be a dead end.

Coleridge's criticism of association begins with the philosophical conviction that a mechanism functioning by necessary causes and necessary effects can have no ultimate moral meaning. That conviction entails the moral belief that a real moral meaning, grounded by an autonomous certainty, inheres in all human acts. The philosophical problem is to make that moral principle appear to the observing mind without compromising the autonomy of the principle. Structurally, the moral sense interrupts the apparently enclosed system that association describes. As we have seen in the experiments with Hartley and the Wedgwoodian double touch, the interruption shows that the normal perceptual faculties have gone wrong by mistaking one thing for another. In one instance the interruption results from the inconsistency of the associative process with itself. In the other, the interruption is the result of the supervention of one faculty (the will, the eye) on another (volition, the touch). In each case normal operation of a morally neutral faculty leads into error; the interruption of the moral sense forcibly brings home that error, which is revealed (seen) as the duplicity of mere association. Thus the criticism of association produces the corollary that the amoral is necessarily associated with the immoral, and that the origin of evil can be attributed to the duplicity of association:

> I will at least make the attempt to explain to myself the Origin of moral Evil from the *streamy* Nature of Association, which Thinking = Reason, curbs & rudders/how this comes to be so difficult/Do not the bad Passions in Dreams throw light & shew of proof upon this Hypothesis?—Explain those bad Passions: & I shall gain Light, I am sure—A Clue! A Clue!—an Hecatomb a la Pythagoras, if it unlabyrinths me.—Dec. 28, 1803—Beautiful luminous Shadow of my pencil point following it from the Candle—rather going before it & illuminating the word, I am writing. 11 °clock/—But take in the blessedness of Innocent Children, the blessedness of sweet Sleep, &c &c &c: are these or are they not contradictions to the evil from *streamy* association?—I hope not: all is to be thought *over* and *into*—but what is the height, & ideal of mere association?—Delirium.—But how far is this state produced by Pain & Denaturaliza-

tion? And what are these?—In short, as far as I can see any thing in this Total Mist, Vice is imperfect yet existing Volition, giving diseased Currents of association, because it yields on all sides & *yet* is—So think of Madness:—O if I live! Grasmere, Dec. 29, 1803.[42]

Experience shows that the streaminess of association eddies into the misdirection of bad passions, which only the conscious rudder of reason can redirect into the proper current. Streaminess (amorality) somehow changes into the bad (immorality) unless it is directed by the rudder (the will, which makes a moral choice possible). Although the transition from a duplicitous streaminess to a vicious badness may broadly account for the presence of evil, it does not explain the actual dynamics of the transition: the nature of the *origin* of evil is still obscure. Besides, as Coleridge observes, that limited model seems to violate the empirical blessedness of "Innocent Children" and the experience of "sweet Sleep"—both natural associative states, but neither afflicted with bad passions. To avoid the contradiction, Coleridge shifts the parallel from sleep to delirium, which is "the height, & ideal of mere association." But the analogy will not serve the ends for which it was formed. Delirium may indeed lead a man to lunatic ravings in the same way that mere association may carry him to immoral acts; yet delirium is a sickness that must be the consequences of some evil, and, therefore, a deliriously immoral association cannot be without *its* stimulus. "But how far," Coleridge asks, "is this state produced by Pain & Denaturalization? And what are these?" What could they be

---

[42]*CN* I, 1770. Coburn regards "the Origin of moral Evil" as a reference to the origin of evil for mankind, and she associates this with Coleridge's 1796 note to himself to include among "My Works" "The Origin of Evil, an Epic Poem" (*CN* I, 161c). To that reference I would add *CN* I, 1619, where Coleridge meditates on "the whole business of the Origin of Evil." It is nonetheless impossible to determine finally whether Coleridge meant the origin of evil in mankind or the origin of evil actions in man, primarily because he, like Hartley, considered the two acts to be completely analogous: the former paradigmatic of all later falls; the latter an opportunity to learn the nature of the first fall through close observation of its indefinite repetitions. Hence the difference between dreaming and waking, with their analogous mental operations of association and reason, is equivalent to the difference between a Coleridgean paradise and the post-lapsarian world. It would be wrong to deny the analogy just because Coleridge's dreams are never wholly innocent; rather, we should note that the dreamy innocence of paradise is interrupted by its "proper" passions.

except the intrusion of something not-natural and painful *ab extra?* But all that has been opposed to or placed outside of mere association is reason. Can it be that the rudder that corrects the stream is the same barrier that deflects the blessed? Perhaps as the amoral under certain (what?) conditions becomes the immoral, so does the moral under certain (uncertain?) conditions act immorally.

The two descriptions of association in the above passage are inversions of each other; or at least they are made to look like inversions of each other through the orientation that Coleridge imposes by means of the metaphors "streaminess," "rudder," "bad," and "natural." Gradually the inconsistencies of this scheme with an already inconsistent experience press Coleridge to a more structural model. In January of 1804 he writes "That *Interruption* of itself is painful because & as far as it acts as Disruption/" (*CN* I, 1833). The antinomian inference produced by this conclusion would lead to the overthrow of the hard won moral distinction between the self-interrupting stream and the interruptive rudder. The overthrow of that distinction would entail the corollary that such moral distinctions among interruptions are only achieved by the fabrication of a metaphorical apparatus that stabilizes an inconsistency which cannot be literally captured—a situation analogous to the way Coleridge metaphorizes young Hartley's question by the addition of the apparatus of the mirror, a displacement of the interruption of the "and then" to an abstract and stable level. Implicated in such a series of inferences, the paradigm undergoes a drastic change. Instead of the stern guidance of streamy association by a reasonable rudder, we have an inconsistent overthrow-overthrowing by a valueless interruption.

That process is depicted in the passage from which the quotation on interruption was extracted:

> But I awoke with gouty suffocation this morning, 1/2 past one / & as soon as Disease permitted me to think at all, the shallowness & falsity of this Solution flashed on me at once / I saw, that the phaenomenon occurred far far too early—in early Infancy, 2 & 3 months old, I have observed it / & have seen it in Hartley, turned up & lay'd bare to the unarmed Eye of merest common sense. That *Interruption* of itself is painful because & as far as it acts as

Disruption / & then, without any reference to or distinct recollection of my former theory, I saw great Reason to attribute the effect
wholly to the streamy nature of the associating Faculty and especially as it is evident that *they most* labor under this defect who are
most reverie-ish & streamy—Hartley, for instance & myself / This
seems to me no common corroboration of my former Thought on
the origin of moral Evil in general.

The passage dramatizes the problem it addresses. Having
framed an explanation of the painfulness of duty, Coleridge has
gone to bed. His sleep is interrupted by a gouty suffocation;
then his mental numbness is interrupted by the "flash" of an
insight, which interrupts the logic of his earlier argument. The
insight? *"Interruption* of itself is painful." *"And then"* another interruption: the "great Reason," which instructs him to attribute
"the effect wholly to the streamy nature of the associating Faculty." The "effect," then, is the pain, but what is the cause? It could
be the streamy nature of association, but to maintain that would
be to lose whatever ground has been gained by the distinction:
both cause and effect would be due to the streaminess of association, and we would be left with the embarrassing paradox of
a morally irresponsible activity being morally responsible.
Streamy association can only be the enabling condition of the
cause, and the cause must be the interruption that diverts the
stream of association. But that inference presses the observer to
the conclusion that interruption, which is conditioned by association and is also the cause of pain in association, is somehow
both inside and outside of the stream: not a rudder, not a
stream, not a thing, and not a state, interruption is merely the
difference of moments. Although Coleridge wants to ascribe to
this interruption pain and the origin of evil, he might as well, as
the evidence shows, attribute to it pleasure and good also, in all
degrees and both at once, for interruption is both the painful
awakening and the flash of insight, both reason and denaturalization—it "is" the "and then" that distinguishes young
Hartley from yon mountains.

There is no mention of the will in this analysis of association,
although "will" would seem to be the most likely name for the
interruption that makes a difference. But interruption is conditioned, and Coleridge wants the will, *causa sui,* to be uncon-

ditioned. Interruption is inconsistent with itself, and the will must be absolute in its consistency. Interruption is without moral attributes, and the will is the certain ground of morality: the difference that the will makes is, above all, a moral difference. Interruption is useless as a philosophical concept because both as phenomenon and as name it lacks *value*. Although the will is the name for value in Coleridge, it is, *nomina sui*, the name for value that cannot be named: to name it is to phenomenalize it, to interrupt it. The writing of the will is a symbolic and foreign addition which entraps its authoritative voice in an equivocal text.

In entry 1170 we have seen Coleridge resisting a logical inference so that he might not have to think "*over* and *into*" the problem of evil again. Of course, Coleridge did think over and into the problem again and again. Coleridge never *overthrows* Hartleian association, but he does continually interrupt it in a manner like that by which *B* interrupts *A*, *C* interrupts *B*, &c. in the machinery of Hartley's system. Although that interruption displays the inconsistencies of association, it does not constitute a positive, philosophical, and moral refutation of the theory. In one of his brief skirmishes with Hartley in a notebook entry of 1808, Coleridge designates the requirement for such a refutation and indicates that such a refutation is still necessary. "1. The Will. Hartley, & association, confuted—(2.) We are seeking moral conviction. What is *conviction*? Certainty—Then *a priori* notions explained & proved—It comes all to this, we being men, for *us* while we are men this must be believed—we cannot be men; we contradict our own nature, if we do not—i.e. if we require further proofs—"(*CN* III, 3583). Although number one looks like the notation of a projected argument, the questions and answers of number two makes it clear that the simple statement "the Will" is meant to *be* the confutation of Hartley and association. This is so because "we are seeking moral conviction" absent from the system of association. The existence of the will interrupts the explanatory power of association by substituting the certainty that association leaves out of the reckoning. The will can be called a moral interruption. But as soon as it is so called, we can see why Coleridge does not so call it: that description or any description opens up a difference in a source that

[94]

must be prior to all differences. The will cannot be explained, "For if the will be unconditional, it must be inexplicable / for to understand a thing is to see what the conditions of it were, & causes—. But whatever is in the Will, is the Will, & therefore must be equally inexplicable / —"(*CN* III, 3559). To state anything beyond "the will" is to condition it. Best not to write the will at all, for as whatever is in the will is the will, so whatever is outside the will is not the will—and that writing is inside and outside the will. Best to rest at the fountainhead of intuition. Yet if that be conviction, it is without moral consequence. The problem that Coleridge faces in refuting Hartley is the same that Hartley himself recognized in the preface to his work: the moral expression of the grounds of morality is a dangerous addition to those grounds, one which jeopardizes certainty in its very expression. Moral action is the risk of moral conviction.

# [3]

# The Marginal Method of
# the *Biographia Literaria*

N. B. To make a detailed comparison in the manner of Jerome
Taylor between searching for the first cause of a Thing &
seeking the fountains of the Nile—so many streams each with
their junction &c—&c—at last, it all comes to a name—
—Coleridge, *Notebooks*

If we accept Coleridge's assertion that Hartley's doctrine is
confuted by the will, in vain do we search for such a confutation
in the *Biographia Literaria,* the scene of Coleridge's last and most
lengthy engagement with Hartleian theory.[1] Argumentative
when one would expect exposition, aphoristic when one longs
for argument, the chapters also contain large amounts of material borrowed without citation, chunks of prose extracted from
Coleridge's own writings, unprovoked and unjustified defama-
tion of the living and the dead, and one Plotinian "o altitudo,"
which craftily forestalls objections with something like a judgment on all merely mortal curiosity. Amid all this restless prose,
however, there appears no attempt to establish the free will
either ontologically or epistemologically. In order to determine
how the profusion of the peripheral bears on the absence of the
central we will not only need to take the text at its words but also
to inquire into the provenance and plan of those words—to ask
from where and why they have been taken.

---

[1]An index of the diminution of Coleridge's interest in *Hartleian* association is
the text of the 1818 *Philosophical Lectures,* ed. Kathleen Coburn (London: Pilot
Press, 1949), which incorporates many passages from the philosophical sections
of the *Biographia,* but which includes only one passing reference to Hartley, and
which takes for granted that the significance of association begins and ends with
Aristotle.

Coleridge begins Chapter V with an affirmation of "the natural difference of *things* and *thoughts*" (*BL* I, 66). The latter "inward experiences" have been historically arranged, he says, into "three separate classes, the passive sense, or what the schoolmen call the merely receptive quality of the mind; the voluntary; and the spontaneous, which holds the middle place between both." He then cites Sir James Mackintosh's opinion[2] that the British empiricists made the only advance in the study of the spontaneous sense since the ancients, and that

> the law of association as established in the contemporaneity of the original impressions, formed the basis of all true psychology; and any ontological, or metaphysical science not contained in such (i.e. empirical) psychology, was but a web of abstractions and generalizations. Of this prolific truth, of this great fundamental law, he declared Hobbs to have been the original *discoverer*, while its full application to the whole intellectual system we owe to David Hartley; who stood in the same relation to Hobbs as Newton to Kepler; the law of association being that to the mind, which gravitation is to matter. [*BL* I, 66-67]

As the tone indicates, Coleridge mentions Mackintosh only to differ. Two differences emerge. First, Mackintosh's conviction that the empiricists' psychology has priority over any other metaphysics constitutes a "chasm" so wide between the two thinkers that Coleridge despairs of the powers of discourse to bridge it. He devotes most of Chapters V through VII to a refutation of the reduction, by British empiricists and Hartley in particular, of inner experience to a single mode and advocates instead the Aristotelian model of multiple causes. The second difference concerns historical priorities, and it is the one that Coleridge immediately addresses. He first disputes Hobbes's "claim" either to have deduced the principle of association or to have built anything on the principle he announced and advocates instead the precedence of Descartes. Then comes a discussion of the history of association before both Hobbes and Descartes. Coleridge mentions the opinions of Philip Melanchthon,

[2] Delivered in 1799 in a series of lectures entitled "Lectures on the Law of Nature and Nations."

Vitus Amberbach, and Ludovico Vives, and applauds Aristotle's ideas on the subject, which are, he says, theoretical, not hypothetical—that is, they are "unmixed with fiction" (*BL* I, 71). The chapter ends with an attack on the originality of Hume's essay on association, which, in passing, implicates Mackintosh in the discovery and subsequent suppression of Hume's copy of Aristotle's *Parva naturalia* as annotated by Aquinas—proof for Coleridge of Hume's servile and unacknowledged dependence on the angelic doctor.

The facts about Coleridge's facts have long been known.[3] His attacks on Hobbes and Hume are inaccurate. His treatment of Aristotle, though largely accurate, is not his own, but was taken *variatim* from J. G. E. Maass's analysis of the theory and the history of association in his *Versuch über die Einbildungskraft*, published in 1797.

As the unacknowledged borrowing from Maass necessarily raises the question of Coleridge's plagiarism, his unfounded allegations regarding Hobbes and Hume may make us less responsive to any likely excuse. The standard of stern judgment has been set by Norman Fruman in his righteous scrutiny of Coleridgean sins.[4] Another, more suggestive approach has been taken by Thomas McFarland, who, though equally sensitive to the problem of plagiarism, is more sympathetic to Coleridge than Fruman. In Coleridge's defense McFarland contends that "the very multiplicity of instances . . . suggests the explanation, bizarre though it may seem, that we are faced not with plagiarism, but with nothing less than a mode of composition—composition by mosaic organization rather than by painting on an empty canvas."[5] Although McFarland admits that the extent of the borrowings in the *Biographia* from Maass, Leibniz, and especially Schelling stretch his theory of *ut mosaica philosophia* to the limits, his ingenious defense should, nonetheless, convince that

---

[3]These facts are best presented in the notes to the edition of the *Biographia Literaria* prepared by Henry Nelson Coleridge and completed and published by Sara Coleridge in 1847. This edition forms the third volume of *The Complete Works of Samuel Taylor Coleridge*, ed. W. G. T. Shedd (New York: Harper, 1884).

[4]See Norman Fruman, *Coleridge, The Damaged Archangel* (New York: Braziller, 1971), *passim*.

[5]Thomas McFarland, *Coleridge and the Pantheist Tradition* (Oxford: Oxford University Press, 1969), p. 27.

one of the major obligations in the *Biographia* is determining the precise character of Coleridge's composition before judging his offense. To take up the issue of composition here requires a consideration of the unexpected prominence of James Mackintosh, whose lectures are the text for many of Coleridge's charges and the pretext for the discussion of association itself. Why *should* Coleridge begin an 1815 discussion of association with an attack on opinions delivered in lectures eighteen years before?

Not only does Coleridge refer to those lectures, he echoes what seems to be a response to them that he had already recorded in 1801: in the philosophical letters to Josiah Wedgwood, Coleridge had taken up the Kepler-Newton, Hobbes-Hartley comparison and energetically discounted it (*CL* II, 686).[6] We may suppose that his lingering contempt for Mackintosh's reputation as a sagacious arbiter of philosophical controversies may have had something to do with Coleridge's decision to choose him as antagonist in the *Biographia*,[7] as his haste in composition must have had a good deal to do with the petty nature of some of his objections. The precedent of the Wedgwood letters suggests that in his hurry to get something down on association, Coleridge may have consulted either his old manuscript (in the hands of Poole) or perhaps only his tenacious memory and, seizing on the dispute between Locke and Descartes, substituted Hobbes for Locke in the hope of furnishing himself with a vehicle to convey his thesis. By refurbishing Mackintosh for the occasion, Coleridge could take a position that he loved: a conservative revisionist and a reluctant controversialist. More important, however, is the fact that, as he told to Southey in 1794, Coleridge could not write without a "*body* of *thought*" (*CL* I, 137), whether it be the embodiment of thought in a personality to whom he could direct *ad hominem* arguments or conversational poems, whether it be the body of thought that a text such as

---

[6]Coleridge does not in the letter specifically attribute the comparison to Mackintosh.

[7]The contempt is well documented. In May 1800, Coleridge writes to William Godwin of "the great Dung-fly Mackintosh"; in October of that year he concludes a scurrilous verse satire (part of the *Skeletoniad*) on the Scotsman in a letter to Humphry Davy; in October 1801 he writes that, "as to his [Mackintosh's] conversation, it was all uncommonly *well-worded*; but not a thought in it worthy of having been worded at all" (*CL* I, 588, 633; II, 771).

Mackintosh's lectures or his own letter might supply, or whether it be the embodiment of a first principle—he needed a "sensible bulk," to use Addison's phrase,[8] to guide his philosophical imagination and to which he might affix his comments. If the letter to Southey expresses the ebullient side of that need, this later note reveals its pathos: "My nature," Coleridge confesses, "requires another Nature for its support, & reposes only in another from the necessary Indigence of its being" (*CN* I, 1679). Bounty and indigence, ebullience and pathos—the *Biographia* encompasses both modes. In fact, they have become indistinguishable.

Coleridge's use of Maass in Chapter V also shows his persistent and overdetermined need for the support of "another nature." The main criticism that Coleridge directs against Hartley's theory is that it, like Hobbes's, "*must* have reduced all its forms to the one law of time" (*BL* I, 69), as the empiricists have in general reduced all the forms of inward experience to the one class of spontaneity. Against that reduction Coleridge sets the Aristotelian theory of multiple "occasioning causes" of association, almost exactly as it is presented by Maass in his book: "1st, connection in time, whether simultaneous, preceding, or successive; 2nd, vicinity or connection in space; 3rd, interdependence or necessary connection, as cause and effect; 4th, likeness; and 5th, contrast" (*BL* I, 72).[9] In sum, Coleridge's entire argument could be viewed as nothing more than a simple elaboration of the German's discussion of Aristotle. There is no doubt of Coleridge's familiarity with Maass. He had read *Versuch über die Einbildungskraft* and annotated it thoroughly, probably well before writing the *Biographia*; his marginalia show a firm understanding, even an assimilation of the German's arguments.[10] The evidence also shows, however, that he did not need to plagiarize Maass any more than he needs to contest Mackintosh.

[8]Joseph Addison, *Critical Essays from the Spectator,* ed. Donald F. Bond (Oxford University Press, 1970), *Spectator* 420, p. 204. Addison uses the phrase to describe the matter that the imagination or fancy requires to prevent its loss in "a kind of chasm."

[9]As Shawcross points out in his note to this passage, Aristotle actually presents only four such occasioning causes: "interdependence or necessary connection" is added by Coleridge to Aristotle and Maass.

[10]Selections from these marginalia are reproduced in the Sara Coleridge *Biographia,* in the notes to pages 214-15.

The nearest anticipation in Coleridge's writings of this specific criticism of Hartley is a notebook entry of 1811:

> One fruitful remark on or against Hartley's *one* Law of Time for Association is that in different moods we naturally associate by different laws—as in Passion, by Contrast—in pleasurable states, by Likeness—&c. To be able to shew the possibility of explaining these things verbally with Time—as Cause & effect always coming together, therefore remembered by *Time*—does not prove the *fact* that they are so—on the contrary, we clearly feel the difference in our own minds & know well when we remember a thing by accident & passively, & when actively—This important distinction of active & passive Remembrance is among the many Omissions of Hartley's System—[*CN* III, 4059]

The contrast of the "one Law of Time" with the "different laws" closely resembles the governing distinction that Coleridge argues in the *Biographia*. But does the distinction here depend on an acquaintance with Maass's work? Coleridge gives no indication. One problem in judging the influence of Maass is that Coleridge's writings yield few clues regarding his reading of the German philosopher. The only recorded mention of Maass prior to the *Biographia* is a puzzling note in 1809, where "Maas" is referred to as a source for a projected ode on the dream vision of Galileo (*CN* III, 3585). That entry does place Coleridge's awareness of Maass before the above note on the one law of association, but it does not suggest a date which we can call the earliest contact. Speculation here must rely on the most uncertain evidence, which is Coleridge's undated annotation of Maass's book. In one note, Coleridge takes issue with Maass's "division of things into matter (sensation ab extra) and form." He comments that, "If then form be not an external active power, if it be wholly transfused into the object by the esemplastic or imaginative faculty of the percipient, or rather creator, where and wherein shall I find the ground of my perception, that this is the Rose and that the Lily."[11] That note is certainly not early Coleridge. The use of "esemplastic," whether or not the word

---

[11]Sara Coleridge *Biographia*, pp. 214-15 n.

was derived specifically from Schelling,[12] is evidence of Schellingian influence. *If*, then, we assume that this comment was added to the margins of Maass during a *first* reading, there is some reason for setting the extreme limit of Maass's influence at January 1, 1806, which is the date of Coleridge's first mention of Schelling (*CN* II, 2784).

Such a reconstruction of dates is exceedingly fragile. Yet that fragility reflects the lack of evidence that Maass had any influence on the development of Coleridge's formal criticism of association. On the contrary, the evidence is strong that Coleridge did not at all need Maass to tell him that the one law of association is insufficient to account for all mental activity. We may refer to Coleridge's letter to Southey in 1803, where he argues that "association depends in a much greater degree on the recurrence of resembling states of feeling, than on Trains of Ideas" (*CL* II, 961). If we follow Coleridge to chart his development toward an organic model, we are likely to emphasize his insistence on feeling as opposed to ideas; but if we take our perspective on this passage from the *Biographia* and notebook entry 4059, what is striking is the claim that resemblance is a mode of association every bit as significant as the simple contemporaneity of ideas. This letter might be offered as compelling evidence that the vaunted overthrow has taken place and that Coleridge has progressed beyond the doctrine of association, were it not that he had already made the same distinction between kinds of association considerably before the 1801 letter to Poole.

In January to March of 1800, Coleridge attended five of Mackintosh's second series of lectures on "The Laws of Nature and Nations." Coleridge did not complete the series, evidently because the lectures were the cause of more irritation than edification, an irritation that shows in Coleridge's sketchy notes.[13] But at least one comment suggests that the time was not com-

[12]For differing views of the derivation of esemplastic, see Sara Coleridge *Biographia*, p. 272 n; where the editor attributes the origin of the term to Schelling's *Ins-Eins Bildung*, and also Shawcross, *BL* II, 249, where the editor attributes its coinage to Coleridge alone.

[13]For example: "Talked a great deal of Nonsense about *judgement* & used a most false example of a Parent's Love to a worthless Infant—might as well have talked of the love to unroasted meat—" (*CN* I, 634).

pletely wasted. He writes: "M's Explication of Likeness as only a species of Contemporaneity to me vague & unmeaning—" (*CN* I, 634). Thus a full year before his so-called overthrow of Hartley, Coleridge had formed the basic distinction that he was to elaborate in his chapters on Hartley in the *Biographia*: resemblance is a kind of association distinct from rather than subordinate to contemporaneity. This goes far toward accounting for Coleridge's resurrection of Mackintosh in the *Biographia*; instead of inserting an anomalous reference to a dated lecture in the course of making a new argument, Coleridge is reusing an argument that he had outlined fifteen years before.

Nevertheless, we cannot yet conclude either that we have explained Coleridge's use of Mackintosh in the *Biographia* or that we have located the origin of Coleridge's critique of Hartley, for two months before he attended Mackintosh's lectures Coleridge inscribed this query in his notebook, without apparent context, motive, or immediate consequence: "May not Time in Association be made *serviceable* & evidence Likeness" (*CN* I, 577). It is in this note—half statement, half question—regarding the serviceability of time that we can come closest to the germ of Coleridge's later criticism of Hartleian association: before Mackintosh, before the overthrow of Hartley, before the letter to Southey, before the note in 1811, and long before the *Biographia*. The evidence suggests that Coleridge's other comments on association, beginning with his response to Mackintosh's lectures and concluding with the critique in the *Biographia*, are fundamentally repetitions of the insight that Coleridge noted in 1799. There are modifications of the statement, certainly—the substitution of feelings for ideas, the tentative application of the distinction to memory, the multiplication of the causes of association beyond the resemblance-contemporaneity distinction—but none of them alters the basic position that the one law of association must yield to an association governed by several causes. Importantly, the provenance of that distinction, as well as its several recapitulations, has nothing to do with an overthrow of association engineered from without; it is directed toward the discrimination of associations from within, effected with pre-Kantian philosophical tools. The history of Coleridge's dealings with association shows both that Coleridge did not consider his argument regarding its modes at all relevant to an overthrow of association and that neither Mackintosh nor Maass were essential to the formulation of that argument.

The distinction of causes, though available to Coleridge as a proposition from 1799, was not stated as an argument until the writing of the *Biographia* in 1815. Until then it is reproduced only in notes: notes on Mackintosh's lectures, notes on experience, notes on reading. When the case is finally argued for publication, that method of presentation is continued. Coleridge takes one small step forward by taking one long step back: he represents the texts as pretexts for his notes. Not only does Coleridge not need Mackintosh or Maass to make his argument, he does not *use* them to make an argument so much as he annexes the body of thought—Maass's text, Mackintosh's lectures—into his manuscript to supply a sustaining text that he can cover with marginalia: notes, interpolations, and revisions.

To call Coleridge's borrowing plagiarism is indeed profitless: the moral blanket smothers the unarguable vitality and complexity of the text. We must mince our words as Coleridge minced his. Yet the moral remission involved in the label "mosaic composition," the suggestion that Coleridge is simply a self-effacing, skillful craftsman, is equally misleading. Although Coleridge has appropriated passages from other writers, every word in the *Biographia* has become his. A book is not a mosaic. Words are not brightly colored stones, which the artist finds and then arranges on a background; even the crude facsimile of the most clumsy plagiarist alters its source by mediation and displacement. Moreover, Coleridge scarcely seems to have composed the *Biographia,* if by compose we mean the act of an intending consciousness bringing disparate materials into equilibrium. To recuperate Coleridge's disturbing prose by means of a metaphor from the visual arts is to suppress the crucial discursive advance he has made beyond Hartley's wishful sketching and to end inevitably by cataloging Coleridge as just another emblematic figure in philosophy's great picture book. One benefit of close attention to Hartley's metaphors for philosophical writing is the ability to see that, though Coleridge found writing as problematic as the associationist, by the time of the *Biographia* he read and wrote that problem in a way that requires us, if we

intend to adhere to Coleridge's discourse rather than to tran-
sume it, to trope his writing *as* writing. The *Biographia* is not a
book of philosophy. Coleridge wrote none. What Coleridge
practices is not mosaic composition but marginal exegesis, not
philosophy but commentary.[14]

In his discussion of Coleridge's kinship with Friedrich Jacobi,
McFarland addresses the peculiar character of marginal commentary when he is faced with the problem of accounting for
the fact that Coleridge hardly ever mentions Jacobi, and that
when he does, it is primarily in marginal comments with a distinctly disapproving tone. To explain this McFarland seconds W.
Schrickx's "plausible hypothesis about the special emphasis of
marginalia": "Schrickx argues that it is 'natural for those who
enrich books with their marginal comments rather to disagree
with or counter views of others and to impose their own than to
express enthusiasm for the author who is being annotated.'"[15]
McFarland uses that hypothesis to support his own conviction of
a special sympathetic relationship between Coleridge and Jacobi.
In other words, he plausibly employs Schrickx's hypothesis to
justify the presumption of marginal comments as inherently
equivocal. The hypothesis of equivocalness is plausible because
a structural equivocation is built into the annotative situation: an
apparently single voice is doubled by the addition of the note.
Once added to the margins of the text the comment makes it uncertain what the text *is*. The original text may presume inalienable priority, but the marginal comment always threatens the
reduction of the original text to a pretext for commentary—
commentary, however, which could not be where it "is" were it

[14]In his essay "The Marginal Gloss," Laurence Lipking identifies the gloss by
contrasting it to marginalium, a term, he notes, that was "introduced by Coleridge." "Marginalia—traces left in a book—are wayward in their very nature,"
he says; "they spring up spontaneously around a text unaware of their presence." According to Lipking, the "marginal gloss, however, responds to another
frame of mind: the need to spell everything out" (p. 612). I am deploying
marginalium in ways that include some of the textual features that Lipking
would associate with the gloss. The extension is, I think, justified by the subject,
Coleridge's prose, where notions of spontaneity and forethought, of part and
whole are highly problematic, and where it is necessary to hypopoeticize a marginal method that is the discursive vehicle of that problematic.

[15]McFarland, *Pantheist Tradition*, p. 133. The quotation from W. Schrickx is
from "Coleridge and Friedrich Heinrich Jacobi," *Revue belge de philologie et d'his-
toire*, 36, pt. 3 (1958), 841.

not for the margins provided. The marginalium is, thus, both enrichment and deprivation of its host, just as it is, equivocally, neither inside nor outside the text. Marginalia exploit the articulations of sense and signification where respires the text's mortality.

Considered as discourse a marginal method is similarly equivocal: philosophical goods are transported by a rhetorical vehicle. The beginning of Chapter VI, where Coleridge launches his specific criticisms of Hartley's system, furnishes a good example. Coleridge has two targets: the hypothesis of vibrations and the reduction of the laws of association to the single law of contemporaneity. The only logical criticism that Coleridge applies to Hartley, one of "a hundred possible confutations," is taken from Maass's analysis of the mechanical hypothesis:

> According to this system the idea or vibration $a$ from the external object A becomes associable with the idea or vibration $m$ from the external object M, because the oscillation $a$ propagated itself so as to re-produce the oscillation $m$. But the original impression from M was essentially different from the impression from A: unless therefore different causes may produce the same effect, the vibration $a$ could never produce the vibration $m$; and this therefore could never be the means by which $a$ and $m$ are associated. [*BL* I, 74-75]

Coleridge employs two other deductions by Maass to answer possible objections to the first. Those deductions are refutations in kind of the scientific propositions that Hartley enumerated in the first chapter of *Observations on Man*. Coleridge does not, however, leave imagination to starve while reason luxuriates in its proper paradise: he ornaments the margins of Maass's syllogisms with his own polished enthymemes—metaphorical illustrations of the German's confutations. The method is effective: the deductions convince; illustrations such as the metaphor of the stone soup (*BL* I, 75) persuade.

Equally persuasive is Coleridge's summary comment on the consequences of Hartley's "material hypothesis":

> Thus the principle of *contemporaneity*, which Aristotle had made the common *condition* of all the laws of association, Hartley was constrained to represent as being itself the sole *law*. . . . Again, from

[106]

this results inevitably, that the will, the reason, the judgement, and the understanding, instead of being the determining causes of association, must needs be represented as its *creatures,* and among its mechanical *effects.* Conceive, for instance, a broad stream, winding through a mountainous country with an indefinite number of currents, varying and running into each other according as the gusts chance to blow from the opening of the mountains. The temporary union of several currents in one, so as to form the main current of the moment, would present an accurate image of Hartley's theory of the will.

Had this been really the case, the consequence would have been that our whole life would be divided between the despotism of outward impressions and that of senseless and passive memory. [*BL* I, 76-77][16]

Coleridge has responded to Hartley's attempt to give a philosophical description of things as they are with an interpretive sketch of what things *might* be like if Hartley's account were accurate. First, he compares Hartley to Aristotle; then he comments on the inevitable consequences of Hartley's theory; then he asks us to conceive an image; *then* he says, "Had this been really the case." If *what* had really been the case? If the mind had really been a stream winding through a mountainous country? For a moment the reference floats: the clear image seems to displace the priority of the difficult concept of contingency that it is meant to represent. That grammatical slippage is paralleled by the rhetorical displacement which Coleridge uses the image to effect. He employs his metaphor as a device to invert his opponent's own position and to turn his arguments against him: the stream image enables Coleridge to associate the associative model with caprice rather than necessity. By removing the metaphor from its "natural" connection, he achieves a remarkable *tour de force.* Yet the consequences of that rhetorical subversion are as ephemeral as those involved in the momentary grammatical displacement. Because of its rhetorical character Coleridge's criticism is inadequate as a refutation; instead, his removal of the

---

[16]As Shawcross notes, Coleridge's remark that "our whole life would be divided between the despotism of outward impressions and that of senseless and passive memory" is taken directly from Coleridge's marginalia on Maass. Cf. Sara Coleridge *Biographia* I, 228 n.

image from its proper context, his "denaturalizing" of the metaphor, suggests that it can be reappropriated to serve antithetical ends: without the anchor of the autonomous will, Coleridge's turn is liable to a similar overturning.[17]

Coleridge's rhetoric has its effect. But that effectiveness has its cost. One of the costs of a marginal method is the complication of the writer's relationship to an ambiguous text or an undisclosed truth, a relationship similar to the Hartleian dyad of decoder-code. The decoder, like the annotator, may be conceived to be in the margins of the text that he is analyzing, and that position is likewise equivocal; but he intends his situation to be only provisional: when he solves the code and establishes the true text, he will have relieved the text of its obscurity and relinquished his own ambiguous position. The marginal commentator, however, relies on the bulk of his text to relieve *him* of the responsibility for systematic discourse, as the rhetorician's persuasive aims relieve him from the need for syllogistic rigor. The shift from a deliberate, scientific argument of inductive or deductive proof to a mobile, fragmentary discourse of persuasion provides the annotator with a kind of (illegitimate) freedom that the decoder does not have: the annotator has no ground to defend because his room—margins, interlinear spaces, gaps between words and letters—is provided for him by his host. The resourcefulness of the commentator derives from a tactical freedom to exploit aggressively any source of argument, which, in turn, depends on his fundamental distance from any general

[17]One is tempted to call this rhetorical maneuver the fallacy of the distinct image, or perhaps even the fallacy of clarity. Coleridge refers to it when he describes those "individuals (Laodiceans in spirit, Minims in faith, and nominalists in philosophy) who mistake outlines for substance and distinct images for clear conceptions." *The Statesman's Manual*, in *Lay Sermons*, ed. R. J. White, *Collected Works*, 6 (Princeton: Princeton University Press, 1972), Appendix D, 93. Hereafter *LS*. See also *BL* I, 91, 189-90. A criticism of the same fallacy from a different point of view appears in one of Ludwig Wittgenstein's comments on the concept of "game": "One might say that the concept 'game' is a concept with blurred edges—'But is a blurred concept a concept at all?'—Is an indistinct photograph a picture of a person at all? Is it even always an advantage to replace an indistinct picture by a sharp one? Isn't the indistinct one often exactly what we need?" *Philosophical Investigations*, trans. G. E. M. Anscombe, 3d ed. (New York: Macmillan Company, 1968), I, 71. In this case the distinctness of the "outline" of Coleridge's image blurs the clarity of the concept which it has been invented to affirm.

premise, just as the rhetorician's persuasiveness is derived from his method's distance from any ultimate origin or end. The anxiety of the marginalist is owed to the fact that his resourcefulness is always derived, his freedom licensed, as it were, by his host—the authority on which he obsessively relies and which he compulsively disrupts. Prosperous in its poverty, sportively impertinent yet embarassingly intimate, the marginalium never quite fits; but once intricate with the text it cannot be cleanly removed. Rather like some weeds: "In the after editions, I pruned the double epithets with no sparing hand, and used my best efforts to tame the swell and glitter both of thought and diction; though in truth, these parasite plants of youthful poetry had insinuated themselves into my longer poems with such intricacy of union, that I was often obliged to omit disentangling the weed, from the fear of snapping the flower" (*BL* I, 3).

To adopt another metaphor (or another metaphor for metaphors), the politic aggressiveness of the marginalist may be attributed to the contingency of living in a borrowed home: the security of a sheltering text is crossed by the unsettling awareness that it is someone else's text. Inhabiting margins is "expropriation, being-away-from home, but still in a home, a place of self-recovery, self-recognition, self-mastery, self-resemblance: it is outside itself—it is itself."[18] *Almost* itself because not quite still a home—or, rather, not quite a still home because borrowed. One must constantly maneuver to maintain one's place until one has a place of one's own. For Coleridge the possible cessation of the anxiety that shadows every turn of the pen attends the fantasy of a home he will never have:

'My dear young friend, . . . suppose yourself established in any honorable occupation. From the manufactory or counting-house, from the law-court, or from having visited your last patient, you return at evening,
>Dear tranquil time, when the sweet sense of home
>Is sweetest—"

[18]Jacques Derrida, "White Mythology," trans. F. C. T. Moore, in *New Literary History*, 6, no. 1 (Autumn 1974), 55. Derrida applies this description to metaphor. The metaphor of the borrowed home is one that Derrida quotes in the same place from Du Marsais, *Traités des Tropes* (chap. 2, p. 10).

to your family, prepared for its social enjoyments, with the very countenances of your wife and children brightened, and their voice of welcome made doubly welcome, by the knowledge that, as far as *they* are concerned, you have satisfied the demands of the day by the labor of the day. Then, when you retire into your study, in the books on your shelves you revisit so many venerable friends with whom you can converse. Your own spirit scarcely less free from personal anxieties than the great minds, that in those books are still living for you! Even your writing desk with its blank paper and all its other implements will appear as a chain of flowers, capable of linking your feelings as well as thoughts to events and characters past or to come; not a chain of iron, which binds you down to think of the future and the remote by recalling the chains and feelings of the peremptory present.' [*BL* I, 153-54]

But the text exacts day labor, home denied. Although Coleridge wishes to write the philosophy of the owner or proprietor who capably and lawfully executes his will within his rightful domain, as unbidden guest, lacking the franchise of a home, his working prose imitates (imitates and refines) the contingency it attacks. In Chapter VI, Coleridge's remarks on the probable lawless consequences of the Hartleian hypothesis are followed by a magisterial gesture toward precision: "There is in truth but one state to which this theory applies at all, namely that of complete light-headedness; and even to this it applies but partially, because the will and reason are perhaps never wholly suspended" (*BL* I, 77). He begins the next paragraph in this way: "A case of this kind occurred in a Catholic town in Germany a year or two before my arrival at Göttingen, and had not then ceased to be a frequent subject of conversation." We recognize the rhetorical appeal to the example, which is intended to clarify and fortify the argument. But it is also evident that the example does not fit neatly into a formed argument: we cannot be entirely certain what "this kind" of case is, an instance of uncontrolled delirium or a case of light-headedness which shows that the reason and will are never wholly suspended. Coleridgean distinctions dance away their rigor. The equivocation in the reference here reflects the discontinuity between the sections of the refutation and highlights the jerry-built transitions between annotations, linked by neither floral nor iron chain but by their equivocal reference to the host text.

What follows is a psychological whodunit. An illiterate maid-servant "was seized with a nervous fever; during which, according to the asseverations of all the priests and monks of the neighbourhood, she became *possessed*, and, as it appeared, by a very learned devil. She continued incessantly talking Latin, Greek, and Hebrew, in very pompous tones and with distinct enunciation." Fortunately the woman is visited by a young physician who is "determined to trace her past life step by step" (*BL* I, 78) and who eventually tracks her pedantic ravings to the nocturnal ambulatory readings of a scholarly former master— traced so satisfactorily "that no doubt could remain in any rational mind concerning the true origin of the impressions made on her nervous system" (*BL* I, 79). In other words, the case can be explained in strictly associationist terms: there is no mention of the will or reason. The equivocal reference of "this kind" has, in its correction, given way to an equivocalness more crucial. Why has Coleridge bothered to tell a story, which, if it performs any function, reinforces the position of his adversary, albeit in a pathological extreme? Has the impulse to give a good rhetorical example been interrupted by Coleridge's desire to tell one of *his* stories? Is the story irrelevant to the context, or is the chapter on Hartley only a pretext for the opportunity to insert this anecdote?

The combination of a grammatical slippage between one paragraph and the next with the logical slippage that the anecdote introduces into the argument opens up the text to these questions and encourages the reader to search for the relevance of the illustration elsewhere than in its simple rhetorical function. The theme of the story is possession. A maid, illiterate and "known" to be a heretic, lives in a home which is not, of course, her own. She possesses nothing. Not only is she possessed by her master, she comes to be possessed by a very learned devil. An investigator discovers, however, that she is guiltless of diabolical communion and completely the victim of her circumstances. The moral may be taken from Chapter VII of the *Biographia*: "God only can know, *who* is a heretic" (*BL* I, 84). Although one may be tempted to associate Coleridge, the writer, with the dogged investigator, it is actually the maidservant who in her feverish glossolalia most closely resembles the writer. We may recall the remark from Chapter IX of the *Biographia*, often quoted in

defenses of Coleridge's borrowings, where he says that he regards "truth as a divine ventriloquist" (*BL* I, 105). This story is a
case of ventriloquism in which, truer to experience, a person is
ventriloquized not by truth but by learning, truth's simulacrum.
One of the major themes of the *Biographia* is also possession:
Coleridge's possession of his ideas before his contact with Schelling's works, his account at the end of Chapter IV of his being
possessed by the genius of Wordsworth, his mention of how
Kant "took possession of [him] as with a giant's hand" (*BL* I, 99),
his possession by the learned devil of Schelling in Chapters XII
and XIII. We may, at one level, read this anecdote as the dis-
guised expression of an excuse and a wish. Coleridge excuses
himself as being guiltlessly taken over by forces beyond his control, and he imagines the advent of a romantic physician who
will exorcise his demons and thus free him from the charge of
heresy by a rational explanation of their cause. Living in a borrowed home, a house of language where one is subjected early
and often to a barrage of words, one becomes transformed into
a vehicle for a volatile, fragmentary discourse which consists of
sentences "coherent and intelligible each for itself, but with little
or no connection with each other" (*BL* I, 78). It is notable that
when Coleridge looks for an excuse he eagerly adopts the Hartleian model of mind (ideas can be tracked "step by step") and
expression (either possession or ventriloquism); conversely,
when he has done something good, *he* wants credit for it. It is apt
that the maidservant is overpowered by books, and not just
books but sacred books and their commentaries, which in a
bizarre process of promiscuous self-reproduction seem to im-
print themselves on the woman's mind, willy-nilly appropriating
her to their margins. Yet in this place Coleridge provides,
however underhandedly, the tools to deconstruct those ethical
excuses. If we take Coleridge seriously we can take the story one
step farther along. Although rational investigation shows that
the girl's ravings are wholly mechanical, *we know* that the "will"
and the "reason" are never entirely suspended—we know because Coleridge has told us so. Somewhere within, the woman
desired to be possessed: she cannot be entirely guiltless because
the activity of the learned machinery received its blessing somewhere in her mind. The converse implication is also true. The

most willed, reasonable action of the woman or the physician is in some way conditioned and cannot be completely to his or her credit. Who can tell the rudder from the stream? In truth, Coleridge can be considered as both patient and physician, the demystifier of his own supposed possession whether by Hartley, Kant, Schelling, or anyone else. No one can fully possess anything—certainly not language, least of all himself. Everyone lives in a borrowed home in the economy of the Coleridgean text because no one has a home of his own. That is not the "lawless consequence" of Coleridge's writing but its characteristic equivocation, which puzzles the bond between act and consequence. The indefinite repetition of the Coleridgean "I AM" in the chamber of the text resounds our sense of voice and echo.

Coleridge deploys various *topoi* besides the illustration to give point to his criticism of association, such as persuasive definition: "the despotism of the eye"; the *occupatio*: "we will pass by the utter incompatibility of such a law"; *reductio ad absurdam*: "the whole universe cooperates to produce the minutest stroke of every letter"; hyperbolic pathos: "the poor worthless I." The one among them that most clearly demonstrates the equivocalness of his method appears in Chapter VI, where he assists Maass's criticism of Hartley's vibrations by comparing the function of the nerve in Hartley's theory to "the flint which the wag placed in the pot as the first ingredient of his stone-broth, requiring only salt, turnips, and mutton for the remainder!" (*BL* I, 75). The implicit claim of this metaphor is that the material factor is deficient in explanatory power without the superaddition of active, vital ingredients to the material model. To give life to matter life must be added. That comparison is not a new one in Coleridge's writings; it was used in lecture five of Coleridge's 1795 Lectures on Revealed Religion, a defense of Priestelian unitarianism:

> Thus I have heard a very vehement Trinitarian explain himself away into a perfect Humanist! and the thrice strange Union of Father, Son and Holy Ghost in one God, each Person full and perfect God transmuted into the simple notion that God is Love, and Intelligence and Life, and that Love, Intelligence and Life are God! a Trinity in Unity equally applicable to Man or Beast! Thus

you are told of the wonderous Power of the Cross, yet you find that this wonder working Sacrifice possesses no efficacy unless there be added to it everything that, if God be benevolent, must be sufficient without it. This is the mysterious cookery of the Orthodox— which promises to make Broth out of a Flint, but when you are congratulating yourself on the cheapness of your proposed Diet, requires as necessary ingredients, Beef, Salt and Turnips! But the Layman might say—I can make Broth out of Beef, Salt and Turnips myself. Most true! But the Cook would have no plea for demanding his wages were it not for his merit in dropping in the Flint.[19]

The same comparison is used by the trinitarian Coleridge to characterize a uniformitarian concept of man that had earlier been used by a unitarian Coleridge to ridicule a trinitarian position. Whether defending Priestley or attacking him, the parable of the mysterious cookery is equally serviceable because though it appears to be the commonest of sense, it has no sense except as a rhetorical dislocation of the argument to which it is affixed. The flint metaphor works well as a criticism of Hartley's premise because it would work well as a criticism of any philosophical premise (what is the free will but the flint . . . ?) or as a criticism of metaphysics itself (what is Being but the flint . . . ?). The flint metaphor's omnipersuasiveness derives from its almost imperceptible distance from any essential truth. Indeed, Coleridge's practice indicates that the flint metaphor may be not only a metaphor for all the metaphors in the stone soup of the *Biographia*, but also for all philosophical metaphors, which are the flints to which the (metaphorical) herbs and meat of the (metaphorical) truth must be added. Is it the metaphor or the truth, then, that is additional? The sophisms that the commentator detects in the text are recapitulated on the margins in a finer tone.

The conclusion of the Hartley section exhibits Coleridge's argument and method at the breaking point. He reduces the errors of association to "one sophism as their common genus: the mistaking the *conditions* of a thing for its *causes* and *essence*; and the process by which we arrive at the knowledge of a faculty, for the faculty itself" (*BL* I, 85). Although Coleridge fortifies this distinction with examples, they assist him no more than to distinguish the Aristotelian species of association, which categorizes the various immediate causes of combination, from the simpler Hartleian kind, which attributes association solely to contemporaneity. One reduction, however, is to open to another. What is the cause of the Aristotelian causes? Coleridge does not phrase that question, but he elicits it when he admits that the Aristotelian categories "cannot be indeed *separated* from contemporaneity; for that would be to separate them from the mind itself" (*BL* I, 87). In other words, the notion of an integral consciousness (the ego, the self which is somewhere present to itself) depends on the premise of the contemporaneity of the mind— its temporal identity with itself. Hence it would appear that it is *essentially* accurate in respect to Coleridge's own ontology to hold the contemporaneity of the mind as the *condition* and final *cause* of all acts of the mind; the discrimination of final from efficient causes does not alter the necessary connection. Coleridge recognizes that to *really* progress beyond necessitarian association requires, somewhere along the line, the rejection of contemporaneity, but he also sees that that would entail an admission of a constitutive or deconstitutive difference, which would in turn jeopardize the primordial unity of being that grounds all principle and all philosophy, that keeps the arbitrary play of the will within bounds. It is only in the decomposition of a tyrannous unity of consciousness that freedom can be located, if at all, although to locate it "there" would be to reduce freedom to a deconstitutive interruption of all certainty, including the certainty of freedom itself. Too close attention to the ground of freedom would lead to questions arising in an endless series, and freedom would be submitted to that ceaseless, discontinuous change from which Coleridge recoils. Such a closure of metaphysics is the terminal hazard that Coleridge's method constantly struggles to evade. That it is foreseen and feared makes all the difference in his prose. As he has displaced the text with marginalia, philosophy with rhetoric, logic with metaphor, so here he substitutes a dispute over efficient causes for the central question. In the service of a greater certainty Coleridge swerves into equivocation. He saves the metaphysics of will by losing it in willful commentary. The chapter closes with a wish that has only marginal significance:

> Sound logic, as the habitual subordination of the individual to the species, and of the species to the genus; philosophical knowledge of facts under the relation of cause and effect; a chearful [sic] and communicative temper disposing us to notice the similarities and contrasts of things, that we may be able to illustrate the one by the other; a quiet conscience; a condition free from anxieties; sound health, and above all (as far as relates to passive remembrance) a healthy digestion; *these* are the best, these are the only ARTS OF MEMORY. [*BL* I, 87-88]

Coleridge acts out the dilemma that Hartley had already expressed, that "it is difficult to explain Words to the Bottom by Words; perhaps impossible." He does so by, in effect, giving up a quest that might open up an infinite and infinitely debilitating regress. For that search, however, Coleridge has simply substituted its proper metaphor, a thoroughly marginal method. Entirely rhetorical, Coleridge's own metaphors have no philosophical content. But his rhetoric has philosophical significance just because it traverses the boundaries of philosophy. Because Coleridge's rhetoric is added to a philosophical argument, because his marginalia are inserted in the text, they make the point that philosophy, susceptible to interruption, is equivocal, that it has margins. That point is, of course, without substance.[20] Coleridge's marginal method may indeed suggest that Hartley's system (or Schelling's system[21]) has inconsistencies, but such a criti-

[20]There is no sage in the stone soup of the *Biographia*. The Coleridge of the period of the *Biographia* and the 1818 *Friend* is, to rephrase F. R. Leavis, at the fine point of discourse. The eventual blunting of that point can be associated with Coleridge's waxing ardor for the mysteries of trinitarianism, which corresponds to the congealing of his rhetoric into the oracular style of the 1825 *Aids to Reflection*, a style which, as John Holloway has indicated, strongly influenced the rhetorical posture of the Victorian sage (*The Victorian Sage* [1953; rpt., New York: Norton, 1965] p. 4).

[21]Coleridge uses Schelling in the *Biographia* in a way similar to that in which he uses Maass and Mackintosh. Schelling's words furnish plausible certainties that are the pretexts for the annotator's own desired certainties. At one point in Thesis VII Coleridge uses Schelling's argument as an authority for freedom of the will, but then he extends that authority in his own remarks to privilege the will before and beyond philosophy: "The self-conscious spirit therefore is a will;

cism can be annexed to any system—to philosophy itself. All philosophical certainties have inconsistencies and interruptions; all texts have margins.

---

and freedom must be assumed as a *ground* of philosophy, and can never be deduced from it" (*BL* I, 185). Although Coleridge considers the will only to remove it from consideration, it is nonetheless rendered equivocal. That peremptory and gnomic assertion would serve as well for a harmless corollary to Hartley's model, which similarly privileges a similarly absent divinity, as it would for a confutation of it. And in an addition to Schelling in Thesis IX, Coleridge furnishes a summation that could have been written by Hartley or Coleridge during his Hartleian period: "We begin with the I KNOW MYSELF, in order to lose and find all self in GOD" (*BL* I, 186). That just such a process had been "*demonstrated* by Hartley" was the stimulus to Coleridge's rhapsody in the 1796 "Religious Musings."

# [4]

# The Literary Life of
# a Man of Letters

Alexander—Mount Athos—a city in his hand—/. Pitt
impertinent Efflorescence of Rhetoric
a synodical Individuum—
a cracked Looking-glass—such is man's mind—Spinoza
Something deeper than his Lead can fathom—
To overdoe in expiation
under the broad-seal of nature—
blind man with the Dagger—C. Lamb—Sunday, March 23—
    1800—
Nescimus quid agunt; sed scimus per quales agunt. Augus-
    tine—

—*CN* I, 102-110

I

At the end of Chapter V of the *Biographia* Coleridge solicits
the patience of his readers as, he says, "I thus go 'sounding on
my dim and perilous way'" (*BL* I, 74). The quotation, one of
many instances in the *Biographia* where Coleridge invokes the
metaphor of the wayfarer, has been traced by Shawcross to the
Third Book of Wordsworth's *Excursion,* where it appears in the
long, autobiographical speech of the Solitary. The citation is apt,
as is its immediate context:

Then my soul
Turned inward,—to examine of what stuff
Time's fetters are composed; and life was put
To inquisition, long and profitless!
By pain of heart—now checked—and now impelled—
The intellectual power, through words and things,
Went sounding on, a dim and perilous way!

[118]

And from those transports, and these toils abstruse,
Some trace am I enabled to retain
Of time, else lost;—existing unto me
Only by records in myself not found.

[695-705]

Whether or not we are prepared to accept the Solitary's judgment on the past inquisition of his life, that it was "long and profitless," as Coleridge's melancholy comment on his own present self-examination, surely that the "intellectual power's" "dim and perilous way" sounded "through words and things" resounds as a dark echo of the earlier optimistic affirmation of the "natural difference of *things* and *thoughts*" and reinforces a skepticism regarding the intervening argument in Chapter V. Moreover, the Solitary's reflections on his past illuminate the method of Coleridge's text. The Solitary cannot paint what then he was; the time of "toils abstruse" was a time of vacancy that left no impression of his self in himself. It is legible only in traces, recoverable in records. Such records—old essays, notebook entries, letters, perhaps—are the kind of material out of which Coleridge devises the refutation of Hartleian associationism in Chapters V through VII and are evidence of a similar vacancy lodged where the self, subject and author of autobiography, might be.

As Coleridge's attempted refutation of Hartley is only marginally related to the proof of the free will, so are the Hartley chapters and their synecdoche the *Biographia Literaria* itself marginally related to the author's life and an authentic autobiography. The Hartleian section of the *Biographia* is an attempt to close off Hartley's influence, to construct and conclude a Hartleian *period* in Coleridge's intellectual life. It is meant to do double duty: to confute Hartley would be both to shape a progressive plot in Coleridge's philosophical career and to establish the will that is the basis of the self and the only fountainhead from which an authentic autobiography could flow. This parallelism structures the *Biographia,* which plots the possible convergence of career and life. Not an autobiography, the literary life is propaedeutic toward one. But, like the Solitary, Coleridge in the present of his writing, his "dim and perilous way" through associationism, finds nothing in himself to further his project. The problem of the will or, elsewhere, of genius and of the imagination, is the problem of the life. Coleridge's text is poised over the question of whether he can be the author of a life or must remain the writer in a biographia literaria, existing to himself and his reader only by records in himself not found.

Either to answer or to elaborate that question requires some preliminary estimation of what the *Biographia* is. Even to begin with the assumption that it is a book may be tendentious. Scholarship has still not completely settled the question whether what Coleridge calls his "immethodical miscellany" (*BL* I, 64) was either conceived of or composed as an autonomous work complete in itself or was instead the eccentric result of Coleridge's disjointed labor on a modest preface to his book of poems, *Sibylline Leaves*.[1] The uncertainty regarding the *Biographia's* genesis is compounded by its conduct. The problem of plagiarism has commanded most critical attention, but numerous local promiscuities have embarrassed or irritated readers of the *Biographia* since its publication; among them: the notorious "letter from a friend" in Chapter XIII, which aborts the promised elaboration of the theory of the imagination; the occasional attribution of *sententia* to sources where they cannot be traced; the unsettling enrichment of the language by capricious coinages; puzzling, often alarming leaps in logic or obliquities in argument; a suspiciously flagrant figurativeness; the disturbing gusto displayed in the use of footnotes to crack jokes, explore etymologies, or open entirely novel areas of inquiry. There seems to be no suitable explanation for such errancies. The conventional explanations of haste in publication or ill health do not satisfy: no critical clinician has been able to reduce Coleridge's alternately exuberant and bemused dislocation of argument to the merely symptomatic. Chaste reason and subtle rhetoric play just enough part in the construction of the *Biographia* to prohibit the wholesale ascription of inconsistencies and excess to either blindness or deceit. Nor can the text be easily recuperated into a genre that would predicate and thereby contain its idiosyncrasies: philosophical essay is least satisfying; autobiography is crucially de-

---

[1]For a discussion of the evidence see Daniel Mark Fogel's essay "A Compositional History of the *Biographia Literaria*," *Studies in Bibliography*, 30 (1977), 219-34.

ficient; the label menippean satire ill fits Coleridge's text, which, unlike its offspring, *Sartor Resartus*, lacks any cues of generic self-recognition. The *Biographia* is a source of anxiety for itself and for established critical tradition. It takes as its subject the possibility of the unified book: the fundamental stability of the grand chiasmus that the text is unified because it is the product of an integral consciousness and that consciousness is unifed because it produces integral texts. At the same time the *Biographia* flirts recklessly with the idea of the book, as though unity were not an anchoring reality but a floating object of desire and as though the desire for unity involved a lapse from the mental and moral integrity which the book supposedly incarnates. The theme of the *Biographia* is its test as book.

## II

Criticism that promotes the unity of the *Biographia* and the integrity of its author offers the choice of taking the text in one of two general ways. First, Coleridge's goal may be considered to be the definitive criticism of Wordsworth, a propaedeutic preface for the anticipated philosophical poem. It follows that Coleridge needs both to establish Wordsworth as a poet sufficiently important to warrant such high argument and to prove his own authority as critic to establish both the principles of Wordsworthian genius and the standards by which that genius is to be judged.[2] Alternatively, Coleridge's purpose may be considered to be the full elaboration of the theory of the imagination. In order to accomplish that Coleridge must both instantiate the imagination through reference to the poetry of Wordsworth and substantiate that faculty both by philosophical argument and rhetorical suasion.[3] Both of those teleological readings are

---

[2]See, for example, George Whalley, "The Integrity of the *Biographia Literaria*," *Essays and Studies*, 6 (1952), 87-101. A compatible conception of the *Biographia*'s unity is advanced by Richard Mallette in "Narrative Technique in the *Biographia Literaria*," *Modern Language Review*, 70 (1975), 32-40.

[3]See M. G. Cooke, "*Quisque Sui Faber*: Coleridge in the *Biographia Literaria*," *Philological Quarterly*, 50 (1971), 208-29. Two recent studies of the *Biographia*, Lawrence Buell's "The Question of Form in Coleridge's *Biographia Literaria*," *ELH*, 46, no. 3 (1979), 399-416, and Kathleen Wheeler's *Sources, processes, and methods in Coleridge's 'Biographia Literaria'* (Cambridge: Cambridge University Press, 1980), were published after the completion of this manuscript.

essentially the same. Both invest heavily in the last part of Coleridge's initial statement of intent, "to define with the utmost impartiality the real *poetic* character of the poet, by whose writings" the controversy over poetic diction "was first kindled and has been since fuelled and fanned" (*BL* I, 1-2), though the former weighs more heavily the actual poet, whereas the latter insists on the generalizing tendency within the phrase "real *poetic* character." More fundamentally, both readings agree on the need for and presence of a generative origin in the *Biographia* which certifies its ideal wholeness and ultimate intelligibility. And for both readings that origin is vitally implicated in the celebration of Wordsworth's poetic genius in Chapter IV.

The stage for the celebration of Wordsworth's imagination is fashioned in Chapter II, in which Coleridge exploits Horace's ancient sarcasm "'Genus irritable vatum'" (*BL* I, 19) (the irritable race of poets), as the pretext for his contrary programmatic claim that the true poetic genius is the least irritable of men, that he is, in fact, "creative and self-sufficing," and "lives most in the ideal world in which the present is still constituted by the past" (*BL* I, 20, 30). Far from being passively subject to an irritating or bewildering swirl of impressions, the poetic genius exhibits what Coleridge calls "a sanity of mind . . . between superstition with fanaticism on the one hand, and indifference and a diseased slowness to action on the other" (*BL* I, 20)—between that compulsively forceful type of mind defined as "commanding genius" and its antithesis, the mind whose impulse to realize its conceptions is paralyzed by their very vividness. The importance of this genial place is such that on the integrity and sanity of absolute genius depends the integrity and sanity of the mind itself. "The poet," Coleridge writes later in the *Biographia*, "described in *ideal* perfection, brings the whole soul of man into activity, with the subordination of its faculties to each other, according to their relative worth and dignity" (*BL* II, 12). The absolute genius, who incarnates the ideal perfection of the poet, not only puts the whole soul of man into activity but also, and more fundamentally, indemnifies a wholeness of soul which *can* be put into activity.

The mutual implication between genius and soul or mind approaches apotheosis in the fragmentary comments on the imagination in Chapter XIII. The constitutive powers of genius

are there absorbed into the active, unifying faculty of the secondary imagination, which, for Coleridge, owes its claim to be
more than theoretical to its embodiment in genius. The fact of
genius is the reality of a mind autonomous and whole, a mind
endlessly capable of combining and modifying ideas into ideal
creations which can be blent with feelings and affections. The
powers of this mind are analogous to those of the deity itself, for
though genius is classified according to a horizontal relation
midway between the extremes of superstition and dejection, the
value of genius lies in its vertical continuity with the transcendental. Partaker of the "highest and intuitive knowledge," which
Coleridge identifies with what Wordsworth calls "'The vision
and the faculty divine'" (*BL* I, 166), the genius is also a moral
agent in the world by means of the language with which he
expresses his ideal creations. Link between deity and man, soul
and body, mind and language, the genius, like the symbol, as it is
defined in the contemporary *Statesman's Manual*, is constituted
by "a translucence of the Eternal through and in the Temporal";
he "always partakes of the reality which [he] renders intelligible;
and while [he] enunciates the whole, abides himself as a living
part of that Unity, of which [he] is the representative."[4] Imagination as genius, genius as symbol—this consubstantiality, itself
symbolic, represents Coleridge's fullest answer to the dilemma
of the will as a power that must be both fully autonomous and
completely moral, conditioning without being conditioned. By
its instantiation in the genius, the free will is substantiated as it
could be in no other way.[5] The very existence of a mind at one
and the same time wholly self-sufficient and yet gloriously creative is itself a moral act insofar as it substantiates the essential
communion of the transcendental with the immanent that is the
scope of the will but which has proved the stumbling block to its
discursive demonstration and has baffled all Coleridge's attempts
to validate the moral integrity of the human mind. In the genius
"the man and the poet lose and find themselves in each other,
the one as glorified, the latter as substantiated" (*BL* II, 123).

[4]*LS*, 30.
[5]An affirmation of Coleridge's project, which relates the imagination and the
will to "an individualist myth of potentiality," appears in Michael G. Cooke, *The
Romantic Will* (New Haven: Yale University Press, 1976), pp. 1-29.

As the moral integrity of mind depends on the real existence of absolute genius, so does the proof of absolute genius in the *Biographia* depend on the "real *poetic* character" of William Wordsworth. The analogical world view endlessly begets metaphors for identity; here it divulges a hypopoesis that in its potential for reassurance and anxiety both structures and deconstructs the *Biographia:* on the absolute genius of William Wordsworth depends the moral integrity of Samuel Taylor Coleridge.[6]

Coleridge situates genius in his enthusiastic description of the "emergence" of Wordsworth's "original poetic genius above the literary horizon" (*BL* I, 56). Elaborating on the signs by which that original poetic genius was so "evidently announced," he adds to the metaphor of the rising sun those of the plant and the butterfly (*BL* I, 56-57) to express the process of unfolding, molting, and developing undergone by the poetic genius in its early stages. But the truly salient moment is that when the interest of evolution erupts into the astonishment of revelation. Coleridge describes "the sudden effect produced on [his] mind" (*BL* I, 58) by Wordsworth's unforgettable recitation of a manuscript poem:

It was the union of deep feeling with profound thought; the fine balance of truth in observing, with the imaginative faculty in modifying the objects observed; and above all the original gift of spreading the tone, the *atmosphere*, and with it the depth and height of the ideal world around forms, incidents, and situations, of which, for the common view, custom had bedimmed all the lustre, had dried up the sparkle and the dew drops. "To find no contradiction in the union of old and new; to contemplate the ANCIENT of days and all his works with feelings as fresh, as if all had then sprang forth at the first creative fiat; characterizes the mind that feels the riddle of the world, and may help to unravel it. To carry on the feelings of childhood into the powers of manhood; to combine the child's sense of wonder and novelty with the appearances, which every day for perhaps forty years had rendered familiar;

[6]See Richard Harter Fogle in *The Idea of Coleridge's Criticism* (Berkeley: University of California Press, 1962), p. 71; Thomas McFarland, "The Symbiosis of Coleridge and Wordsworth," *Studies in Romanticism*, 2, no. 4 (1972), 263-304; and Angus Fletcher, "'Positive Negation': Threshold, Sequence, and Personification in Coleridge," *New Perspectives on Coleridge and Wordsworth: Selected Papers from the English Institute*, ed. Geoffrey Hartman (New York: Columbia University Press, 1972), pp. 148-49.

'With sun and moon and stars throughout the year,
And man and woman;'
this is the character and privilege of genius, and one of the marks
which distinguish genius from talents. And therefore is it the prime
merit of genius and its most unequivocal mode of manifestation, so
to represent familiar objects as to awaken in the minds of others a
kindred feeling concerning them and that freshness of sensation
which is the constant accompaniment of mental, no less than of
bodily, convalescence. Who has not a thousand times seen snow fall
on water? Who has not watched it with a new feeling, from the time
that he has read Burns' comparison of sensual pleasure
'To snow that falls upon a river
A moment white—then gone for ever!'
In poems, equally as in philosophic disquisitions, genius produces
the strongest impressions of novelty, while it rescues the most
admitted truths from the impotence caused by the very circumstance of their universal admission. Truths of all others the most
awful and mysterious, yet being at the same time of universal interest, are too often considered as *so* true, that they lose all the life
and efficiency of truth, and lie bed-ridden in the dormitory of the
soul, side by side with the most despised and exploded errors."—
THE FRIEND*, p. 76, No. 5 [BL I, 59-60]

Here, if ever, Coleridge presents an origin. Formally, the passage seems intended to furnish the original experiential basis for
the later theoretical treatment of the powers of the imagination
and for the subsequent application of that theory in a return to
Wordsworth's poetry, poetry which will be judged according to
Wordsworth's original standard. Besides its structural status as a
beginning, the passage is about origins and the conditions of
origination. The instances are various: the originating power of
the original poetic genius is compared to the absolute integrity
of the "first creative fiat" of the deity; the original work of the
poet provokes in the auditor a re-creation of the original "sense
of wonder and novelty" of the child at the same time that it
originates in him a "mental convalescence" through a reconstitu-
tion of a lost "freshness of sensation." Moreover, the passage
also recollects the origin of Coleridge's now strained intimacy
with Wordsworth: as the old is united with the new, the familiar
invigorated by the novel, so Coleridge's literary life finds its vital
origin in the transformation of the recent stranger into an old
friend.

Although the significance of this moment as both celebration of the integrity and power of the original act and as establishment of a standard by which to identify absolute genius and its original works is clear, the passage is, nonetheless, peculiar. For a moment that contains so much of Coleridge's literary theory and portends so much more, the presentation is remarkably careless. Although the empirical reality of the recitation is important, Coleridge takes no pains to locate the moment with any precision: he rather vaguely mentions an unpublished manuscript the same in "stanza and tone of style" to the "'Female Vagrant,' as originally printed in the first volume of the 'Lyrical Ballads'" (*BL* I, 58)—a stanza and style which he later casually identifies as Spenserian—but the only date he gives for the reading is a statement of his age at the time, a statement which all editors have agreed is inaccurate. Since Coleridge never referred to such a recitation either in his letters or his notebooks, precise dating is difficult. His first contact with the "Female Vagrant" came in a version of the poem that would eventually be published in 1842 as "Guilt and Sorrow"; the recitation must have occurred some time between August of 1795 and March 1796. The difference between August and March reflects, however, a difference between two quite distinct versions of the poem, now called respectively "Nights on Salisbury Plain" and "Adventures on Salisbury Plain."[7] Given the overlap, it is altogether possible that Coleridge has, in recollection, conflated his reaction to the two versions or confused a reading of the manuscript of one poem with the recitation of another. Indeed it is entirely possible that in recalling this moment of origin Coleridge has invented the recitation, one, after all, like so many others that would follow in his intimacy with Wordsworth. Each of those possibilities entails the consequence that for the purposes of his argument in Chapter IV Coleridge has to some extent imagined the poem itself. Regardless of the relative probability of individual hypotheses, the uncertainties surrounding both poem and recitation equivocate the fact of the origin as Coleridge recounts it.

[7]See Stephen Gill's introduction to *The Salisbury Plain Poems of William Wordsworth*, ed. Gill (Ithaca, N.Y.: Cornell University Press, 1975).

The passage echoes with equivocations. Note that to describe his original experience of Wordsworth's original genius Coleridge employs a passage which he has already used in his 1809 periodical *The Friend*. To make that connection demands no detective work, because Coleridge rather uncharacteristically encloses the passage in quotation marks and notes the spot in *The Friend* from which the passage was taken. He even attaches a footnote to justify its use:

> *As "the Friend" was printed on stampt sheets, and sent only by the post to a very limited number of subscribers, the author has felt less objection to quote from it, though a work of his own. To the public at large indeed it is the same as a volume in manuscript. [*BL* I, 60]

In the spirit of Coleridge's scholarship, we, in turn, can note that Coleridge reuses a good deal of the same passage in *The Statesman's Manual*, a work written after the *Biographia* but published earlier.[8] What can be made of the choice of this warmed-over passage to describe this putative origin?

First, it can be inferred that Coleridge liked the passage. And understandably so, for it is a fine piece of writing, which begins in the sublime style but which ends by fastening itself firmly to the earth through a homely but effective metaphor. Coleridge could justifiably feel that the passage was worthy of being resurrected from its grave in *The Friend*. Or it could be that Coleridge felt that this was a definitive statement of genius and that by applying it to Wordsworth's poetry he could most emphatically affirm the genius of the poet. Neither of those explanations satisfactorily addresses, let alone resolves, the discordant effect that the quotation has in context, however. Each is inadequate just so far as it fails to explain the effect that having to hypothesize motives has on the putative integrity of the passage. Neither hypothesis bears within it the recognition of the critical role that the repetition of the passage plays in provoking an hypothesis. Before the invention of any explanatory hypothesis, it is mere repetition that is *first* indicated by those quotation marks—an

[8]*LS*, 25. Shawcross notes that the "same thought is recorded in almost the same language in *A.P.* [*Anima Poetae*] 1803 (p. 41) [*BL* I, p. 225].

original repetition supplementing the origin which endows with
significance features of the text that would be otherwise unre-
markable and opens it to chains of conjecture and layers of
commentary.

Take, for example, the poetic quotations that Coleridge deploys in the passage. They have long been identified: the first is
from Milton's sonnet "To Mr. Cyriack Skinner upon his Blindness"; the second is taken from Burns's "Tam O' Shanter." In
reading the periodical version of *The Friend* the quotations may
pass unnoticed, lost in the vagaries of the argument or the
obscurities of the style. But in reading the *Biographia* it should be
marked that when repeated and applied to Wordsworth the
association of Milton and Burns suddenly *means* something:
those poets are two acknowledged influences on Wordsworth's
poetry; moreover, they are also influences that correspond to
what Coleridge identifies as antagonistic poles in Wordsworth's
work: the pole of the Miltonic philosophical poet and that of the
humble lyricist or dramatic poet who professes to speak "the real
language of men." Indeed, by endorsing Burns's genius in his
quotation, Coleridge not only traces the split within Wordsworth
but adumbrates his later response to it in Chapter XXII, where
he asserts that, far from being a rustic exemplar, Burns is the
marvelous exception who proves the general rule of the inability
of the "very delicate" and "very rare plant" of poetic genius to
take root in rural soil (*BL* II, 106). I am not claiming that this
criticism is buried in this passage or necessarily implied, but the
repetition of the quotations does make them more interesting
than they would otherwise be. That quickening of interest *may*
adumbrate a criticism; at the very least it acts as an irritant that
deflects attention from the integral power of Wordsworth and
slightly disturbs the placid continuity of the original moment,
something like the effect of creeping breezes on a mountain
pond. That these two influences and aspects of Wordsworth
precipitate out so quickly after the assertion of the "fine balance"
of Wordsworth's poetry may unsettle the reader's assurance that
such a balance is actually there. Certainly if we add to the quotations from Milton and Burns the fact that Coleridge gives as one
of the two specific characteristics of the recited poem its
"Spenserian stanza which always, more or less, recalls to the

reader's mind Spenser's own style" (*BL* I, 59), we have an account of Wordsworth's genius resonant with the genius of others—influences more or less in the auditor's mind and only more or less unified in the ideal world of Wordsworth's poetry. Notably, Coleridge's use of the word *Spenserian* here antedates any other usage of the word listed in the *OED*. Is this the "original" use of *Spenserian*, then, pointedly to characterize Wordsworth's style in his wholly original poetry?

Once a reader begins unraveling poetic language it is difficult to know when to stop, as Coleridge was well aware. Is it not uncannily circumstantial that the two lines that Coleridge repeats here as apparent reinforcement of his topic of genial restoration are respectively from a poem and a passage which treat conditions of complete and irreversible loss? The passage in "Tam O'Shanter" from which the lines are taken concludes with the proposition that "Nae man can tether time nor tide" (l. 67). In the Milton sonnet, where vision is sacrificed to "the noble task" of defending liberty, the success of which more than compensates for the inexorable approach of blindness, the glory of the poet's sacrifice depends on the finality of his loss. Coming to the Milton from Coleridge we can, I think, catch both the familiar accent of Coleridgean dejection over loss of power—a theme in the *Biographia* as well as in the poetry—and a surprising affirmation of the conditions of sacrifice: there is something more important than vision; genius isn't everything. Regardless of how we read the story of these allusions out in the text, they seem to qualify thematically both the optimism of the passage in which they appear and to deflect the singleminded attention on Wordsworth's overpowering genius. Regardless of whether we choose to read these allusions out at all, the glimpse of the possibility of unraveling has *already* begun unraveling the apparently univocal affirmation of the origin.

This investigation might have begun with the simple observation that Coleridge's decision to justify his self-quotation in a footnote suggests that he is uneasy about it, that perhaps he has a bad conscience about deflecting attention, no matter how slightly, from Wordsworth, the speaking poet to Coleridge, recollector and writer. That deflection certainly does seem inconsistent with the intention of the passage and with the effacement of self that Coleridge, auditor of and vehicle for Wordsworth's genius, has practiced throughout Chapter IV. But if that inconsistency is the problem, the footnote proves a dubious solution, for it clearly diverts even more attention to Coleridge the writer. It makes an issue—or, more precisely, an issue of an issue: No. 5 of the 1809 *Friend*. By emphasizing the obscurity of *The Friend*, Coleridge in the same gesture publicizes it. Moreover, though the 1809 *Friend* may effectively be in manuscript for all its currency and availability, as Coleridge claims, the reader knows that he had firm plans to complete and republish *The Friend* by the time he had begun writing the *Biographia*. The reader knows because among the many references to *The Friend* scattered throughout the *Biographia* are two footnotes (*BL* I, 147 and 164) which announce the imminent republication. By calling attention in Chapter IV to the choice expressions to be found in *The Friend* Coleridge not only publicizes a stillborn manuscript, he advertises his new book.

If we act on this publicity and consult *The Friend*, we discover another good reason for Coleridge's hypothetical uneasiness. *Friend* No. 5 is devoted to a fervid defense of the author's inveterate preoccupation with difficult metaphysical topics both in this periodical and in other of his writings. Coleridge asks, "How shall I avert the scorn of those Critics who laugh at the oldness of my Topics, Evil and Good, Necessity and Arbitrement, Immortality and the ultimate Aim."[9] He answers with the passage we are considering—a declamation, then, which is not merely a celebration of the powers of genius but is both a defense and promotion of Coleridge's *own* genius. Transferred to the *Biographia*, this passage defends, promotes, and realizes Coleridge's genius. Coleridge simultaneously promotes a defense of his genius from *The Friend* and actualizes that genius in the communication of the genius of Wordsworth. The quoted passage is a commentary on its own function in the *Biographia*. It finds in the ability to feel and unravel, to carry on and combine, the character, the privilege, and the distinguishing marks of genius.

[9]*The Friend* (1809), ed. Barbara E. Rooke, *Collected Works*, 4 (Princeton: Princeton University Press, 1969), II, 73.

Feeling Wordsworth's power, unraveling it, and carrying it on to a wider audience in a manner that represents familiar objects, such as Wordsworth's poems, so as to awaken in the minds of others a kindred feeling concerning them, Coleridge impresses on the page the distinguishing marks of his own genius: the authority to determine genius and the power to communicate its truth to the world.

The inclusion or intrusion of the quoted passage produces a familiar Coleridgean movement: the apparent effacement of self before the genius of Wordsworth or anyone else, a theme magnified here by the apologetic tone of certain digressive remarks, turns out to be no self-effacement at all, but instead a subtle maneuver which looks a great deal like self-aggrandizement.[10] The shape of that maneuver and its subtlety can be most clearly seen as it bears on the Wordsworth-Coleridge relationship and the problem of genius in a passage following Coleridge's taxonomy of genius in the beginning of Chapter II. There he introduces Shakespeare as the first member of the fraternity of absolute genius, a club from which Coleridge feels himself constitutionally excluded, but of which Wordsworth will be one of the most illustrious members. Coleridge's aim here is to show that genius, even Shakespeare's genius, is compatible with a sense of personal greatness. The text he uses from Shakespeare to show the poet's sense of his greatness and thereby doubly to reinforce the profundity of Shakespeare's genius is not a passage from the plays or from the longer narrative poems but Sonnet 81, "Your name from hence immortal life shall have," wherein Shakespeare's greatness is proved by his ability to make immortal his *friend.* That is, Shakespeare exercises his genius and advances his greatness by promoting the greatness of his friend, in the transparent fiction that the friend will be immortal whereas the poet himself must die. The analogy of that relationship with the relations existing

[10]See Reeve Parker's discussion of this maneuver in chapter 7 of *Coleridge's Meditative Art* (Ithaca, N.Y.: Cornell University Press, 1975), where he concludes his interpretation of the apparently adulatory "To William Wordsworth" by asserting that Coleridge therein "avenged himself on his friend by enriching their relationship with a poem that recorded his own egotistic and transcendent ideal" (pp. 239-40).

between the Coleridge of the *Biographia* and his friend Wordsworth is uncannily close.[11]

A possible conclusion might be that Wordsworthian genius is Coleridge's figure, that Coleridge, for his own ends, fabricates Wordsworth the genius and exploits that figure within the analogical play of his literary life. Yet to have a figure normally requires the presumption of one who figures, of an intentionality somewhere, somehow recoverable; and once absolute genius, the very symbol of the intending consciousness, is subjected to the illegitimate freedom of the text, lost is the ground which permits the hypothesis of an integrity of mind that *has* its own ends, that is ontologically capable of fabrication and morally culpable for exploitation. Wordsworthian genius may be a Coleridgean figure, but it is hardly Coleridge's figure. Although it is important to read this passage in Chapter IV, to notice the quotation marks and to track the language to *The Friend,* where it supports Coleridge's claim to genius, the duplicity of this repetition should not be mistaken by precipitately ascribing its origin to the author of *The Friend,* and thereby encouraging the comfortable conclusion that one has thereby *placed* Coleridge's unsettling genius. The one sure thing that can be said about the *Biographia* is that Coleridge's literary life is the story of Wordsworth's genius—a sharp saying that cuts both ways. It is possible to indicate that duplicity by prying loose what can be considered Coleridge's central proposition about genius,[12] that the "prime merit of genius and its most unequivocal mode of manifestation [is] so to represent familiar objects as to awaken in the minds of others a kindred feeling concerning them and that freshness of sensation which is the constant accompaniment of mental, no less than of bodily convalescence." Prime, unequivocal. But whose equivocation is it, the writer's, the reader's, or the genius's, that accounts for the shimmer of the figurative in the phrase "freshness of sensation" and the uneasiness in the meta-

[11]Coleridge gives three examples of geniuses: Shakespeare, whose sense of his greatness appears in the celebration of his friend; Spenser, who remained gentle despite the "unjust persecution" he, like Coleridge, endured; and Milton, who remained calmly self-possessed even though, like the author of the *Biographia,* he was in his "latter days: poor, sick, old, blind, slandered, persecuted" (*BL* I, 23).

[12]See M. H. Abrams, *Natural Supernaturalism* (New York: Norton, 1971), p. 379 and *passim.*

phor of "mental convalescence"? Convalescence? From what sickness? And why not health?

Coleridge's first use of such language that I know of occurs in a 1798 letter to his brother George: "Laudanum gave me repose, not sleep: but YOU, I believe, know how divine that repose is—what a spot of inchantment, a green spot of fountains, & flowers & trees, in the very heart of a waste of Sands!—God be praised, the matter has been absorbed; and I am recovering a pace, and enjoy that *newness* of sensation from the fields, the air, & the Sun, which makes convalescence almost repay one for the disease" (*CL* I, 394-95).

What can be safely said about the association of these two passages, one celebrating genius, the other a drug? Which stimulant has priority? Should it be stated that genius has the effect of a drug or that the drug has the effect of genius? If we accept Coleridge's weighting in the *Biographia*, "mental, no less than physical," the physical seems to have precedence; at least physical convalescence is far more familiar. In its attack on illness and in its production of a convalescence midway between illness and health the drug seems to have furnished Coleridge with both the experience of fresh sensation and the material for metaphor. But if this precedence, experiential or material, be granted, how can the manifestation of fresh sensation be an unequivocal sign of genius? How can one be immediately and absolutely certain that the vision one takes as the effect of original genius is not merely the effect of another drug? The possible reply that convalescence is just metaphorical when applied to genius does not remove the equivocation installed in the passage by the incorporation of a metaphor here at this supposedly unequivocal point. It is not necessary to argue either an epistemological or ontological priority for the physical in order to insinuate that here the mere anteriority of the physical to the mental, the vehicle to the tenor, unsettles the supposed epistemological and ontological priority of genius: it is as if metaphor produces genius rather than genius metaphor.

Notions of priority and agency become even more ambiguous once we engage the fact that what provokes physical convalescense is not merely another drug but laudanum, not medicine but an anodyne. An anodyne, of course, does not cure illness but relieves pain; the convalescence it provokes is always metaphorical since it will never produce literal health. Moreover, this anodyne, laudanum, is an opiate. The anodyne suppresses pain and provokes a metaphorical convalescence that is as much of health as can be expected; it is the genius of the opiate, however, to figure that convalescence with the pleasurable vision of its proper paradise—a figure made possible by an invigorating respite from the numbing monotony of painful sensation. Crucially, though, this figure of blessed health, like Kubla Khan's walls and towers, includes within its fold, as part of its pleasure, the marks of its transience: the overtaking of the oasis by the surrounding sands, the certain fall from a paradisal convalescence back into dull, everyday pain. Its figure remarks the transience of the anodyne itself. The marks of its transience are the inscription of its otherness: the possibility of a benign wholeness, the figure of convalescence, is made possible by the incorporation of the anodyne, which at the same time limits that possibility to the figurative not only because it is transitory but because of its ineradicable otherness. This foreign thing gives one (almost) oneself; self-possession is (im)possible through the incorporation of the other. And besides being transitory and foreign, the opiate is also addictive. Under its dispensation the possible autonomy of self-possession can only be understood as the function of a habit; freedom is both constituted and regulated by the mechanical rhythm of need. The incorporation of laudanum thus marks the difference of the Coleridgean convalescence from both sickness and health; convalescence will inevitably subside into a pain become indistinguishable from the effects of withdrawing from the anodyne—a pain that is but the deferral of another dose of the opiate. Convalescence, as figured in Coleridge's text, is thoroughly hypopoetical because it is the place where one imagines the fact and position of health, a place whose fact and position is itself the fanciful effect of the supplementation of pain by the anodyne.

Although I have called this paean to the convalescent powers of laudanum Coleridge's "first use" of the *locus amoenus* which he employs to describe the effect of Wordsworth's genius, Coleridge's *first* use is not Coleridge's at all, but Wordsworth's, who in his "Salisbury Plain" begins the long excursus that ends the

1793-94 version of the poem with this valediction of the traveller and the female vagrant:

> Adieu ye friendless hope-forsaken pair!
> Yet friendless ere ye take your several road,
> Enter that lowly cot and ye shall share
> Comforts by prouder mansions unbestowed.
> For you yon milkmaid bears her brimming load,
> For you the board is piled with homely bread,
> And think that life is like this desart broad,
> Where all the happiest find is but a shed
> And a green spot 'mid wastes interminable spread.
>
> [415-23][13]

If, reading Coleridge, we have read the turns of this figure aright and find in Coleridge's celebration of this place an installation of it within the ritual mechanics of need and withdrawal, we also read Coleridge's echo of Wordsworth's glad vision as a remark that resituates the green spot which Wordsworth nostalgically ventures as a symbol of a possible home within the poignant allegory of succession and loss where it "belongs":

> "Some mighty gulf of separation passed
> I seemed transported to another world:
> A dream resigned with pain when from the mast
> The impatient mariner the sail unfurled,
> And whistling called the wind that hardly curled
> The silent seas. The pleasant thoughts of home
> With tears his weather-beaten cheek impearled:
> For me, farthest from earthly port to roam
> Was best; my only wish to shun where man might come.
>
> "And oft, robbed of my perfect mind, I thought
> At last my feet a resting-place had found.
> 'Here will I weep in peace,' so Fancy wrought,
> 'Roaming the illimitable waters round,
> Here gaze, of every friend but Death disowned,
> All day, my ready tomb the ocean flood.'
> To break my dream the vessel reached its bound

---

[13]As reproduced in Gill's edition, pp. 21-38.

And homeless near a thousand homes I stood,
And near a thousand tables pined and wanted food."

[370-87]

The dream of another, altogether better world, of an inviolable resting-place, the dream broached by Wordsworth, is broken as the poem reaches its bound in the echo of its auditor, the critic who in recalling that dream, in the very act of apparently passing the mighty gulf separating them in space and time, reinscribes it between inverted commas, thereby marking the poet's resignation to a pain that is the lapse between the prospective refuge and the lost serenity of a perfect mind.

Having read the origin of the *Biographia* in Chapter IV, we can reread its beginning in Chapter I, where Coleridge seems to be consciously foreshadowing the encounter with Wordsworth and where he adumbrates its ritual mechanics. He fondly recollects the effects of the "genial influence" of William Lisle Bowles's poetry, which he credits with having withdrawn him temporarily at least from the "preposterous pursuits" of metaphysics, given an infernal venue by means of a quotation from Book II of *Paradise Lost*. Coleridge's grateful memory of this time as a "long and blessed interval, during which my natural faculties were allowed to expand, and my original tendencies to develope themselves: my fancy, and the love of nature, and the sense of beauty in forms and sounds" clearly anticipates the waning of Bowles's healing power and another descent into the metaphysical underworld. So much is also suggested by Coleridge's self pitying, "Well were it for me, perhaps, had I never relapsed into the same mental disease; if I had continued to pluck the flower and reap the harvest of the cultivated surface, instead of delving in the unwholesome quicksilver mines of metaphysic depths" (*BL* I, 10). In one sense and from a certain bracing distance, Bowles is the type for which Wordsworth is the antitype; and in that sense the *Biographia*, like *Paradise Lost* and *The Prelude*, forecasts a future happier far—an ideal world prepared by the redemptive discovery of a truly philosophical poet, the hero who will rescue Persephone from her cyclic fate. That perspective explains Coleridge's complacent use of "instead" here to wedge apart lightsome pleasures from infernal indulgence as informed

[136]

by his foresight of a reconciliation of those extremes in the harmony of head and heart. But complacency is surely a hazard for both writer and reader. From up close Coleridge's text is neither hell nor the fair fields of Enna. In the intimacy of his engagement with Wordsworth, a poet of both more depth and more cultivation than Bowles, we read a Coleridge whose flower plucking (poppies, perhaps?) *is* a delving—a figure for whom the blessed interval of the convalescent turn toward the light is the mere interruption in the machine that articulates the rhythm of lapse/relapse.[14]

### III

I can imagine Wordsworth reading Chapter IV and putting to Coleridge the question that the latter puts, rhetorically, to the anonymous critics of the reviews: "[H]as the poet no property in

[14]Coleridge is more explicit in connecting this lost serenity with convalescence in his notebooks. At one point he writes: "Strange contradiction of Being!—When I am *miserable I can forget my misery but at soon as I* begin *to be happy* at the first dawning of convalescence, then *comes upon me such an agony of love & recollection that I call out for misery in order not to be miserable*" (*CN* III, 3441 [words in italics deciphered from Coleridge's code by the editor]). At another: "All convalescence a resurrection & palingenesy of our youth—One loves the Earth and all that lives thereon with a new Heart—But oh! the anguish to have this aching freshness of Yearning—& no answering object—only remembrances of faithless change and unmerited alienation—" (*CN* III, 4083). Coleridge's writings show the pervasive influence of his physical illnesses. I am not the first to point that out. Coleridge was: "Images in sickly profusion by & in which I talk in certain diseased States of my Stomach / Great & innocent minds *devalesce*, as Plants & Trees, into beautiful Diseases / Genius itself, many of the most brilliant sorts of English Beauty, & even extraordinary Dispositions to Virtue, Restlessness in good—are they not themselves, as I have often said, but beautiful Diseases—species of the Genera, Hypochondriasis, Scrofula, & Consumption!" (*CN* I, 1822). Yet if we seek for what Kenneth Burke calls "correlations between styles and physical disease," we must keep in mind what few students of Coleridge besides W. J. Bate and Thomas McFarland (see "Coleridge's Anxiety" in *Coleridge's Variety*, ed. John Beer [Pittsburgh: University of Pittsburgh Press, 1975], pp. 134-65) have acknowledged, "that the true locus of assertion is not the *disease* but in the *structural powers* by which the poet encompasses it" (Kenneth Burke, *The Philosophy of Literary Form* [1941; revised and abridged, New York: Vintage Books, 1961], p. 16). Moreover, in the case of Coleridge there is the added complication that he is both poet and critic. "I appear to myself," he writes, "like a sick Physician, feeling the pang acutely, yet deriving a wonted pleasure from examining it's [sic] progress and developing it's causes" (*CL* I, 133). Coleridge's prose is the stage (or clinic) on which he thus appears to himself.

[137]

his works?" (*BL* I, 29). The *Biographia* is that text where one may imagine Wordsworth asking Coleridge's questions in a voice that we had always taken to be Coleridge's own. The appropriateness of such imagining returns once again the thematics of the *Biographia*: what kind of book is it? whose property is the text? what proprieties does it observe? That return argues that the phrase "The real *poetic* character of the poet" will not satisfy the critical need for an integrating principle. Coleridge never promised that it would. At the beginning of the *Biographia Literaria* where he states his purpose, Coleridge implies that the poetic character of the poet, though ideally standing on its own, cannot be understood in this case without explicating its relationship to another issue, the nature of poetic diction: "But of the objects, which I proposed to myself, it was not the least important to effect, as far as possible, a settlement of the long continued controversy concerning the true nature of poetic diction, and at the same time to define with the utmost impartiality the real *poetic* character of the poet, by whose writings this controversy was first kindled and has been since fuelled and fanned" (*BL* I, 1-2). To understand the poetic character of the poet is tantamount to understanding the true nature of poetic diction, which in turn will require the settlement of a controversy between the poet and his critic—a settlement that will be completed, the metaphor suggests, when the critic has extinguished the flames kindled, fuelled, and fanned by the poet's writings.

"Has the poet no property in his works?" The question of poetic genius is the question of the poet's property in his works and in himself. The two come to the same thing in a virtual tautology: everything that belongs to the genius he possesses; everything he possesses belongs to him. The genius's property is proper to him; and the genius validates the propriety of property in the entirely valid *amour-propre* of his absolute self-possession. Instantiated in the genius, the intimate connection of property and propriety can also be confirmed by the history of the English language. In a footnote on the formation of words Coleridge informs us that until the time of Charles II the different senses of the two words were combined under the single spelling "propriety." Coleridge has introduced this philological commentary to justify his desynonimization of imagination and fancy, which, though conscious, partakes of "a certain collective, unconscious good sense working progressively to desynonimize those words originally of the same meaning, which the conflux of dialects had supplied to more homogeneous languages, as the Greek and the German: and which the same cause, joined with accidents of translation from original works of different countries, occasion in mixt languages like our own" (*BL* I, 61). But the example of property and propriety constitutes a special case within this context, as it does for the book as a whole.[15] Although Coleridge asserts that the "original likeness" of the desynonimized words has been generally "worn away by the progressive good sense of the language," property and propriety are deployed in the *Biographia* as part of a genealogical and genial strategy that will insist on the retrieval not only of their likeness but their essential identity.[16]

As Coleridge's note indicates, the desynonimizing of propriety and property has a specific history. The loss of synonymity corresponded to the major shift in the constitution of the British state that occurred in the seventeenth century: the challenge to and decline of the authority of the sovereign, which began with regicide, was partially redressed by the Glorious Revolution of 1688, but has advanced with deplorable velocity ever since. On the synonymity of propriety and property rests the possibility of restoring that lost authority which Coleridge associates with the last age of sovereignty.[17] Congruent with that historical vision is a social concern vitally interested in preserving the places where the alliance of head and heart is still delicately

[15]Joel Weinsheimer ably explores some of the implications of Coleridge's concept of synonymity from a perspective different from my own in his essay "Coleridge on Synonimity and the Reorigination of Truth," *Papers on Literature and Language*, 14, no. 3 (1978), 269-83.

[16]When in *On the Constitution of Church and State* Coleridge addresses the question of the property that forms the "legitimate objects" of the power of the state he coins the term "Proprietage" to indicate that resynonimizing of property and propriety (*CCS*, ed. John Colmer, *Collected Works*, 10 [Princeton: Princeton University Press, 1976], 82 and 108).

[17]Although Coleridge has no fondness for the memory of Charles I, he never condones regicide, which severs from the state its "head and arm" (*CCS*, 82). Perhaps his most concise and telling statement of the mutual implication between the form of government and the shape of thought is this: "1680—the birth of our Constitution, the death of our philosophic mind!" (*CN* III, 3951).

maintained by the synonymity of property and propriety. The epitome of such a place is the English county parish, which Coleridge celebrates in Chapter XI: "That to every parish throughout the kingdom there is transplanted a germ of civilization; that in the remotest villages there is a nucleus, round which the capabilities of the place may crystallize and brighten; a model sufficiently superior to excite, yet sufficiently near to encourage and facilitate, imitation; *this*, the unobtrusive, continuous agency of a Protestant church establishment, *this* it is which the patriot and philanthropist, who would fain unite the love of peace with the faith in the progressive amelioration of mankind, cannot estimate at too high a price" (*BL* I, 155). Although the clergyman's unobtrusive establishment can be used to exemplify aptly the general social benefits of the synonymity of property and propriety, such exemplification itself necessarily obtrudes on the harmonious whole from a perspective outside its symbolic space. The hint of nostalgia in Coleridge's eulogy is magnified not only by his expressed regrets over his youthful rejection of the church as a career (*BL* I, 158-59), but also by his sociological observations on the ambiguous status of a church which is currently under attack from all sides, even from its supposed beneficiaries, the farmers who now clamor against church property. The increasing agitation to disestablish the church is a particularly alarming example of an unconscious *bad* sense working not only to dislodge the church from its place in society but to sever all the cultural, political, social, and religious bonds that unite the various distinct parts of the nation into one harmonious whole. For Coleridge the genius is that individual whose symbolic and symbolizing place in the nation (in the language) is as the "good sense" which insures that desynonimization is "progressive" rather than merely dissociative, as the power which reverses those unconscious associations that both reflect and contribute to the general decline suffered by the traditional symbols of authority. Sovereign by virtue of his absolute property in himself and his complete propriety of self, the genius is the ideal monarch of the ideal commonwealth, who will restore the principle of sovereignty to king and country and will dissipate the confoundment of distinct meanings in order to distribute the "reversionary wealth in our mother tongue"—a wealth that is true wealth because, backed as it is by a sovereign at one with his imagination, it can never be exhausted. The progress and value of desynonimization can only be judged according to those "absolute synonymes" (*BL* I, 63 n.) which constitute the inalienable capital of the language. At issue in the controversy between Coleridge and Wordsworth over poetic diction is the sovereign synonymity of propriety and property. At stake is the establishment that endows meanings with meaning. What makes the controversy crucial for Coleridge is that the very genius whose imaginative power and moral integrity has been hypopoeticized as the source, manifestation, and agent of "progressive good sense" has perversely broached the severest challenge to the identification of propriety and property.

Coleridge is precise about the nature of the controversy between him and Wordsworth. "My own differences," he says, "from certain supposed parts of Mr. Wordsworth's theory ground themselves on the assumption, that his words had been rightly interpreted, as purporting that the proper diction for poetry in general consists altogether in a language taken, with due exceptions, from the mouths of men in real life, a language which actually constitutes the natural conversation of men under natural feelings" (*BL* II, 29). Coleridge obviously strays from Wordsworth's actual language, which is much more qualified than he represents it.[18] He deliberately overstates Wordsworth's argument because he is less interested in it for what it is than for what it does or may do. Coleridge interprets Wordsworth's position as part of a tendency which, however equivocal its expression, has unambiguous significance in its relation to issues of the utmost importance not only for poetry but for language, metaphysics, culture, and politics. The density of the analogies to which Coleridge has committed himself works like a lens to arm his vision so that tendencies in ambiguous language appear with a deadly clarity; he acts to prevent fraying in an area even as apparently peripheral as poetic diction lest

---

[18]For discussions of Coleridge's manipulation of Wordsworth's argument see Stephen Maxfield Parrish's *The Art of the Lyrical Ballads* (Cambridge, Mass.: Harvard University Press, 1973), *passim*, and Don Bialostosky's article "Coleridge's Interpretation of Wordsworth's Preface to *Lyrical Ballads*," *PMLA*, 93 (1978), 912-24.

it lead to the unraveling of the entire fabric woven on the genius's loom.

For Coleridge, Wordsworth's theory is either pointless or, if pointed, harmful: "My objection is, first, that in *any* sense this rule is applicable only to *certain* classes of poetry; secondly, that even to these classes it is not applicable, except in such a sense, as hath never by anyone (as far as I know or have read) been denied or doubted; and, lastly, that as far as, and in that degree in which it is *practicable*, it is yet as a *rule* useless, if not injurious, and therefore need not, or ought not be practised" (*BL* II, 29-30). After summarizing some of the conventional reasons for introducing low and rustic life into serious poetry, Coleridge quotes from Wordsworth to show that his motives are neither conventional nor acceptable. Coleridge's supervening reason for rejecting the standard of rustic life, resonant for the thematics of the *Biographia,* is that "for the human soul to prosper in rustic life, a certain vantage-ground is pre-requisite" (*BL* II, 32). "Education or original sensibility," the alternative prerequisites he identifies, synonymous with propriety and property respectively, are themselves synonymized under the rubric of the "vantage-ground." Only the ownership of the ground makes possible any vantage; the vantage from which one can oversee far and near, past and future, makes the property worth owning. The only true ground for Coleridge is a vantage ground: to own is to have a vantage as to have a vantage is to own. If one strikes "rustic life" from the sentence just quoted, the analogical force of the metaphor is released: the human soul can only prosper on high ground. But the odd quality of this central metaphor is that though at its ultimate and necessary extension it summons forth the prerequisite of a transcendental God (origin and educator), who is *the* vantage ground, because it is a metaphor, because the prospering of the human soul requires some touch with the fact of the world, at its limit the figure will literalize itself in an extravagance of myth, like that of Sinai in Exodus, which was so analomous in yet necessary to Hartley's history of language. For Coleridge too, the one exception to his strictures against rustics occurs in a necessary literalization of his metaphor that exemplifies the economy it represents: "Whatever may be concluded on the other side, from the stronger local attachments and enterprising spirit of the Swiss, and other mountaineers, applies to a particular mode of pastoral life, under forms of property that permit and beget manners truly republican, not to rustic life in general, or to the absence of artificial cultivation."[19] The Swiss are the fabled exceptions who prove the rule because, literally sharing the vantage ground of the Alps, they hold a place prior to desynonimization of propriety and property, education and original sensibility. To insure that his economics are not confused with a sentimental naturalism Coleridge contrasts the cultivated, enterprising Swiss with the "peasantry of North Wales," Wordsworth's poetic subjects for whom "the ancient mountains, with all their terrors and all their glories, are pictures to the blind and music to the deaf" (*BL* II, 32). The Welsh peasants may be in but they do not own the mountains: psychologically natural, their passions are "incorporated with the beautiful and permanent forms of nature"; socially natural, they possess no vantage ground. Psychologically and socially, the Welsh peasantry are insufficiently advantaged; the poet's misguided investment in their meager lives will produce no abiding interest either for himself or his readers.

Whatever interest may be derived from rural characters or incidents is wholly accidental; adherence to the rustic as the standard of the real in effect means adherence to no standard at all. Conversely, Coleridge identifies *his* standard as properly permanent and universal. He adopts "with full faith the principle of Aristotle, that poetry as poetry is essentially *ideal*, that it avoids and excludes all *accident*; that its apparent individualities of rank, character, or occupation must be *representative* of a class; and that the *persons* of poetry must be clothed with *generic* attributes, with the *common* attributes of the class; not with such as one gifted individual might *possibly* possess, but such as from his situation it is most probable before-hand that he *would* possess" (*BL* II, 33-34). Coleridge uses Aristotle against Wordsworth in Volume II of the *Biographia* as he had used him against Hartley

[19]The attribution of such qualities to the Swiss was a well-established convention. See Alan D. Mckillop, "Local Attachment and Cosmopolitanism—The Eighteenth-Century Pattern," in *From Sensibility to Romanticism*, ed. Frederick W. Hilles and Harold Bloom (New York: Oxford University Press, 1970), pp. 191-218.

in Volume I, not as a positive statement of belief, but as one tactic in a defensive strategy. His primary aim is not to attack Wordsworth's indecorous penchant for ascribing noble sentiments to low characters but to defend against the subversion of the principle of decorum involved in the poet's refusal to subscribe to the stabilizing function that class plays in ordaining limits of possibility and probability.[20] Coleridge chastises Wordsworth's wanton genius in the name of Aristotle's decorus genius: poetic genius also (it is the whole tendency of the *Biographia* to affirm), no matter how "absolute," belongs to a class and must take its place "with the *common* attributes of the class; not with such as one gifted individual might *possibly* possess." For genius to err against propriety in its representations is to violate the principle that sustains genius as a class, to undermine its very vantage ground.

The Wordsworthian tenets to which Coleridge objects—the standard of the real language of men, the denial of any essential distinction between the language of prose and metrical composition—imply the poet's descent from the god-given prominence that endows him with special power over his language and that entails weighty responsibilities in the exercise of that power. Rather than accept the place of genius which belongs to him and to which he belongs, Wordsworth displays a decisive distrust of the very notion of the vantage ground, which in the Preface he disdainfully associates with the outworn and disgusting artifice of poetic diction. The poet, he says, "must descend from this supposed height, and in order to excite rational sympathy, he must express himself as other men express themselves. To this it may be added, that while he is only selecting from the real language of men, or, which amounts to the same thing, composing accurately in the spirit of such selection, he is treading upon safe ground, and we know what to expect from him."[21] Coleridge quotes what follows, where Wordsworth distinguishes the

---

[20]Coleridge illustrates his standard of the cultivated style in Chapter XIX, relying especially on the example of George Herbert, who is an "exquisite master of this species of style where the scholar and the poet supplies the material, but the perfect well-bred gentleman the expressions and the arrangement" (*BL* II, 73).

[21]Wordsworth, "Preface to *Lyrical Ballads* (1802)," *Literary Criticism of William Wordsworth*, ed. Paul M. Zall (Lincoln: University of Nebraska Press, 1966), p. 54.

"safe ground" of meter from the caprice of poetic diction: "'The distinction of rhyme and metre is voluntary and uniform, and not, like that produced by (what is called) poetic diction, arbitrary, and subject to infinite caprices upon which no calculation can be made. In the one case the reader is utterly at the mercy of the poet respecting what imagery or diction he may choose to connect with the passion.'" The critic reacts to this claim with predictable alarm: "But is this a *poet*, of whom a poet is speaking?" (*BL* II, 63).

No answer can be made to Coleridge's question that would not be tendentious within a context that has already broached an equivocation in the word "poet." If not necessarily a poet, however, it is certainly *Wordsworth* of whom Wordsworth is speaking in this dense passage; and it is possible to reconstruct a characteristic Wordsworthian crisis in the turnings of the prose. The passage implies that for Wordsworth the pretense of elevation fabricated by poetic diction is a license for poetic caprice. Wordsworth's rejection of poetic diction is motivated both by his contempt for such counterfeiting and by his desire to respect the compact between the poet and his readers. Yet here as elsewhere in Wordsworth the ethic offered as justification reads less like reason than pretext. The sense of heroic sacrifice that plumes his descent obscures a more complex dynamic. Notably, what Coleridge calls "vantage-ground" is for Wordsworth a "supposed height." Now, it must be asked what "supposed" means. The adjective is clearly pejorative: Wordsworth derides the pretense of an especially elevated visionary poet by casually invoking and scornfully discarding the whole assortment of *topoi* pitched forward into tradition from Parnassus. But if we consider the context as dynamic—the text forming and reforming to adjust to concepts so singular that they lie beyond proper context—we might entertain the hypopoesis that "supposed height" does not simply disdain the traditional pretense of privileged poetic elevation but charges that it is the very notion of height when applied to intense passion which is "supposed." That emphasis suggests that Wordsworth introduces and disposes of the metaphor of height as part of a strategy to refresh by dislocation the sense of *beyond* which has been trivialized by indefinite repetitions of the spatial metaphor. Wordsworth destroys the vehicle of the metaphor in order to rejuvenate the power of the tenor; subversion of metaphor is a Wordsworthian tactic to thwart the limitations of language. Thus Wordsworth descends to "safe ground" rather than stay at a "supposed height" not merely out of an ethical impulse but because poetic height is *really* a visionary actual about which nothing can be supposed and about which only Wordsworth knows. Because the visionary actual is no place at all, the poet literally does not belong there, in that non-place which has neither property marker nor index of propriety. Wordsworth's visionary actual, which I have had to invent in a passage where it cannot appear, is, unlike Coleridge's Reason or even his God, utterly without content, utterly inhuman, utterly without utterance—hence the potential for, even the necessity of, its being capriciously translated into the infinite variations of language. The poet vacates the visionary actual not because it is dangerous ground but because it is no ground at all.

By referring Wordsworth to this hypopoetical region, which I have called the visionary actual, I have not escaped the trap of placing him within this passage from the Preface. But that is a problem in my writing, not in Wordsworth's. Wordsworth makes it impossible to conceive that he has ever been in a visionary place or that he has ever returned. What *can* be conceived is that he has been as far as we can imagine ourselves going— which is conceived *as* we imagine ourselves going, being evacuated, that is, from our place as reader. Wordsworth's approach to the visionary actual halts at a verge marked by the intensification of the feeling of the complete submissiveness of reading, a dramatic threat of attenuation toward complete self-loss. The visionary actual is adumbrated in the reader's impression of a total writing completely indifferent to any reading—a schizophrenia of the text blind to all compacts, wherein the sole engagement of writer and reader is like an impersonal conflict that subtends no ideology, promises no spoils, and gives no quarter.

Coleridge will not read Wordsworth this way. He makes of himself the ideal reader of an ideal Romantic poetry through his will to read only what reinforces the myth of the vantage ground. His need to have Wordsworth take root on that height is a corollary of his will to believe that the height exists and that man—particularly the poet, who is the perfection of man—belongs there. The vision of the visionary that Wordsworth's Preface supplies, as not an elevated, translucent symbol but as a species of total writing, would make it difficult for the reader, even an ideally gifted reader, to distinguish between the creations of the poet and the products of the printing press, where language, "mechanized as it were into a barrel organ, supplies at once both instrument and tune" (*BL* I, 25)—the very cultural enervation against which the genius is supposed to stand as vital antithesis. Dread at Wordsworth's descent from his vantage ground and anxiety over Wordsworth's *supposition* of that ground combine to explain the apparent excess of Coleridge's response, which explodes the one bit of "safe ground" that Wordsworth had hoped to secure: "But is this a *poet* of whom a poet is speaking? No, surely! rather a fool or madman: or at best of a vain and ignorant phantast! And might not brains so wild and so deficient make just the havock with rhymes and metres as they are supposed to effect with modes and figures of speech?" (*BL* II, 63). The poet who leaves his summit retreats not to safe ground but to streamy association; he who should act as rudder becomes just another momentary interruption in the uncharted flow. Coleridge finds in the poet's substitution of the delusive standard of the "real" for the certain privileges proper to his vantage ground a dark sign that substitution may be the engine of language, that one's own words are capable of being exchanged with anyone else's. As a consequence, then, of his repudiation of authority Wordsworth not only neglects his duty to others but perversely attacks himself. "In short," Coleridge comments, "were there excluded from Mr. Wordsworth's poetic compositions all, that a literal adherence to the theory of his preface *would* exclude, two-thirds at least of the marked beauties of his poetry must be erased" (*BL* II, 84). The very marking of beauties would be proscribed by a theory which would eliminate the poet in the reduction of poetry to little more than the marks mechanically supplied by a superadded meter. Wordsworth's Preface promises no philosophical poem; instead it threatens to consume the genius that the poet is nourished by. Coleridge's criticism of Wordsworth is legitimated as an attempt to protect the poet from self-mutilation.

Coleridge explains the eccentric direction that Wordsworth's writings have taken in a manner that recalls Hartley's comments on the difficulty of observing the afterimage of a candle flame (see above): for Wordsworth "the too exclusive attention to [truths] had occasioned its errors, by tempting him to carry those truths beyond their proper limits" (*BL* II, 95). Coleridge's literary life suffers from Wordsworth's too exclusive attention and is sacrificed to the need to redefine for the poet the proper limits of the truth. To define those limits is to forecast Wordsworth's true book, the "FIRST GENUINE PHILOSOPHIC POEM" (*BL* II, 129), which will be both monument to Wordsworth's genius and fulfillment of Coleridge's criticism. In order to make that book possible Coleridge must substitute his preface for Wordsworth's own in the faith that a single substitution of principles will forever quell promiscuous substitution: "If Mr. Wordsworth have set forth principles of poetry which his arguments are insufficient to support," Coleridge exhorts, "let him and those who have adopted his sentiments be set right by the confutation of those arguments, and by the substitution of more philosophical principles" (*BL* II, 95). Coleridgean substitution is, as we have seen, not a matter of simple aggrandizement, however. Here the move which substitutes Coleridge's principled preface, his literary life and opinions, for Wordsworth's erroneous sentiments has as its corollary the substitution of Wordsworth's philosophical poem for Coleridge's own volume of poems, the pretext for the preface of the *Biographia*. Wordsworth's preface yields to Coleridge's; Coleridge's poems give place to the Wordsworthian poem. In Coleridge thinning substances away to shadows permits shadows to be deepened into substance. This process could be conceived of dialectically if we were to "elevate the Thesis from notional to actual, by contemplating intuitively this one power with its two inherent indestructible yet counteracting forces, and the results or generations to which their inter-penetration gives existence, in the living principle and in the process of our own self-consciousness" (*BL* I, 198)—could be so conceived if it were not that what we read is no counteraction of forces but a substitution of books in a structure which does not obey the logic of dialectic but conforms to the figure of the chiasmus: Wordsworth to Coleridge, Coleridge to Wordsworth. And this chiasmus prefaces another text which will be substituted for both Coleridge's volume and Wordsworth's philosophical poem: Coleridge's "*great book on the* CONSTRUCTIVE PHILOSOPHY'" (*BL* I, 200),[22] the central book for which all other books are merely prefatory, the unequivocal statement which articulates the margins of the *Biographia* as the promise of a final substitute.

Discursively, the chiasmus of Coleridge to Wordsworth, Wordsworth to Coleridge has the characteristics of a double bind: Wordsworth is both the poetic genius who must have property in his own work and the poet whose work subverts notions of property and propriety; in his assertion of the place of property and propriety in Wordsworth Coleridge must risk impropriety by challenging Wordsworth's sole property in his own work. Coleridge recognizes the bind and attempts to escape it by exploiting a distinction first raised in his discussion of the supposed irritability of genius. There he answers the carping of those who cite instances of excited temperament in men of accepted genius as evidence of genius's inherent irritability by claiming that what "is charged to the *author,* belongs to the *man,* who would probably have been still more impatient, but for the humanizing influences of the very pursuit, which yet bears the blame of his irritability" (*BL* I, 24). Coleridge will work to disengage cleanly the serene genius from the irritable man. Wordsworth the man writes in prose; and his theoretical errors are to a great degree attributable to the essential contingency of prose, a disability which has been exacerbated by a general cheapening of language and trivializing of thought. The man, the prose, may be in error, but the error is correctible by reference to a genial orientation which Wordsworth obeys even in his wandering. Coleridge applies to Wordsworth's proclaimed intention to submit to the real by selecting the real language of men the same logic he has earlier applied to Hartley's association mystification of the free will: "I conclude," he writes, "that the attempt is impracticable; and that, were it not impracticable, it would still be useless. For the very power of making the selection implies the previous

[22]See "The Symbiosis of Coleridge and Wordsworth," in which Thomas McFarland comments, "Wordsworth's great philosophical poem was really to have been a version of Coleridge's own *magnum opus*" (p. 300).

possession of the language selected" (*BL* II, 43). Wordsworth's error lies in mistaking his own powers. True poet, he possesses all within himself; deluded theorist, he mistakes the light within as a light bestowed, his power of creation as a mere instrument of selection—whereas in truth the latter operation already presumes the creative capacity that makes selection possible. Error is interpreted as accident which may happen to (may be written by) the man but which does not destroy the authority of the poet, who cannot escape the force of his own disposing will, or descend from the vantage ground which is his gift and his given. An impulse to abdicate can, after all, occur only to a monarch; occur like a shadow, a preface: "And I reflect with delight," Coleridge writes, "how little a mere theory, though of his own workmanship, interferes with the processes of genuine imagination in a man of true poetic genius, who possesses, as Mr. Wordsworth, if ever man did, most assuredly does possess,

'THE VISION AND THE FACULTY DIVINE'" (*BL* II, 45).

Although Coleridge's logic corrects the error of the theory, it does not explain why there should be any such interference in the processes of genuine imagination. We return to the logical labyrinth that has baffled Coleridge's quest for the free will: if the man is to be characterized as a vagrant, prosy error, the man cannot be held responsible for his merely characteristic mistakes. If true agency can be imputed only to the poet, so must error; but if error be imputed to the poet how can the absolute integrity of genius be maintained?

Coleridge confronts the existence of error within the poetry of Wordsworth in Chapter XXII, where the urgency of his theodicy is most pronounced, where his discriminations are most sophisticated, and where the exchange between Coleridge and Wordsworth can be brought to at least a tentative resolution. He begins with a distinction aimed at sharply delimiting the object of his criticism: "In a comparatively small number of poems he [Wordsworth] chose to try an experiment; and this experiment we will suppose to have failed. Yet even in these poems it is impossible not to perceive that the natural *tendency* of the poet's mind is to great objects and elevated conceptions" (*BL* II, 95-96). Coleridge illustrates this unfortunate disjunction between choice and natural tendency with the concluding lines from the 1805 poem "Fidelity":

"Yes, proof was plain that since the day
On which the traveller thus had died,
The dog had watched about the spot,
Or by his master's side
*How nourishd here for such long time*
*He knows, who gave that love sublime,*
*And gave that strength of feeling, great*
*Above all human estimate!*"

About these lines Coleridge asks, "Can any candid and intelligent mind hesitate in determining, which of these best represents the tendency and native character of the poet's genius? Will he not decide that the one was written because the poet *would* so write, and the other because he could not so entirely repress the force and grandeur of his mind, but that he must in some part or other of *every* composition write otherwise?" (*BL* II, 96). That rhetorical embrace of the reader should not tempt him to overlook the crucial shift that occurs in Coleridge's terminology as he attempts to accommodate his criticism to the apparent intrusion of error on the poem itself: poet *as* genius becomes *poet's* genius. The shift to the genitive relation marks a slippage in both the concepts of poet and genius; what has been heretofore an identity, the poetic genius, has become relative, the poet's genius. In the interest of preserving the integrity of genius Coleridge condenses all the varieties of error associated with the man into the character of the poet, whose error, it seems, is not accidental but is the error of choice, of willing to write in a certain way. Error emerges from the *he* that would, the *he* that in willing can only "repress the force and grandeur *of his mind*" (again the genitive). Force and grandeur form a tendency more native than the *he* which wills and who in willing can only be willful. As Coleridge tracks evidence of error deeper into the poet's work he simultaneously intrudes deeper into the mind, stripping away the ever burgeoning accidental, traversing the familiar Coleridgean territory on the shifting margins of will and willfulness to locate an area of genius which belongs to the poet but over which the poet cannot exert any proprietary control without repressing a natural tendency—a tendency which "must" emerge because in its nativeness it obeys only the law of its own impersonal process. In protecting the autonomy of property against the possible caprice of its supposed owner Coleridge converts Wordsworthian property into a Wordsworthian commodity whose property it is to belong as much to the principled critic as it does to the willful poet. The more attributes Coleridge's poet, like the Christian God, attracts to his indefinitely flexible genitive (genius of, force and grandeur of, property of, propriety of) the more ghostly becomes the essence to which the attributes relate and, consequently, the more is effaced "the sacred distinction between things and persons" (*BL* I, 137) which the poet, like the deity, is imagined to uphold.

This effacement can be traced in the telling simile the critic employs to explain Wordsworth's disease of the will. Coleridge claims that "his only disease is the being out of his element; like the swan, that, having amused himself, for a while, with crashing the weeds on the river's bank, soon returns to his own majestic movements on its reflecting and sustaining surface" (*BL* II, 96-97). Coleridge has begun with the expansive gesture of indemnifying the moral integrity of the mind by demonstrating its embodiment in the absolute self-possession and infinite fecundity of poetic genius. Here, defending against a subversive willfulness in the name of limits and of native tendency, he reaches for an analogue of that noble genius in the swan, a creature whose majesty consists in floating peacefully on a pond where it is sustained by its own reflected image. We can recognize in this emblem of genius a version of the self-possessive reflection that is constitutive of self-consciousness; but here, crucially, the noble identity of subject and object has been reduced to nothing more than a specular reflection in which "self" has no place. The emblem of the swan represents a mirror stage where all that is recognizably human has been canceled for the sake of a prehuman serenity of reflection—the accurate image of a love great above all human estimate. As Wordsworth must be eliminated to certify the Wordsworthian, so must the human be eliminated in the emblem of a love sublime.

What the swan simile confirms in my speculations on the poet's genius, Coleridge's use of Wordsworth's "Fidelity" confirms in my speculations about the swan simile. Coleridge asks his reader to make two comparisons; the second, which we have seen, between two halves of the same stanza; the first, between a single stanza and the rest of the poem:

"There sometimes doth a leaping fish
Send through the tarn a lonely cheer;
The crags repeat the raven's croak,
In symphony austere;
Thither the rainbow comes—the cloud—
And mists that spread the flying shroud;
And sunbeams; and the sounding blast,
That if it could would hurry past;
But that enormous barrier binds it fast."

The comparison implies that the two passages which Coleridge
approves are of the same character. But can any candid and
intelligent mind hesitate in determining a difference in diction
between the former and the latter? This passage on the mountain scene is both more concrete and more metaphorical than
the lines in praise of "love sublime," which consist wholly of
abstract pieties. I suggest that what makes the mountain passage
Wordsworthian for Coleridge is its similarity to the more sedate
swan image: everything—fish, cheer, rainbow, cloud—remains
in its element. But perhaps it is more precise to say that everything here, unlike in the swan's pond, is *confined* to its element by
the awesome reflective powers of the concentering place: the
fish leaps forth but falls back into the tarn; the raven's spontaneous croak is returned to it not as a flattering reflection but as
a haunting echo; the hurrying weather enters, never to depart,
its sounding blast returned on itself as it is forcefully stationed
by the enormous barrier of the crags. Coleridge's simile and
Wordsworth's scene are each images of the mind, but the tame
beauty of the critic's figure cannot subdue by prepossession the
daunting splendor of the poet's. In its sublime display of solitary, forceful grandeur majestically echoing and reflecting itself, this "huge recess" savages the placid narcissism of the
swan's mirroring to disclose, like the view from the summit of
Snowdon in *The Prelude*, "the type of a majestic intellect," symbol
of the awful, ruthlessly inhuman powers of the mind. The passage is sharply different in manner and effect from the concluding lines Coleridge italicizes, which do not display the sublime
but use diction associated with sublimity to reinforce the stated
reverence for the deity and to bring the poem decorously to an
uplifting close. That Coleridge quotes the two passages but fails
to discriminate between them, raises the question of what he is

repressing in his discussion of Wordsworth's repression. We might profitably pursue that question by rephrasing it: What makes possible or perhaps necessary the transition in the poem from the sublime diction of the first passage to diction of the sublime in the second?

One answer beckons: death. "Fidelity" tells of a mountain shepherd who, halted by a strange bark, discovers a dog in rocky terrain. Struck by the dog's odd motions and its unusual cry— evidence that it is out of place—he suddenly becomes aware of the place where he is: "It was a cove, a huge recess / . . . Far in the bosom of Helvellyn, / Remote from public road or dwelling, / Pathway, or cultivated land; / From trace of human hand."[23] Then follows the quoted description of the shepherd's view of the recess where he stands for a while, "not free from boding thoughts." The shepherd's "boding thoughts" are apparently fulfilled when the dog leads him to the remains of a human skeleton. Appalled, the discoverer looks round for clues to explain the sight. There follows the peculiarly Wordsworthian turn, which identifies the weightiness of this story:

> From those abrupt and perilous rocks
> The Man had fallen, that place of fear!
> At length upon the Shepherd's mind
> It breaks and all is clear:
> He instantly recalled the name,
> And who he was, and whence he came;
> Remembered, too, the very day
> On which the Traveller passed this way.
>
> [42-49]

The immediate explanation for the skeleton is obvious: a man has fallen from the rocks. That that "history" does not satisfy the shepherd's need for explanation becomes apparent when "it breaks, and all is clear: / He instantly recalled the name." The "instantly" follows and seems to cancel the "at length," an indefinite period of indeterminate emotions and mental adjustments; the instant not only produces the name but also the recollection

---

[23]*Wordsworth's Poetical Works*, ed. E. DeSelincourt (Oxford: Clarendon Press, 1947), vol. 4, lines 16, 20-24.

of as much of the personal history of the traveller as the shepherd could have known, more, probably, than he was aware he ever knew. His curiosity is satisfied. But that satisfaction is defective. There is a problem with the lines; the reference of "it" is not entirely clear: is the breaking "it" the catalog of clarifying biographical detail that, like a tide of facts, spills across the shepherd's mind, or is the wash of detail made possible by the breaking up and clearing away of something else, a blockage both more massive and more terrifying?[24] The ambiguous "it" generates the impulse and the indeterminate "at length" clears the space for speculation.

The nature of that possible block, both massive and fearsome, may be suggested by noting what has been left out of the shepherd's inquiry and solution: the reason the traveller ascended to the remote height and the cause of his fall. Reasons and cause can be easily derived from romantic convention: he climbed, one assumes, because of a fascination with the sublimity of the setting and, once on top, was overtaken by a sudden vertigo which caused his misstep and fall.[25] Both the simplicity of the action and its dramatic possibilities are such, however, that the avoidance of explicitness here by both the poet and his shepherd spokesman bodes all the more significant. The "it" gains a massiveness in the ambiguity of its reference that precision could not give. Indeed, I would suggest that the "it" *stands* for an ambiguity of reference, the reference of the skeleton on the ground, and that *its* weight on the shepherd's mind derives from the possibility of a fall not physical but psychical.

To credit that hypothesis one must cultivate a sensitivity to the

---

[24]For a discussion of the dynamics of blockage and flooding see Neil Hertz's "The Notion of Blockage in the Literature of the Sublime," in *Psychoanalysis and the Question of the Text, Selected Papers from the English Institute, 1976-77*, ed. Geoffrey H. Hartman (Baltimore: The Johns Hopkins University Press, 1978), pp. 62-85.

[25]Convention jibes with Wordsworth's own account of the event that apparently inspired the poem. In an 1805 letter to Sir George Beaumont he reports on the finding of the corpse and mentions that the man's name "appears to have been Charles Gough, several things were found in his pockets: fishing Tackle, Memorandums, a Gold Watch, Silver Pencil, Claude Lorraine Glasses &c. &c" (*The Letters of William and Dorothy Wordsworth: The Early Years, 1787-1805*, ed. Chester L. Shaver [Oxford: Oxford University Press, 1967], p. 612). The Lorraine Glass identifies the connoisseur.

ominous in the poem. Note that the discovery of the skeleton has been anticipated during the shepherd's view of the huge recess by his "boding thoughts," which foretell disaster and in doing so track a path through the supposedly traceless wilderness, a path of identification.[26] Gazing on the cove, the shepherd supposes himself to the traveller's place on the heights above: the portent of disaster is only possible through an identification with one who will fall or who has fallen; it echoes in a lower place and in a different key the vertigo of the traveller on the heights. That portent remains fanciful—the hasty fiction that the mind creates to explain the eccentricity of the dog—and the identification theatrical, until the imagined fall is translated into reality by the discovery of the skeleton. The rapidity with which the discovery follows the boding both endows the association of the two moments with an almost causal logic and challenges the theatrical distance which has structured the implicit identification. With the realization of the imagined the distance between observer and victim precipitously closes. In finding the corpse at the end of the path the shepherd not only learns that the boded fall has actually occurred but discovers his own ambiguous participation in it. It is as if the shepherd has fallen along with the traveller, as if disaster has been produced and imitated by the power which has predicted it.[27] The sight of the skeleton is appalling because the very bizarre testimony of the imagination's power in the echo of reality is the loss of power over the imagination, which takes on a life of its own by divulging the image of one's own death. The skeleton of the dead man is the image of the shepherd's loss of self. "At length" he stands over the skeleton, hovering dizzily between the imaginary and the real, recess and

[26]Coleridge had personal experience of a similar kind of boding, as he attests in this letter from 1811: "For all prophecies are the first effects of some Agent, whose presence is not yet seen: as I have heard a friend calling to me by the echoes of his voice among our rocks in Cumberland, before I heard the voice itself or saw *him*" (*CL* III, 303). The echo is a prophecy of a friend. But suppose that between the hearing of the echo and the appearance of the person, the speaker stumbles on the rocks and dies. Such a supposition, always marginally present in Coleridge's accounts of echoes, is the premise of "Fidelity," where the echo of the mind becomes the bode of death.

[27]An effect characteristic of the sublime moment. See Thomas Weiskel, *The Romantic Sublime* (Baltimore: The Johns Hopkins University Press, 1976), pp. 12-14.

corpse, self and other: fall with is the precarious ledge over fall into. That dizzying indeterminacy, like that of "echoes that beget each other amongst the mountains" (*BL* I, 193), can only be traced (but *can* be traced) in the shepherd's recovery from vertigo and a possible fall into the dead man, the catastrophe of which would be complete self-loss. Identification with the dead man is defended against by the compulsive production of a stabilizing meaning—meaning as biography, literal evidence of a fixed difference between other and self—which breaks over the shepherd like a hermeneutical providence and rescues him from the vertiginous prospect of self-loss.

To have tracked the shepherd to this point is to justify my initial premise of the "bosom of Helvellyn" as symbol of Mind. The interpretation is warranted not because of any specific mental content of the emblem but, on the contrary, because it has no specific content at all. The huge recess is a place which in its sublime self-reflection indifferently blends sound and echo, physical and psychical, reality and image, shepherd and traveller, into an austere symphony where the note of the human is not distinguishable from the terrible harmony of the sounding and resounding blast. If this bosomy place has maternal associations they are with a voracious maternity that precedes and prevents the emergence of the self with its individual mind. In this place, type of an intellect both majestic and inhuman, conventional identities and differences are, one and all, unsentimentally blanketed by a "flying shroud." The huge recess, Mind, is a place of fear for shepherd, for poet, and for reader because at its edge arise thoughts which teeter on the brink of a cavity of endless echoes and reflections, thoughts which eclipse the autonomy of the consciousness from which they emerge. The indefinite "it" breaks on "the Shepherd's mind" in order that the shepherd's mind may not break on it.

That interpretation would be a great deal to hang on an "it" if the poem simply ended with the preservative recollection of the traveller's biography. But the poem does not end there; not quite *all* is yet clear. The poet describes all that has been told thus far as merely sad preliminary for what follows: "But hear a wonder, for whose sake / This lamentable tale I tell! A lasting monument of words / This wonder merits well." The lasting monument of words which will be raised in the poem is not to be dedicated to the dead man but to the living dog who for three months had been a dweller in that "savage place." The monument comprises those concluding lines whose devotion Coleridge underwrites, lines which in their elevated diction rise above the rest of the poem in order to memorialize a reassuring fidelity and to reverence properly a place yet more exalted whence came the nourishment that sustained the dog and the strength of feeling that bound it to its dead master's side. Raising monuments always means a burial of some kind, however, and in this instance memorializing the dog's fidelity has the effect of covering up the actual behavior of the dog, who has, significantly, *not* remained right by his master's side. "The Dog had watched about the spot, / or by his master's side." Moving back and forth from the site of the fall to the skeleton is faithful, to be sure, but slightly more than faithful. The dog seems somehow to share the shepherd's fascination with the spot, the place of fear; indeed, his movement mimics the movement of the shepherd's imagination between recess and skeleton which, I have argued, the "at length" represses. Evidence for the repression lies in the mimicry; evidence for the mimicry lies in a further repression, whereby the poet becomes the shepherd's accomplice. There is no safe ground in "Fidelity." Roving in this "savage place" the dog dwells in an uncertainty not only uninhabitable by shepherd or poet but one that neither can even afford to recognize because of the thoughts it bodes. Can the mind bear to recognize the image of its dynamics in the troubled movements of a dog— an image of more than mechanical, less that purposive restlessness which compounds the indeterminacy of the relations among huge recess (type of intellect), dead man (antitype of corpse) and rapt observer (typist and/or typed, intellect and/or corpse) by displaying them as the nexus between canine prowling and human reflection? What could this recognition mean? Where could it lead? Nowhere in "Fidelity." The return of the repressed indeterminacy in the dog's movement is transfigured by a sublime leap in which the poet, indistinguishable from shepherd in this vaunting act of sublimation, cancels the dog's disturbing prowl by memorializing it as Fidelity—a strenuous abstracting which facilitates the elimination of the indeterminacy disclosed in the human by identifying the odd subhuman behavior as fidelity and attributing it to suprahuman agency, to the transcendental power that comprehends and justifies all the fearsome elements of the poem: huge recess, skeleton, and canine obsessiveness. The dog is, in effect, sacrificed both that he might be faithful and that fidelity might be. The dog breaks upon the poet's diction and all is, finally, clear.

Coleridge's undiscriminating approval of the two parts of the poem he quotes has the effect of flattening out both into the same kind of thing, called Wordsworthian diction, and thereby both effaces the passage in the poem from one point to another and sublimates the indeterminacy encountered in that passage. Coleridge is the ideal reader of "Fidelity" (of Wordsworth's poetry) because he eagerly capitulates to the invitation the poem makes to take the monument of words as pretext for forgetting the indeterminacy it subdues. But the *Biographia* shows that in reading Wordsworth the ideal reader is also the most antithetical reader, for just as Wordsworth's repudiation of poetic diction licenses our skepticism about the altitude at which the poem ends, so does Coleridge's uncharacteristic crudeness in his comments on diction return us to a neglected poem and make the sublimations in the poem legible. Both his praise and his censure remind us that in Wordsworth we must not only read diction but read *for* diction, and Coleridge's clear error in collapsing the description of the cave and the monument to fidelity into a single, high Wordsworthian diction marks out the place (or displace) of error in this poem and, by implication, in Wordsworth's poetry.

"Fidelity" errs toward certitudes, whether of biographical detail or monumental assurance—an error that emerges from a groundless fear and that can be followed from the natural supernaturalism of the cove to the naturalism of the shepherd's response to the corpse to the supernaturalism of the monument. But the ideal reader is God's spy in the poem. By collapsing dictions Coleridge attempts to make the huge recess the pious equivalent of the monument to fidelity and to make both symbols of the same transcendent power: the former an emblem of the self-possession of genius, the latter of the divinity which grounds the former. Coleridge intends here, as in the diction controversy at large, to prove that Wordsworth's fears are groundless. But the effect of the critic's supererogatory sublimation is to call attention to the failure of the poet's own defense, as if, despite the proferred consolation, the critic reading the text were subject, like the shepherd in the poem, like the poet writing the poem, to boding thoughts which lead to preposterous, dizzying inconclusions. It is as if Coleridge's criticism of Wordsworth here and throughout the *Biographia* were a struggle to recover from a vertigo consequent on a trespass on a mind which is its own place and displace (no place at all) a self-reflecting, awful scene, dangerous to the mental traveller who ventures too close.[28]

Coleridge's strategy may be intended piously to erase fearfulness and savagery, but his insistence on these two moments as congruent and equivalent to the true Wordsworth (whom the critic has "at length" recalled is not Coleridge) both betrays the self-interested supposition behind that truth and discloses the savagery of a reverence that commits the poet to a place, a diction, which can only be attained by sacrificing the most subtle passages of his poetry to what Coleridge considers to be the force and grandeur of his mind. Throughout the *Biographia*, as here and in the genius passage of Chapter IV, Coleridge sublimates the indeterminacy of Wordsworth with the teleological intent to erect in its stead a monument of words which he calls the Wordsworthian, a trace of a record not in himself found. The difference between Wordsworth and the Wordsworthian is the difference between a dog compelled, one knows not why, to traverse a savage place and a swan tranquilly taking its pleasures on a reflecting pond.

What Coleridge says of Gray's "imitation" in "The Bard" of a passage in Shakespeare's *Merchant of Venice* might be aptly applied to Wordsworth's shifting dictions in "Fidelity": "all the propriety was lost in the transfer" (*BL* I, 12). As his criticism of Wordsworth shows, for Coleridge propriety becomes an issue on the verge of its complete loss. That verge is the terrain not only

---

[28]For another clear example of this struggle see Coleridge's criticism of "The Thorn" in Chapter XVII. I discuss that criticism in "Wordsworth's Misery, Coleridge's Woe: Reading 'The Thorn,'" *Papers on Language and Literature*, 16, no. 3 (1980), 268-86.

of Coleridge's encounter with "Fidelity" but of the *Biographia* as a whole, which turns on the issue of propriety and which attempts to return all propriety lost in various deplorable transfers—some plainly mistaken, some suspiciously devious, some almost unaccountably bizarre—to where it belongs. One explanation for the eccentric method of the philosophical criticism of the *Biographia*—both its overall autobiographical disposition and its local *ad hominem* diversions—is that propriety cannot, without the most reckless impropriety, be neatly abstracted for analysis, however much that would pacify the querulous understanding, because propriety belongs to the man, it *is* his self-possession; to transfer propriety from the person to the arid discourse of the understanding would be, regardless of the benevolence of one's intentions, to assist in the dispossession that reason and imagination would reverse.

IV

Coleridge's reading of Wordsworth dramatizes the attrition of those genial resources on which he relies to resynonymize property and propriety while preserving "the sacred distinction between things and persons" (*BL* I, 137). What is at stake for Coleridge in the latter distinction is indicated in Chapter XI, where he poignantly advises the aspiring author that he "be not *merely* a man of letters!" (*BL* I, 158). That admonition could serve as slogan for the whole of the *Biographia*, which is that text in the tradition wherein the possibility of becoming "merely a man of letters" is taken literally, and feared. In beginning the *Biographia*—before he mentions "politics, religion, and philosophy," or refers to Wordsworth—Coleridge states his intent to defend himself against the demeaning consequences of having become, involuntarily, a man of letters. He complains that it has been his "lot" to have had his name introduced "in conversation, and in print" with more frequency than he can explain—and, apparently, more misrepresentation than he can tolerate. Before all, Coleridge describes the *Biographia* as "exculpation" from unspecified accusations he has suffered as man of letters (*BL* I, 1). To be a man of letters is not only to have one's name introduced in print and thereby have it removed from one's person but also to have the name taken for the man, a capture no less straitening for being metaphoric: it is, indeed, a peril that threatens the soul. "[D]ue interest and qualified anxiety for the offspring and representatives of our nobler being" come to "authorize acts of self-defence" (*BL* I, 32). By means of his *Literary Life* Coleridge aims to reclaim what has sprung from him in order to save the life behind the literature.

Coleridge attributes the motive for the unprovoked "persecution" (*BL* I, 35) he has suffered to his "habits of intimacy with Mr. Wordsworth and Mr. Southey" (*BL* I, 39). In self-defense he energetically works to absolve Wordsworth and Southey from the most sweeping and irresponsible charges against them, while he cautiously distances himself from them, particularly from Wordsworth, in those areas where they are most vulnerable. Coleridge's identification of the motives of his persecutors, like his confession of what is the hardly sinful sin of "careless indifference to public opinion" (*BL* I, 31), is already an absolution of himself from any responsibility for his persecution. He does admit that early in his career he innocently "published a small volume of juvenile poems" (*BL* I, 2) and recalls a course of resolutely historical lectures he gave on English poetry, but the former is almost too nugatory to mention, and the latter was, he insists, abbreviated so that he "might furnish no possible pretext for the unthinking to misconstrue, or the malignant to misapply [his] words, and having stampt their own meaning on them, to pass them as current coin in the marts of garrulity or detraction" (*BL* I, 38). No possible pretext is, in the contemporary literary scene, evidently an adequate pretext, however. Once Coleridge has sent either his poems or his critical dicta abroad they become, even the most ephemeral and disinterested of them, blank counters subject to the promiscuous counterfeiting of anonymous reviewers, whose forgeries cheat the credulous readers of such reviews and confound the innocent victim whose fate it is, surprisingly, to find himself in print.

Characteristically, Coleridge interprets his predicament as symptom of a general malady. Although he does on occasion directly attack those most culpable for his own persecution, he also condemns the periodicals for their generally pernicious effect on contemporary readers (a topic treated even more pointedly in *The Friend,* as we shall see). Moreover, his disparaging tag "anonymous reviewers" evokes dangers that not only threaten the unfortunate who enters the arena of contemporary letters but also imperil any man who tries to sustain himself by writing. In Chapter X he quotes another man of letters, Herder, to specify the hazard awaiting the unwitting author: "With the greatest possible solicitude avoid authorship. Too early or immoderately employed, it makes the head *waste* and the heart empty; even were there no other worse consequences. A person, who reads only to print, in all probability reads amiss; and he who sends away through the pen and the press every thought, the moment it occurs to him, will in a short time have sent all away, and will become a mere journeyman of the printing-office, a *compositor*" (*BL* I, 159-60 [STC's translation in note]).[29] According to Herder's grim admonition, the employment of authorship eventually reduces to a merely mechanical transfer in which all propriety and property is irrecoverably lost. By sending away through the pen and the press every thought the moment it occurs to him, the author wastes his capital of head and heart in a profitless prodigality which ends with the loss of all his authority as he finally materializes into a "mere journeyman of the printing-office, a *compositor*." Having signed away his property and having transferred his authority to the instrument of his dissipation, the typical writer is all too ready to settle into the routine vagrancy of the compositor as an eternal wanderer on the face of the page, whose soul, forgetful of home, has only the significance of type capable of being retyped, is subject to endless transformations ungoverned even by Circean whim, is duplicated in indefinite reproductions—echo upon echo of an altogether superfluous voice.

Herder has transformed the myth of metamorphosis into a myth of mechanization. And by means of Herder's myth Coleridge has turned his own problem into the writer's condition.[30]

[29]In his edition of the *Biographia,* George Watson notes that the passage from Herder was extracted, with alterations, from his *Briefe, das Studium der Theologie betieffend* (1780-81), Letter 23 (1956; rpt. New York: Dutton, 1971), p. 133 n. 3.
[30]Coleridge uses a version of this metamorphic machinery to explain his renunciation of the practice of poetry: "From the time of Pope's translation of Homer, inclusive, so countless have been the poetic metamorphoses of almost all possible thoughts and connections of thought, that it scarcely practicable for a

For Coleridge the fear of self-loss, which the German evokes, is made more acute by the fancy that the depletion and dispersion of mind attendant on authorship bodes a subjection to letters so extreme that one's own body is indistinguishable from the body of the text. Coleridge is only half joking in this aside, where he connects the breaks of the text to the pains of the body:

> This effusion might have been spared; but I would feign flatter myself, that the reader will be less austere than an oriental professor of the bastinado, who during an attempt to extort per argumentum baculinum a full confession from a culprit, interrupted his outcry of pain by reminding him, that it was "*a mere digression!*" All this noise, Sir! is nothing to the point, and no sort of answer to my QUESTIONS! *Ah! but*, (replied the sufferer) *it is the most pertinent reply in nature to your blows.* [*BL* I, 110]

Rhetorically, this digression gives the reader the choice either to orient himself with a torturer who, like the anonymous reviewer, can persecute Coleridge remorselessly because he cannot or will not distinguish between letters and man or to refrain from beating the truth out of Coleridge in the sympathetic recognition that the digressive cries of pain are real and wholly pertinent. This oriental interlude also epitomizes the *Biographia* as a whole—a digression that attempts to excuse digressions by charming, impressing, or even confusing the anonymous reader, but most of all by encouraging him to conceive of the man beneath the letters, if only by imagining his pain.

Though Coleridge's rhetoric may be disarming, the *Biographia* does not wholly rely on the reader's capricious goodwill for its self-protection. Coleridge aims to ward off stray blows by anticipating the breaks which are their occasion. Superintending his text is the recuperative motto he adopts from Goethe:

---

man to write in the ornamental style on any subject without finding his poem, against his will and without his previous consciousness, a cento of lines that had pre-existed in other works; and this it is which makes poetry so very difficult, because so very easy, in the present day. I myself have for many years given it up in despair" (*CL* III, 469-70). See also Coleridge's disgust with the mechanical modes of teaching "by which children are to be metamorphosed into prodigies" (*BL* I, 7).

Little call as he may have to instruct others, he wishes nevertheless
to open out his heart to such as he either knows or hopes to be of
like mind with himself, but who are widely scattered in the world:
he wishes to knit anew his connections with his oldest friends, to
continue those recently formed, and to win other friends among
the rising generation for the course of his life. He wishes to spare
the young those circuitous paths on which he himself had lost his
way. [*BL* I, Title page, *verso*]

The motto which Coleridge has affixed to the margin is a figure
for his own marginal life, an auspicious figure of recollection
and renewal which anticipates from a perspective outside the
text the return of his prodigal literary life unharmed to the place
where it originally began. The centripetal promise and the
figurative binding power of the motto supply both the literary
life with a structure and the author with a vantage ground from
which he can benignly offer the young heartfelt advice—advice
which derives its authority not only from the Goethean precedent but also from the author's ability to recognize, invoke, and
submit to authority. The promise to knit anew can be credited
because the promise is itself a knitting. Not merely another
souvenir picked up by the man of letters on his wanderings, the
Goethean motto is a harbinger of home.

Coleridge returns to the figure of the circuitous path at the
beginning of Chapter IV and at strategic places elsewhere in the
*Biographia,* but he exploits it most strikingly in Chapter XI,
where he counsels the young not to forsake a secure career in
the established church because of fanciful scruples and as a
consequence of that error lose their way in letters as he has lost
his. Coleridge's advice recollects not only his own past but also
the biography of Hartley, whose scruples about aspects of the
thirty-nine articles both kept him out of the ministry and in-
directly turned him toward the deviant philosophy of the association of ideas.[31] This interpenetration of the biographical and

---

[31]See the biographical sketch of Hartley written by his son and attached as
preface to the Pistorius edition of *Observations on Man,* p. vi. The leading features
of Hartley's early life—that he was son of a vicar, admitted young to Jesus
College, Cambridge, and intended for a career in the church, which he forsook
for reasons of principle—parallel Coleridge's.

the theoretical is more than a philosophical conviction for Coleridge; it is the existential premise that makes philosophy possible. There is nothing coincidental about the association of error, associationism, and authorship either for Hartley or Coleridge; once the established church, truth, or text has been abandoned or even modified, the best intentions will eventually lead to loss of the certainty of intention's prescriptive power. Both Hartley's philosophy and his philosophizing were poignantly illustrative of that moral logic. Indeed, the words Coleridge uses to enforce his advice in Chapter XI echo the trope with which Hartley described the dangers of figurative language, synecdoche for writing itself. Hartley had warned that "it is not uncommon to see Men, after a long and immoderate Pursuit of one Class of Beauty, natural or artificial, deviate into such By-paths and Singularities, as that the objects excite Pain rather than Pleasure" (*OM*, II, 242-43). Coleridge offers himself as the monitory example of a man who, late in life, "had discovered himself to have quarreled with received opinions only to embrace errors, to have left the direction tracked out for him on the high road of honorable exertion only to deviate into a labyrinth where, when he had wandered till his head was giddy, his best good fortune was finally to have found his way out again, too late for prudence though not too late for conscience or truth!" (*BL* I, 158-59).

Like Hartley's by-paths, Goethe's circuitous paths, and the Solitary's dim and perilous way, Coleridge's labyrinth tropes the truth as being carried beyond its proper limits by an errant desire. All are figures for the deviation from the one track which, if diligently followed, would lead safely from starting post to goal. The writer wanders out of the way not simply in his initial choice of an eccentric career nor in his occasional use of figurative turns in his language, but in the daily exercise of his craft, which is to make tracks of his own on the "passive page" (*BL* I, 35) that lies on his desk—tracks that lead nowhere but to other tracks, which the startled writer, like the shepherd in "Fidelity," comes upon and recognizes as if they were, impossibly, his own. But, it should be recalled, Goethe came back from his circuitous journey. Coleridge too tells his reader that he reached a point in the labyrinth of tracks where he, like a wanderer in mountainous terrain, was overtaken by a perilous giddiness that he providentially survived, perhaps that he might live to warn others not to leave the surveyed security of the high road.

Of all Coleridge's figures that project desire and loss only Herder's dour vision of the typesetting of the mind does not predicate a redemptive return. Herder's warning is the bleakest of the various admonitions against error not merely because it tropes writing as a nightmare metamorphosis of mind from order of spirit into the fact of matter, but because Herder's transformation involves neither enchantress nor intoxicant; it is tooled merely by the machinery of the printing press, disorder of being, which alters out of neither love nor hate and which, indifferent iron, does not obey the golden discipline of myth. Outwitting pessimism, Coleridge takes advantage both of the marginal opportunity for choice implied by Herder and the margins of his page to rescue his chapter from the German's grim vision of mechanization by prescribing an alternative economic model wherein what is sent away never entirely departs: "To which I may add from myself," he comments, "that what medical physiologists affirm of certain secretions applies equally to our thoughts; they too must be taken up again into the circulation, and be again and again re-secreted in order to ensure a healthful vigor, both to the mind and to its intellectual offspring" (*BL* I, 160 n.). Coleridge invents an escape from the fate of the journeyman ever faring forth in the simulacrum of print by inventing a machine that runs on itself, that has its sole extension in the slight, hardly perceptible turn from secretion to re-secretion—a thoughtful machine prudently cogitating its own integrity. One cannot be beaten for natural secretions, especially if they are hygienically recirculated.

What Coleridge adds to Herder in Chapter XI he instaurates in Chapter XIII as the secondary imagination, which "dissolves, diffuses, dissipates, in order to recreate" (*BL* I, 202). Each circulative model has the function of both identifying and indemnifying a processive space safely apart from the labyrinth of letters where a person first loses his way, then loses his memory that there is a way to lose. Both models, physiological and epistemological, promise to protect the author from dispersion because both processes are conceived of as operating without letters; they secure the author in his proper place by the hypo-poesis of an authoring independent of script. The physiological model secures the autonomy of the author because under its dispensation the thoughts he circulates testify to the authority of him who thinks in the compliant witness of their faithful return. The objects of the imagination are, crucially, not specified in Coleridge's definition because imagination's object is imagination itself, its aim the smooth operation of its own restorative processes. The implicit justification of the apparent auto-affection of the physiological model is the economic principle of homeostasis, the conservation of the organism's health, vigor, and life. The imagination is similarly the defense of the self; it legislates a processive space of economical venture and return which circumscribes and cancels all possible losses. As the physiological process is under control of that which thinks, so the circulation of the imagination derives its purposiveness from the presumption of a power within, something reserved from dissolution and recreation, which can send out and bring back. Everything doubles within metaphysics' mirrored nest. As the activity of the imagination presumes a power in reserve, so is the imagination itself a faculty in reserve, a birthright and native tendency that can neither be renounced nor charmed away in any of the empirical transactions to which man or author must submit. Coleridge shares Hartley's analogical faith that biography recapitulates epistemology, though for Coleridge the assurance that biography is ultimately intelligible depends on an epistemology conceived as a venture and return occurring within a place governed by a power in reserve. Becoming a mere man of letters may be prevented because the imagination, insulated from the entropism of association, is both a place to return to and the power to return. One can afford to send one's thoughts abroad because both the sending and the abroad are wholly imaginative. The imagination is the guarantee that Coleridge will return from the circuitous paths of the *Biographia*.

Although the imagination is proposed as a constant epistemological and moral alternative to the tyranny of the association of ideas, the definition of the imagination emerges at the end of a labyrinthine philosophical argument which exhibits the most objectionable features of the association of ideas: an apparent progression that goes nowhere, a dispersion of the author's moral and ontological integrity through the compulsive, unacknowledged use of other's ideas and words. Although the argument is offered as a methodical ascent to the imagination, the farther it proceeds the more it recedes from any evidence that the imagination is at work. Logical progress is countered by a rhetorical regress. The reader does not observe a genius objectively disclosing the source of his subjective power; he tracks the writer, who becomes entangled in the intricacies of his composition as if the man of letters had no defense against the lettering of his texts(s). That suspicion is only partially quelled by the revelation of the imagination in Chapter XIII, since the transition from lettering to imagination is executed not by the author alone but at the behest of one of the best known men of letters in English literature, the fictive correspondent who admonishes Coleridge to cut short the philosophical deduction of the imagination and come, finally, to the point.

Coleridge's correspondent is a man of letters in the conventional sense—he alludes to a classical *topos*, to Milton, and to Coleridge himself—as well as in the literal sense: the man of the letter is strictly a man of letters because he has no existence outside of the text that Coleridge attributes to him, no life outside of the text in which those words appear. The structural function of this providential apparition has been examined by Gayatri Spivak, who gingerly brings a Lacanian model to bear on the relation between the "cut" the letter makes in the philosophical argument and the immediate emergence of the full-fledged statement of the imagination. The pressure of contradiction which, I have argued, can be discerned in the relations between argument and rhetoric afflicts the argument itself, according to Spivak, who contends that Coleridge's philosophical theses in Chapter XII, which begin with the problem of the priority between subject and object, inexorably gravitate towards a gap between knowing and being that is logically irreducible yet metaphysically inconceivable. "And it is in this gap," Spivak urges, "between knowing and being that the episode of the imaginary letter occludes." That occlusion is "the eruption of the Other onto the text of the subject. Read this way, what is otherwise seen as merely an interruption of the development of the *argument* about the imagination may not only be seen as a keeping alive, by unfulfillment, of the desire that moves the argument, but also as the ruse that makes possible the establishment of the *Law* of the imagination."[32] By cutting off the argument the letter liberates the author from his writing and enables the Law, which is the law of the sovereign self, to emerge and dictate according to its God-given prerogative.

It is a characteristic of the text and a problem for the imagination that even if we, confident in the constant supervision of the imagination despite a temporary occlusion, were benevolently to ignore the contradictions of Chapters XII and XIII, there would remain the condition on the imagination's appearance *as theory* that it must manifest itself at a certain point in the text. That engagement with the physical is not only a logical inevitability but also an analogical necessity, whether we consider the imagination under the rubric of law, where the manifestation of the divinity on Mt. Sinai is the corroborative type, or under the rubric of redemption, where the crucifixion of Christ is the paradigm. But let not this necessity of engaging the text be considered as a degradation of imagination's power. It is far otherwise. It is an opportunity for the imagination to manifest itself not as just another theoretical approximation of an ineffable metaphysical gravity but as guarantee, agent, and sign of a return to the constant center, as the authoritative economist of desire. Certainly the manifestation of the imagination in Chapter XIII is meant to be the return of the writer of the *Biographia* to himself: it returns him after years of doubt and disagreement to the original vision of creative possibility he experienced in the dawning of Wordsworth's genius; it returns the intellectual and emotional investment he has made in disputing associationism; it recovers a self that had been lost both to journalistic ephemera and the vicious nominalism of anonymous reviewers. Even more immediately, the imagination returns the author from and even gives teleological sanction to the torturous deviations and plagiarisms of Chapters V through XIII. It is in the course of those latter chapters that the Coleridgean path turns most circuitous;

[32]Gayatri Spivak, "The Letter as Cutting Edge," *Yale French Studies,* no. 55/56 (1977), 218.

there Coleridge's letters begin to letter him in his very defense against becoming a mere man of letters; his voice is almost reduced to just another inflection in the eloquent ventriloquism of the text. Yet providence assumes all losses; the secondary imagination, Coleridge affirms, "dissolves, diffuses, dissipates, *in order to* recreate" (*BL* I, 202; emphasis added): it is the existence of plagiarism that makes the imagination conceivable,[33] as it is only the return of the imagination with its restorative powers that can justify a world where plagiarism exists. The *Biographia* often appears exasperatingly dense not only because of the familiar romantic mimesis of narrative structure and meaning (the imaginative telling of imagination's story) but also because this mirroring has the unsettling effect of producing a literary theorizing which reflects the practice it theoretically deplores, imitates the threat it defends against.

The return of the imagination happens on a letter. As the phallus in Coleridge's notes on touch-double touch is denominated the "mutually assimilant junction between Love and Lust," so might the fictive correspondent be called the mutually assimilant junction between logic and rhetoric or between man and letters. A solution of continuity, it performs the same function and evinces the same hypopoesis as Hartley's infinitesimal elementary body between body and soul. Like the phallus, impotent in its potency, and the elementary body, inexplicable in its explanation, the man of the letter impersonates himself. Unlike either phallus or infinitesimal link, however, the man of the letter has neither empirical nor symbolic affiliations. Leslie Brisman has categorized the intervention of the man of the letter as a version of the interruptive natural man, whose type he identifies as the man from Porlock.[34] But what distinguishes this interruption is that the man of the letter is not from Porlock, nature, or anywhere else; he has no home but his assigned, marginal resting place. He is a man *of* the text that he interrupts—literally a correspondent of the writer. Not natural or supernatural, he is closest to being preternatural—a term employed by Hartley to

---

[33]See Thomas McFarland's discussion of this relation in his essay "The Originality Paradox," *New Literary History*, 5 (1973-74), 469-76.

[34]Leslie Brisman, *Romantic Origins* (Ithaca, N.Y.: Cornell University Press, 1978), pp. 30-37.

characterize the first, liminal stage of vibrations and used spo-
radically by Coleridge to describe a creature or incident with the
character of the uncanny. But preternatural is inadequate because here there is no trace of the thematics of the uncanny or
the daemonic; nor is there any figuration of a threshold. The
letter of the man is the man of the letter—a chiasmus in which
*"substances [are] thinned away into shadows, while everywhere shadows
[are] deepened into substances"* (*BL* I, 199) and which both conceals
and reveals the lapse of dialectic. Indeed, the importance of this
passage in this text is that it marks in the first dialectical venture
of English Romantic thought, the first, ineluctable lapse of dialectic. And after the first lapse there is no other.

To figure the man of the letter as natural man, as eruption of
the Other, or even as interrupter is to overpower it with design.
Rather than so master it one may try, as Coleridge does in his
notebooks, to think the interruption. There, as we have seen, his
meditation on the will eddies anxiously between the prepossesa-
sive metaphors of rudder and stream; at a loss for words, he
admits the literal fact of a difference without a distinction in the
anguished comment that *"Interruption of itself is painful."* The
will in the world is the man in the text. The chiasmic interruption of the man of the letter stages the irreducible, vital pain of
Coleridge's literary life. Whether we conceive of the text as
foundering on a metaphysical contradiction or render the intervention as a passage where the text is halted giddily at the last
articulation of self-loss and self-recovery, it is painfully clear that
the imagination fails to make book, though it is difficult to con-
ceptualize that lapse without recourse to terms subject to the
infinitely elastic prejudice of philosophy and psychology. It is
impossible to imagine that moment without censoring fancy's
play. I would hope to reproduce imagination's crisis by saying
that in Chapter XIII the redemptive path of the imagination,
which the reader has been assured can be confidently followed
out into the labyrinth of language and back to the security of
one's self, comes upon a fault that would be impassable were it
not for the difference of a letter that will vault the traveller
home. Not by argument or revelation is Coleridge delivered to
the imagination, returned to himself, and rescued from the fate
of becoming merely a man of letters; he is saved by a blank coun-

ter which the fancy alights on and letters into a man. The gap between knowing and being is itself already interrupted at its first appearance by the counterfeit of life. That neither gaps nor interruptions are merely what they are constitutes the pain of gaps and interruptions for the sovereign subject, an imaginative pain that is the fancy's literal pleasure.

The fanciful letter in Chapter XIII is interposed as "mere aid of vacancy" (*BL* II, 43); a solution of continuity, its appearance makes possible the self-imposition of the edict of the law, which is, ultimately, the self-imposition of the continuous self. According to Spivak, the self is fathered in Chapter XIII by the legislative imagination which is "rusingly" fathered by the author.[35] The prodigal, we know, can only be restored to grace by a father, and if none is immediately available one can be invented or, what comes to almost the same thing, fathered. Texts may indeed pull themselves up by their bootstraps, but the elevation thus reached is merely a supposed height, with room enough at the top, certainly, for innumerable sons to pretend to receive the law from their supposed fathers and with ample space to fight any number of gloriously dubious battles, but where the trophies of sacrifice and the spoils of war are the same blank counters that furnished the original pretext for escalation and struggle. The break in the text made by the letter turns man of letters into man of the letter into letter of the law—a turn upon turns that will never return the text to where it has been, deviations that subvert not only the metaphysical distinction of subject and object but the psychoanalytic categories of father and son. The interruption of the man of the letter in the logic of the imagination limns the repressed always returning in the imagination, for what the myth of the imagination represses is literally the letter. And when with disarming insouciance it stages its return, the letter appears as its own glib facsimile: the supposed outsider, who is, however, neither outside nor inside, father nor son, but the turn between the two, a deviation that has always been and cannot be canceled from the imagination even in its most hypopoetical form. Although the law of the imagination insists that all can be retrieved, the emergence of

[35]Spivak, "Letter as Cutting Edge," p. 219.

the law is only made possible by a figure which not having been secreted cannot be re-secreted and which in making me what I am leaves me less than I had thought I was. The law of the imagination may suffer logically because its manifestation is spurious, but the self suffers ontologically because it is legislated. Home is the mariner at the end of Chapter XIII, but to come home under the conditions of his return is to remain forever homeless. The man of letters does lead, after all, a literary life.

Any study of the *Biographia* is liable to expend too many words on Chapter XIII and the hypopoesis of the imagination. Its strategic location within the text—as if a center, as if a goal—the peculiar manner of its presentation, as well as the incrustation of exegesis both invite further commentary and insure that no commentary will ever be adequate. Chapter XIII of the *Biographia* is one of the classic places where criticism not only must recognize its incapacity to explain the text fully (an easy, often pious, confession for criticism), but the incapacity of the text to satisfy criticism. The proliferation of commentary on Chapter XIII, including my own, is evidence of a mutual incompatibility between text and criticism which in this case at least mirrors the incompatibility of the text with itself. The interruption of the man of the letter in Chapter XIII may be the most scandalous example of this incompatibility, but the scandal is, again, a function of an overinvestment in this particular place. That the imagination is inadequate to the attention paid to it and that the man of letters need not be charged with a shocking singularity are attested by the repetitions of this pattern of deviation in the text. There are many men of letters appearing in various roles in the *Biographia*. I have already discussed the German maid whose literary interest lies in the bizarre impropriety of her frenzied literacy—a possession by the infinite verbosity of sacred texts. One might examine Gray's Youth, whose manliness waxes and wanes according to the whim of the compositor (*BL* I, 12). There is also Coleridge's version of the narrator of "The Thorn," who in his superstitious repetition of "habitual phrases, and other blank counters" (*BL* II, 42) becomes a man of letters by meaning's default. Preeminent perhaps is the pseudonymous Nehemiah Higginbottom, whom Coleridge invented as parodist of his "characteristic vices" (*BL* I, 17) and to demonstrate his mastery of the languages of poetry and criticism, but whose life in letters he ends because mastery threatens to be mastered by its own invention. The multiplicity of these marginal characters reinforces the urgency while it compromises the feasibility of Coleridge's advice not to become merely a man of letters: it seems to be a common fate. Moreover, the evidence qualifies the emphasis he gives to *merely*; none of the figures encountered in the labyrinth of the *Biographia* is merely a man of letters because to be a man of letters within the conditions of the Coleridgean text is not to be merely something but to be marginally anything.

As the interruption in the path toward the imagination disrupts the myth of return, so does the first appearance of the man of letters undermine the myth of departure. During the course of his recollections of Boyer's "very severe" tutelage, Coleridge refers to his teacher's strictures against inflated, hackneyed diction and gives an example of the facile rhetorizing he condemned:

> Among the similes, there was, I remember, that of the Manchineel fruit, as suiting equally well with too many subjects; in which however it yielded the palm at once to the example of Alexander and Clytus, which was equally good and apt, whatever might be the theme. Was it ambition? Alexander and Clytus! —Flattery? Alexander and Clytus!—Anger? Drunkenness? Pride? Friendship? Ingratitude? Late Repentance? Still, still Alexander and Clytus! At length, the praises of agriculture having been exemplified in the sagacious observation, that had Alexander been holding the plough, he would not have run his friend Clytus through with a spear, this tried and serviceable old friend was banished by public edict in secula saeculorum. [*BL* I, 5][36]

Do we require Lamb's recollection (*BL* I, 206) to detect Coleridge in this young simile-monger, too early come and too singlemindedly devoted to the employment of authorship, for whom

[36]Clytus, who had once saved Alexander's life, was counselor and friend to Philip of Macedon before serving the young emperor in the same capacity. One evening, heated with drink, Alexander became increasingly intemperate in speech and behavior. Clytus chided him repeatedly and was repeatedly ignored. Finally, however, enraged at the elder man's persistent censure, the drunken emperor seized a spear and slew his counselor. His remorse, it is said, was both immediate and enduring.

the entire ocean of schoolboy topics and themes can be turned into a savory soup by the simple addition of the stone of Alexander and Clytus? Coleridge's account gives us a glimpse of the poet as one who does not possess genius but is possessed by the poetical character, a youth of letters. The first style of this youth is enthusiastically rhetorical, boldly derivative; his original tendency is flamboyantly associative. The plain style, native and natural, comes only as the result of a "public edict," one of Boyer's characteristic "irrevocable verdicts" (*BL* I, 5), which terminates the precocious eloquence. Not actually kills, however, but "banishes," and in that banishment lies a mistake, for what is banished (as the story of Oedipus cautions) can sneak back across the borders at a later date. There is, indeed, a slanting and provocative allusion to Alexander and Clytus in the very recollection of Boyer's supposedly beneficent edict, which, like Alexander's spear, is directed against what Coleridge calls "a serviceable old friend." Boyer's righteous thrust is both more merciful and less successful than the Greek's, for what came back to Alexander as remorse returns to Boyer in the economy of letters as a figure subsuming the narrative of its own suppression.

Indeed, the *exemplum* of Alexander and Clytus *can* be turned to various ends. It is an eminently suitable simile for the relations between the young, intemperate emperor of simile and his scolding adviser. Emperors never grow out of the imperial. Note that though Coleridge recalls the stern censures of the persistent Bowyer with approval and even gratitude, his recollection closes on a deadly note: "He is now gone to his final reward, full of years, and full of honors, even of those honors, which were dearest to his heart, as gratefully bestowed by that school, and still binding him to the interests of that school, in which he had been himself educated, and to which during his whole life he was a dedicated *thing*" (*BL* I, 6, my emphasis). Alexander's stroke may be deferred, but it will not be prevented from completing its fatal arc. The quality of memory is twice turned: it revives the dead man but only that, resurrected, the man may be abstracted into a "thing." Alexander still wields the sword and murder is always Clytus' final reward.

The pen would be mightier than the sword. Coleridge's

wholehearted internalization of his master's edict produces an exorbitant superego that would, fantastically, legislate to the law itself: "I have sometimes ventured to think," Coleridge muses, "that a list of this kind, or an index expurgatorious of certain well known and ever returning phrases, both introductory, and transitional, including a large assortment of modest egoisms, and flattering illeisms, &c., &c., might be hung up in our law-courts, and both houses of parliament, with great advantage to the public" (*BL* I, 5). The index expurgatorius is the type of those centering, conservative, symbolic entities—the will, genius, the imagination—which Coleridge proposes in the *Biographia,* the wished concretization of Clytus' censures of the excesses consequent upon the fiercely antinomian delight of conquest, whether it be of strange nations, forever foreign, by a mercenary army, or of an alien reality, forever estranged, by counterfeit signs. But if the index expurgatorius is the type of the consubstantiation of unalterable law and immovable lawgiver, it is also in its fantastic excess the parody of what it typifies.[37] Considered in context, internalization seems to be the wrong word for the imperial intemperateness with which Coleridge appropriates the proscriptions of his mentor. For Coleridge obedience to Clytus is another way of murdering the proscriptive agency; for Coleridge as for Romantic literature in general, submission to authority is a strategy of conquest, ambivalence a kind of power. The index would be meaningless without the potential for verbal anarchy; it is the articulation of a system where, as in the correspondent mechanics of drug addiction, dreams of order

---

[37]A case in point is this description of the writer's toil by the man of letters: "Mr. Gillman, who has written & published a very sensible Tract of Hydrophobia (a prize Essay) observed a few days ago, that till the time that he had been occasionally my Amanuensis he had not the remotest conception of what, how great, and (almost) how endless the difficulties are of composing where the Writer understands, and binds himself to attend to, the three-fold Ordonnance of Sound, Image, and of Logic.—Wherever I corrected a sentence, I described the fault for which it was corrected, generalizing it, and then designated it by a Greek Letter—I looked into half a dozen modern books, and looking here & there for instances of faults which from habit I could not fall into myself, I designated them likewise till I had a tolerably compleat catalogue, a sort of Bis-decalogue of Breaches of the intellectual Commandments.—I then took the first pamphlet, a medical Review, which came into the House after that time— and without the least hypercriticism, in the course of 50 pages I had written the whole Greek Alphabet five times over" (*CL* IV, 692).

merge into nightmares of chaos. In Coleridge's writing ever returning phrases summon forth ever returning indices, irrevocable verdicts that revoke themselves in the marvelous complications of their repetition. Indeed, much of the *Biographia's* unsettling vitality can be attributed to the extraordinary tension of this pervasive, often murderous complicity between phrase and index, the imperial impulse of conquest and the censorial reflex of retrenchment. The aim of indexing, the play of phrasing, the metaphor of the printing press, and the *topos* of Alexander and Clytus all circulate within this summary estimate of contemporary literature culture:

> But now, partly by the labours of successive poets, and in part by the more artificial state of society and social intercourse, language, mechanized as it were into a barrel-organ, supplies at once both instrument and tune. Thus even the deaf may play, so as to delight the many. Sometimes (for it is with similes, as it is with jests at a wine table, one is sure to suggest another) I have attempted to illustrate the present state of our language, in its relation to literature, by a press-room of larger and smaller stereotype pieces, which, in the present Anglo-Gallican fashion of unconnected, epigrammatic periods, it requires but an ordinary portion of ingenuity to vary indefinitely, and yet still produce something, which, if *not* sense, will be so like it as to do as well. [*BL* I, 25-26]

The illustrations do not so much swallow as imitate the thesis: at the wine table of language Clytus' censure is Alexander's provocation; what is poisonous for the mentor is an intoxicant to the emperor for whom the simile of the machine "supplies at once both instrument and tune." In the chiasmic play of the *Biographia* where Alexander becomes Clytus, Clytus Alexander, Coleridge Wordsworth, Wordsworth Coleridge, the letter man, the man letter, no things that stand apart will remain separate; no things joined will remain united.

v

Like the Solitary's tale, Coleridge's "mournful narrative" of error, persecution, and frustrated aspirations "commenced in pain, / In pain commenced, and end[s] without peace: / Yet tempered, not unfrequently, with strains / of native feeling, grateful to our minds" (*Excursion*, Bk. IV, 2-5). The Solitary is pained by the memory of past calamities; Coleridge suffers from present confusion: "[W]e are so framed in mind," he writes, "that all confusion is painful" (*BL* II, 208). In the case of each narrator the correction of despondency depends on the intelligibility of the story he tells, an intelligibility that is threefold. First, the simple telling of the story induces the "consolatory feeling that accompanies the sense of a proportion between antecedents and consequents" (*BL* II, 207). Second, the communication of that narrative to a sympathetic audience makes calamities and confusion intelligible. The Solitary seems to have experienced "some relief" while his auditors "sate listening with compassion due" (Bk. IV, 6-7). For Coleridge the proportions and distinct shapings of narrative, like "the relations of Cause and Effect" are "Eternity revealing itself in the phenomena of Time" (*BL* II, 207). From the perspective of the "mystics" the narrative enables the meditative soul to escape "the dreadful dream in which there is no sense of reality, not even of the pangs they are enduring. . . ." From a perspective "more on a level with the ordinary sympathies of mankind . . . in this same healing influence of *Light* and distinct Beholding, we may detect the final cause of that instinct which, in the great majority of instances, leads, and almost compels the Afflicted to communicate their sorrows" (*BL* II, 208). But the ultimate correction of despondency is not the intelligible proportions of narrative nor the making of one's despondency intelligible to others, but the recognition of the final cause of all autobiographies, whether they be personal or literary lives. Breaking the silence that follows the Solitary's tale, the Wanderer, who in the massive irony of Wordsworth's poem is more fixed than the recluse, corrects his friend and subjects his own moved heart by declaiming.

> 'One adequate support
> For the calamities of mortal life
> Exists—one only; an assured belief
> That the procession of our fate, howe'er
> Sad or disturbed, is ordered by a Being

Of infinite benevolence and power;
Whose everlasting purposes embrace
All accidents, converting them to good.'
[Bk IV, 10-17]

In his "Conclusion" Coleridge, Solitary and Wanderer, corrects himself by finding the intelligibility which is an anodyne for a confusion worse than death in the divine governance of the truly Final Cause, the "effective presence of a Father" (*BL* II, 207). The text closes with a correction that is Coleridge's equivalent of Wordsworth's elevated diction:

> It is Night, sacred Night! the upraised Eye views only the starry Heaven which manifests itself alone: and the outward Beholding is fixed on the sparks twinkling in the aweful depth, though Suns of other Worlds, only to preserve the Soul steady and collected in its pure *Act* of inward adoration to the great I AM, and to the filial WORD that re-affirmeth it from Eternity to Eternity, whose choral Echo is the universe. [*BL* II, 218]

The text ends, but in concluding is suspect. Coleridge's conclusion is suspicious from the structural perspective it supplies. Any reading of the *Biographia* must recognize that this literary life is not a narrative in any conventional sense; only the wish of a reader to escape painful confusion at all costs could fabricate within the divagations of the *Biographia* the "proportionality and appropriateness of the Present to the Past" or ascribe its lapses and improprieties to the final cause of governing genius or god. What we read, the eddying, unpropertied involvement of inhibitory index and dispersive phrase, man and letters, rudder and stream, does not imply resolution or resolver.

Coleridge's conclusion may also be suspected from the thematic perspective provided by his reading of "Fidelity," which insists on an uplifting conclusion not despite the distortion it entails but because the distortion suppresses deviations more harrowing. Coleridge's preface, like the shepherd's surmise, is a concatenation of "boding thoughts" presaging a spot where the writer will arrive or where an event will occur. The huge recess of cultural and social echoes and reflections which provokes the boding thoughts is, for the prefacer, the sign of a similarly huge recess of echoing circulations opening within. Coleridge escapes not fatality but the more frightening prospect of an indefinite fall *toward* fatality in the same manner as the shepherd, by elevating through his "pure act of inward adoration to the great I AM" a sublime "monument of words," which piously silences the text and brings his literary life to a close. The monument of words enables Coleridge to return "some trace" of conclusion, "else lost"; "existing unto [him] only by records in [himself] not found." The best example of what Harold Bloom and Northrup Frye agree is the "natural theology" of Coleridge's literary criticism, Coleridge's last, ardently sublime index neither resolves the painful confusion of the text nor satisfies the "unquenched desire" (*BL* II, 218) which he reintroduces in his "Conclusion" and which leaves the final obeisance to Father Being on a footing as unsettling as his similar prostrations before Wordsworth's genius. Coleridge's reading of "Fidelity" not only warrants a general mistrust of such supposed heights but encourages redirection of the attention elsewhere to resolutions lost or suppressed along the way, to resolutions that reflect rather than sublimate the problems they engage.

Indeed, the Solitary is not the only figure to have preceded Coleridge on his "dim and perilous way." The phrase is first used by Rivers in *The Borderers* to describe his mental state after he learned he had been manipulated into murder:

> three nights
> Did constant meditation dry my blood;
> Three sleepless nights I passed in sounding on,
> Through words and things, a dim and perilous way;
> And, wheresoe'er I turned me, I beheld
> A slavery compared to which the dungeon
> And clanking chains are perfect liberty.
>
> [1772-1778]

Having learned to live in what, in the 1842 version of the drama, are called "disputed tracts" (line 596), Rivers attempts to escape his slavery by exploiting the dimness of the border between words and things. He finds release from his mental affliction by a narrative infliction; he tells stories and stages narrative events which, by mixing word and thing, trouble Mortimer with a painful confusion. Mortimer's struggle to resolve that confusion involves him and others in worse pain, a torment perfected by Rivers' narration of the story of his life, which has become all but identical with Mortimer's own, and is capped by this coldly ironic consolation: "So meet extremes in this mysterious world, / And opposites thus melt into each other" (lines 1529-30). Rivers' maxim, the unacknowledgable precedent for Coleridge's favorite aphorism, "Extremes meet," articulates and dramatizes the warning implicit in the play of Alexander and Clytus: when extremes meet, dialectical semblance borders on murderous complicity; the righteous correction of confusion offered by elevated thoughts is only marginally different from violent self-vindication.

The complicitous divagations of the *Biographia* are crystallized and consummated in the pattern of relations Coleridge has with his anonymous critics, whose unwarranted abuse is the pretext for Coleridge's exculpation. As it develops that exculpation is intricately bound up with Coleridge's intimacy with Wordsworth: his self-defense is simultaneously a defense of that intimacy and a defense against it. Unlike the anonymous reviewers, Coleridge knows he is not Wordsworth because in his intimacy he knows who Wordsworth is better than anyone else, including Wordsworth himself. Nonetheless the captious reviews have provoked Coleridge to isolate all that is merely the result of willfulness or accident in Wordsworth's poetry, and identify it as a source of Coleridge's own pain—pain *by* and *of* association. Coleridge's self-defense anticipates a meeting of extremes, a *rapprochement* between the aberrant potency of anonymous reviewing and the pointed truths of principled criticism: could the machinery of the quarterlies be driven by the impersonal engine of principle there would be produced a criticism whose edicts would be beyond pretext, entirely without accident, whose verdicts would be irrevocable, deadly. The features of that fabulous criticism are drawn in what is perhaps the most bizarre digression in the disputed tracts of the *Biographia*. Coleridge imagines the formation of "any number of learned men into a "body corporate" that will administer literary judgment "according to a constitution and code of laws" grounded "on the two-fold basis of universal morals and philosophic reason." If so organized, such a body will, he says,

> have honor and good wishes from me, and I shall accord to them their fair dignities, though self assumed, not less chearfully than if I could inquire concerning them in the heralds' office, or turn to them in the book of peerage. However loud may be the outcries for prevented or subverted reputation, however numerous and impatient the complaints of merciless severity and insupportable despotism, I shall neither feel, nor utter ought but to the defence and justification of the critical machine. Should any literary Quixote find himself provoked by its sounds and regular movements, I should admonish him with Sancho Panza, that it is no giant, but a windmill; there it stands on its own place, and its own hillock, never goes out of its way to attack anyone, and to none and from none either gives or asks assistance. When the public press has poured in any part of its produce between its mill-stones, it grinds it off, one man's sack the same as another, and with whatever wind may happen to be then blowing. All the two and thirty winds are alike its friends. Of the whole wide atmosphere it does not desire a single finger-breadth more than what is necessary for it sails to turn round in. But this space must be left free and unimpeded. Gnats, beetles, wasps, butterflies, and the whole tribe of ephemerals and insignificants, may flit in and out and between; may hum, and buzz, and jarr; shrill their tiny pipes, and wind their puny horns, unchastised and unnoticed. But idlers and bravados of larger size and prouder show must beware, how they place themselves within its sweep. Much less may they presume to lay hands on the sails, the strength of which is neither greater nor less than as the wind is, which drives them round. Whomsoever the remorseless arm slings aloft, or whirls along with it in the air, he has himself alone to blame; though, when the same arm throws him from it, it will more often double than break the force of his fall. [*BL* II, 88-89]

The passage should come as no surprise. In Chapter I, after reflecting on his excesses in the youthful poetry which first provoked the strictures of critics, Coleridge arrived at the judgment, "my mind was not then sufficiently disciplined to receive the authority of others, as a substitute for my own conviction" (*BL* I, 2). The *Biographia* is a long essay in that discipline, for

Wordsworth, for anonymous critics, for the reader, for Coleridge. If discipline frequently looks like license, it is because the process of substitution has willy-nilly discombobulated the authority to be substituted, an authority invoked precisely to govern the tyranny of substitution. Substitution fosters an indeterminacy among categories and entities—argument and rhetoric, meaning and signification, self and other—which ought to be, must be, distinct. That categorical indeterminacy is the unbearable burden of Coleridge's preface, which aims to preface the true book, but which in its very effort to open the highway weaves off into thickets and byways. Coleridge lays that burden down, obliterates all that is accidental, ephemeral, written, by shrugging off the weight of the proper, eliminating the human. In its depiction of a truly principled criticism, this digression in Chapter XXI reveals that principle has no human countenance. Writing on "First and Last Romantics," Harold Bloom remarks, "As the dream of divination wanes, an obsession with transformations takes its place. The poet, if he cannot dodge his death through prolepsis may delude death by offering it many substitute forms for himself."[38] Coleridge dodges a (wholly) literary life worse than death by fabricating what would be the final substitute. In its circuitous journey the *Biographia* has arrived at the place where preface is transfigured into premachine.

It may be psychologically true that the last act of self-defense is to identify with one's persecutors and that the most extreme form of exculpation is to relinquish all responsibility to an overpowering automaticity, but Coleridge's vision of the critical machine ventures beyond the last acts and extremes of psychology, beyond identification and excuse to an utterlessly impersonal mechanics. If I avoid the paradox at hand, that in the *Biographia* the logic of self-construction is the logic of self-destruction, it is because in the sphere of the critical machine paradox is dangerous; the windmill will tolerate no turns but its own. Even the irony with which Coleridge introduces his vision is no protection against a desire that realizes itself in the image of an impartial power beyond desire, a power which mechanically punishes all

[38]Harold Bloom, *The Ringers in the Tower* (Chicago: University of Chicago Press, 1971), p. 8.

merely rhetorical ploys, which grinds off irony and paradox between its milling stones. The critical machine combines the power of Alexander with the knowledge of Clytus, imposing its severe verdicts without remorse because its verdicts have no more judgment than the inevitable revolution of a wind-spun blade. Beyond good and evil, beyond father and son, beyond possession, beyond the imagined transactions of myth—"it is no giant but a windmill." Whether we read the critical machine as the realization or exhaustion of romance, we perilously mistake it if we read Coleridge's admonition as merely the lamentable extinction of the Coleridgean will to separate persons and things and a capitulation to the object as object; the windmill makes meal of the distinction and acknowledges no submission. The critical machine, unlike Blake's dark Satanic mills with their wheels upon wheels, obeys an ecologic which readily and economically translates the friendly force of the "two and thirty winds" into a steady power. Nothing is wasted; no excess is permitted. There can be no question of the windmill's prominence, no charge that it occupies a supposed height, for anyone can see that "it stands on its own place and its own hillock," and anyone who will *not* see determines his own verdict. As Wordsworth's abdication of the supposed height of poetic diction represents both a recognition and a refusal of a total poetry, so does Coleridge's assumption of the real height where stands the windmill assert, with fearful symmetry, a total criticism. Articulating the varying air, situate on an indubitable hillock, remorselessly executing its principled function, the windmill is the austere parody of the promised "Constructive Philosophy"; the critical machine is the *Biographia*'s true *genius loci*.

True, perhaps; figurative nonetheless. There abides in this consummate place a ghost: the echo of the voice of Sancho Panza, whose quixotic attempt to communicate the truth is a fine instance of romantic excess. The voice that warns of error, though that warning prove futile, mitigates the austere punishment for error, though that punishment be just. That prefatory gentling hopefully marks what may be salvaged from the fierce confrontation of author and machine: a cushion of superfluity, the figure of a friend.

# [5]

# The Method of
# *The Friend*

My first Essay (and what will be at the BOTTOM of all the
rest) is—on the nature and importance of *Principles*.

—*CL* III, 131

For since the re-commencement of THE FRIEND at the 3rd
No., scarcely a fortnight has passed, in which I have not been
compelled to struggle with some fresh and unforeseen difficulty: and more than once what I have taken for an Island
plunged away from under my feet, and left me to providence
and my own efforts, to swim or sink.

—*CL* III, 274

The *Biographia* was not followed by the true Philosophical
Poem, the great work on the Constructive Philosophy, or a
genuine autobiography. It led to *The Friend*. The frequent references to *The Friend* throughout the *Biographia* attest to its greater
importance for Coleridge, an importance indicated by the singular investment of time and material that he dedicated to it in its
several manifestations. Coleridge struggled bravely with dilatory
printers, fickle patrons, and his own wayward habits to put out
the original twenty-seven numbers in 1809-10; he printed a collected edition in 1812; he worked hard to revise the 1818 edition
(which will be my text here[1]) for a successful publication. The
1818 *Friend* includes within it not only original essays but some
of Coleridge's best journalism, selections from his correspondence, and the unadulterated version of an encyclopedia article
on method. Moreover, among Coleridge's published work only
*The Friend* surpasses the *Biographia* in its intellectual range: its

---

[1]Vol. I of the Rooke edition. Hereafter cited in text as *F*.

topics include metaphysics, religion, politics, literature, biography, history, and ethics.

Besides publicizing it, the *Biographia* forecasts *The Friend* in another and more suggestive way. In its "Conclusion" Coleridge identifies the *Biographia,* as we have seen, as a communication of sorrows, an alleviation of grief through representation, release, and distribution. He quotes the Polish Jesuit poet Casimir Sarbiewski to express the way in which "Grief loses its strength in friendly ears and grows ever less when divided and sent to wander through many hearts."[2] That communication of sorrow to a friend has its payoff in *The Friend,* which draws on the assumption that the antecedent communication of sorrow has purchased the philosophical poise and intellectual credit necessary for the deliberate communication of truth, the central, abiding concern of Coleridge's literary career and the rubric that best comprises the problems in logic and rhetoric that I have been investigating thus far. Hartley's associationism gravitates toward the test of the word as authoritative voice, solution of continuity; Coleridge's attempted overthrows of Hartley test the will as a moral, communicable alternative to associationism. The *Biographia* is the test of the book as symbol of a unified consciousness. *The Friend* is the test of that which makes all such tests (im)possible: it is the test of language itself as vehicle of anything but itself, as being capable of communicating true principle or, at the very least, the truth of principle.

I

Not *The Spectator, The Tatler,* or *The Rambler, The Friend* identifies itself as intimate rather than sociable, humble but essential, amicable yet advisory. It is inaugurated with a motto adopted from Petrarch, which, more confident than the Goethean precedent in the *Biographia,* promises "Help to the Struggling, Counsel to the Doubtful, Light to the Blind, Hope to the Despondent, Refreshment to the Weary," but aims "not so much to prescribe a Law for others, as to set forth the Law of my own Mind" (*Friend,* 9 n.). The motto proposes a moral autobiography

---

[2]Watson, *BL,* 280-81, n. 2.

with therapeutic consequences. The text begins with an account of what might be called a therapeutic crisis. Coleridge tells the cautionary "Fable of the Madning Rain," which takes place toward the end of a "golden age . . . when Conscience acted in Man with the ease and uniformity of Instinct; when Labor was a sweet name for the activity of sane Minds in Healthful Bodies, and all enjoyed in common the bounteous harvest produced, and gathered in, by common effort" (*F*, 7). The fable is the story of an old man who repeated to his tribe the words in which a voice from the interior of a cavern had warned him of the advent of a maddening rain. He admonished the assembled innocents to seek shelter in the cave until the storm had passed. At the ominous words, "confused murmurs succeeded, and wonder, and doubt." The people did not follow their Elder's counsel, for "they could attach no image, no remembered sensations to the threat" (*F*, 8). Unheeded, the prophet retired alone to the cave and waited out the rain. On emerging from his shelter, he discovered that the catastrophe had indeed occurred: mankind had given itself over to avarice, idolatry, licentiousness—to madness. The sight bewildered him. But more shocking was the response of this race of madmen to his strange appearance; they interpreted his eccentric sanity as the mark of a madman and an idler, and they subjected him to such harsh usage that "harrassed, endangered, solitary in a world of forms like his own, without sympathy, without object of love, he at length espied in some foss or furrow a quantity of the maddening water still unevaporated, and uttering the last words of reason, IT IS IN VAIN TO BE SANE IN A WORLD OF MADMEN, plunged and rolled himself in the liquid poison, and came out as mad and not more wretched than his neighbours and acquaintance" (*F*, 9).

Although the prophet's career neatly expires in his declamation of its moral, Coleridge adds a commentary in which he explains that the fable contains all the skeptic's objections to his own plan: either he is the "Blind offering to lead the Blind," or he is "talking the language of Sight to those who do not possess the sense of Seeing" (*F*, 10). Characteristically, the implications of Coleridge's tale overbalance the morals that the narrative is said to exemplify. One does not require a myth of the Fall to illustrate the absurdity either of the blind leading the blind or of

talking the language of sight to those who cannot see—as apho-
risms they speak for themselves; as clichés they fail to engage
fully the text they cap. The fable of the maddening rain does
increase the pathos of the morals, and it does enhance the ethos
of moral authority on which the success of Coleridge's therapy
rests—yet it does so to excess. A moral guide no more needs the
credentials of a persecuted prophet to be effective than a literary
theorist needs the credentials of a persecuted poet to be right.
This exemplary excess, the excess of the example, looks like a
defense against unspoken anxieties about moral communication, as if the Friend's "dream of communication" were also a
"dream of failure."[3] The features of the defense adumbrate the
peculiar shape of the Friend's project.

The first moral seems especially inadequate. If this Elder is
"blind," he is nonetheless a blind prophet—of that the fable
allows no doubt. Neither the authenticity of his message, which
comes from a voice speaking from the cavern that holds the
source of the region's life-giving stream, nor the singularity of
his election is questioned by the elder. He may not fully understand what the prediction of madness denotes, but he accepts
without question the authority of the voice to elect him as its
oracle. What *is* overtly questioned in the fable is the possibility
that authenticity and authority can be communicated to those
who have no immediate experience of either; what is covertly
doubted is the morality of any communication at all. Although
the downpour of maddening rain is represented as the primal
catastrophe that separates humanity from its sanity and the people from its elder, that disaster is prefigured by other catas-
trophes that diminish its impact: most proximate, the tribe's
"confused murmurs," which follow the startling warning of the
oracle; earlier, the disturbance caused by the elder-become-
prophet's first ascent of a "small eminence" to speak to the
assembly. The later disturbance is comprehended by Coleridge's

[3]I take the phrase "dream of communication" from the title of Geoffrey Hartman's essay on one of Coleridge's most influential interpreters: "I. A. Richards
and the Dream of Communication," which is collected in *The Fate of Reading*
(Chicago: University of Chicago Press, 1975). Jules Henry writes about the
"dream of failure" in *Culture against Man* (New York: Random House, 1963), p.
296.

second moral of sight speaking to sightless, but the earlier one is not; it is a visible dislocation that disrupts the community and jars the moral symmetry of the fable: a catastrophe not only *in* but *of* the tale. And that disruption is prefigured by an earlier disturbance, the summons of the voice itself. The Edenic condition of this race had been characterized as "dateless as Eternity, a State rather than a Time," a paradise where "even the sense of succession is lost in the uniformity of the stream" (*F*, 7); yet it is a voice from the source of that life-giving stream which, by electing a prophet, introduces the small eminence that disrupts paradisal uniformity and precipitates the succession of murmurs. The original voice at the source does not fully speak until its life-giving words are heard as the death-dealing echo of the catastrophe it supposedly precedes. These recessive prefigurations undermine the neatness of the catastrophic failure to communicate by telling of a prior disruption in the communication itself. The dramatic catastrophe of the fall is a fable within the fable, the hypopoesis that makes possible both the story and *The Friend*.

Hearing those echoes makes possible the isolation in the fable of three levels of anxiety about the communication of truth. First, there is the overt doubt that the proper means can be found by which to communicate that which is not accommodated to the understanding of an audience—that for which it has no images and no remembered sensations. In part, the fable is itself an attempted solution to the problem it represents: by fabulizing the message the foreign is made familiar. Second, there is the pathos of the prophet's fate: the most dreadful consequence of the elder's sacred mission is not his failure to prevent the madness of his fellows (who are, after all, relatively content with their misery); rather it is the terrible fate of one who, marked as a prophet by a providential voice, is made imprudently sane and, because of that distinction, suffers both physical violence and the appalling humiliation of choosing madness.[4] Finally, however, there is a sense in which the violence

[4]Although he reverses the symbolic landscape that Socrates employs in the Allegory of the Cave in *The Republic* by rendering cave as profound source rather than as theater of illusions—a change governed both by Coleridge's switch to auditory rather than visual metaphors and by the interest he takes in the social

of the madmen *is* deserved, if not morally justified, for the
prophet is not only the forecaster of catastrophe, he is the car-
rier of a difference of which the catastrophe, when it comes, is
only the dramatic reiteration.[5] A prophet, the elder is the visible
representation of the secretive speaking voice; his very appearance, regardless of the moral integrity of his intention, regardless of his ability to communicate that intention fully, is the
evident intrusion of a previously unknown duplicity into the
Edenic community—a duplicity which bears the message not of
a catastrophic division between sanity and madness or innocence
and experience, but which accents the more subtle differences
that have been latent in both the community and in its source all
along. Coleridge announces the first consequence as the moral
of his fable, thus justifying his role, setting the extreme limit of
his project, and dramatizing its hazards—while implicating his
reader in the challenge of overcoming all difficulties and dangers. That he would willingly accept the second consequence is
attested by his frequent reference to the lonely heroism of his
own crusade in the face of violent opposition.[6] Coleridge would

and historical effects of truth telling—Coleridge parallels Socrates both in his
appreciation of the "pain and vexation" an access to the truth would occasion
and in his fears for the safety of the prophet who, no longer fit for the world he
has left, would try to communicate the truth to his comrades: "They would laugh
at him and say that he had gone up only to come back with his sight ruined. . . . If
they could lay hands on the man who was trying to set them free and lead them
up they would kill him." (*The Republic*, trans. Francis MacDonald Cornford
[1945; rpt., New York: Oxford University Press, 1966], VIII. 515 and 516.) In
sum, for both Socrates and Coleridge one of the dominant rhetorical aims of the
fable is to justify its metaphoricity.

[5]This oscillation between possible perspectives is both evident and functional
within *The Friend*, but it also marks the duplicity of the fable within Coleridge's
works. The story of the oracle appeared earlier as the introduction to one of
Coleridge's lectures on revealed religion in 1796. The editors of those lectures
comment on the surviving abbreviated form of the fable as it "is introduced
into the lecture as an illustrative prelude to Coleridge's remarks about those
modern 'prophets' of reform who abandon their principles and join the ranks of
their adversaries" (*LRR*, 215 n.). What had been an implicit attack on Burke and
Pitt becomes a defense of Coleridge. Like the metaphor of the stone soup, the
fable seems to have reversed its emotive implications as Coleridge reversed his
allegiances. In this case, however, the tale includes within it the dramatization of
the punishment for such a reversal.

[6]The theme of the embattled crusader, a constant in Coleridge's philosophical
and critical prose (cf. his use of Mackintosh, Hume, and the anonymous critics in
the *Biographia*) is addressed directly in the essay "Genius and Novelty," in which

not, however, accept the last moral of the story because it tends to subvert the notion that there is a moral. That there may be no absolute distinction between sanity and madness, not even one in the relatively simplified context of a fable, and that the emergence of a prophet or oracle merely makes visible an ineffaceable difference operating all along are precisely the amoral positions that he most ardently desires to combat, but ones which he nonetheless introduces in a prose that confuses every speaking forth, that compromises its profession of disinterested benevolence and friendship, and that justifies the persecution it projects.

Only the play of all three morals in the story of the maddening rain can explain the course of *The Friend* from its fabulous genesis. Although in the second essay Coleridge forthrightly asserts that "the objects and contents of his work" are to "refer men's opinions to their absolute principles, and thence their feelings to the appropriate objects, and in their due degrees; and finally, to apply the principles thus ascertained, to the formation of stedfast convictions concerning the most important questions of Politics, Morality, and Religion" (*F*, 16), the project does not get directly underway with the proposition of the principles themselves but hangs, as if fascinated, for thirteen essays over the problem of reference. The existence and virtue of the absolute principles are not questioned any more than the elder questioned the authenticity of the voice from the cavern, but the possibility and means of communicating those principles are, and on the failure to communicate the secret decree of the voice adequately turned the prophet's abject futility and eventual suffering. Reference is invested with a telling doubleness: it is, for Coleridge, both a problem of a relation that exists but is not always perceived and a problem of how to relate or communicate that connection. Everyone has the problem of determining within and for himself the proper reference of opinion to prin-

---

Coleridge defends himself against "the scorn of those critics who laugh at the oldness of my topics" (*F*, 109). Although, as the editor notes, Coleridge seems to have Hazlitt in mind in this case, by pluralizing his former friend and protege into "critics" Coleridge typically abstracts an instance of antagonism into a principle of opposition which he has aroused and will defend against by his principled moral philosophy.

ciple; the special task of Coleridge is to refer men to the importance of that problem and to direct them toward its solution.[7] The conviction that lies behind Coleridge's project is that absolute principles of truth, self-evident to the light of reason, which is "conscious *Self*-knowledge . . . and the organ of the Supersensuous," can faithfully and effectively communicate with the circumstanced, discursive understanding, "the conception of the Sensuous, or the faculty by which we generalize and arrange the phaenomena of perception: that faculty, the functions of which contain the rules and constitute the possibility of outward Experience" (*F,* 156). Such conviction may comfort the philosophic believer closeted in his study, but for the moral essayist faith must go to work. And once morality becomes more than a private affair between an individual, his conscience, and his God, once it becomes a public *issue,* new obligations and problems arise. In the most general terms, to be successful Coleridge must be able morally and amicably to communicate to his readers a moral communication, to verify reason's word within a discourse of reason. In the instance of *The Friend* the difficulty of bringing truth into the everyday is compounded by the prosaic problem of writing about complex philosophical matters in the format of a periodical, a literary form that is ordinarily devoted to information and amusement, not intellectual exertion. From the beginning, then, Coleridge's propaedeutic figure of the Friend is situated as mediator not only between reason and understand-

[7]This task of reference is a duty that Edmund Burke ascribed to the "learned and reflecting part of this kingdom" in *Reflections on the Revolution in France*: "Persuaded that all things ought to be done with reference, and referring all to the point of reference to which all should be directed, they think themselves bound, not only as individuals in the sanctuary of the heart, or as congregated in that personal capacity, to renew the memory of their high origin and cast; but also in their corporate character to perform their national homage to the institutor, and author and protector of civil society; without which civil society man could not by any possibility arrive at the perfection of which his nature is capable, nor even make a remote and faint approach to it" (*Reflections*, ed. Conor Cruise O'Brien [Harmondsworth, England: Penguin Books, 1969], p. 196). The influence of Burke on *The Friend* is pervasive, if not decisive. The example of Burke affects not only Coleridge's judgment of the consistency of his own allegiances but also his arguments about the relation of principle to expedience. The distinction that governs the various differences in argument and rhetoric is that that which for Burke must be maintained is that which for Coleridge must be restored.

ing but also between the private conscience and the public eye, the reader of prose periodicals. To avoid the fatal opposition of an insane sanity and a sane insanity the Friend seeks to find opposites which are not dead antitheses, poles that though distinct can be rightly comprehended as communicating—to find, in other words, extremes that meet.

In Essay II the Friend seeks to discriminate himself and his audience from the general writer and reader by projecting a radically rewarding relationship between amusement and instruction:

> The present Work is an experiment; not whether a Writer may *honestly* overlook the one, or *successfully* omit the other, of the two elements [instruction and amusement] themselves, which serious Readers at least persuade themselves, they pursue; but whether a change might not be hazarded of the usual *order*, in which periodical writers have in general attempted to convey them. Having myself experienced that no delight either in kind or degree, was equal to that which accompanies the distinct perception of a fundamental truth, relative to our moral being; having, long after the completion of what is ordinarily called a learned education, discovered a new world of intellectual profit opening on me—not from any new opinions, but lying, as it were, at the roots of those which I had been taught in childhood in my Catechism and Spelling-book; there arose a soothing hope in my mind that a lesser Public might be found, composed of persons susceptible of the same delight, and desirous of attaining it by the same process. [*F*, 15]

Though instruction and amusement are distinguishable, the Friend's reflection on his own experience has convinced him that, properly understood, instruction and amusement do communicate with each other. That reflection justifies his hazard of a change in the usual order of priorities in the periodical essay. He hopes that the "intellectual profit" he has accrued can interest an audience, fit though few, who will forsake thriftless curiosity and imitate his reflective exercise by going to the "roots" of current opinions, where instruction and amusement meet in the "distinct perception of a fundamental truth, relative to our moral being." The promise of such a true delight both justifies the Friend's high expectations of his audience and au-

thorizes his provisional compromise with a natural and decorous
desire for pleasant relaxation:

> THE FRIEND does not indeed exclude from his plan occasional
> interludes; and vacations of innocent entertainment and pro-
> miscuous information, but still in the main he proposes to himself the
> communication of such delight as rewards the march of Truth,
> rather than to collect the flowers which diversify its track, in order
> to present them apart from the homely yet foodful or medicinable
> herbs, among which they had grown. [*F*, 16]

Promiscuity will be permitted, but only because it can be securely
bundled off from the higher pleasures of a severe chastity.

The order that the Friend discovers among instruction, delight,
and innocent entertainment will govern both the organization
of his essays and the logic of his argument. The book will be
a progressive march of truth punctuated by pleasant interludes,
toward clear and distinct perceptions of fundamental truths
that can be applied to the formation of steadfast principles of
conduct. One of the supervisory metaphors for this arrangement appears at the end of the first stage of *The Friend's* advance, the first "Landing-Place"—so named because it recalls
the magnificent spiral staircase in "THE GREAT HOUSE" of
the Friend's youth, an ascent "relieved at well-proportioned
intervals by spacious landing-places" (*F*, 148). One's difficult
climb to the top is relieved by places to relax and rewarded by
an elevated, delightful view of the whole structure.[8] This emblem
of the harmonious ascending spiral corresponds to an even
more potent figure for the dynamics of *The Friend*, the metaphor
of the stream. When Coleridge sought to evoke the paradisal
state of mankind in his introductory fable, he described it, as we
have seen, as a "State rather than a Time" in which "even the
sense of succession is lost in the uniformity of the stream." The
source of that stream, the fable tells us, is in that cavern where
the elder hears the providential voice, the fountain of truth

---

[8]The spiraling staircase is a fit emblem of that spiraling ascent to a place
correspondent to but higher than one's starting point which M. H. Abrams has
identified as the "typical design of Romanticism's high argument." See *Natural
Supernaturalism* (New York: Norton, 1971), pp. 183-87.

from which, the Friend later instructs us, a life-giving stream flows progressively onward:

> In fine, Truth considered in itself and in the effects natural to it, may be conceived as a gentle spring or water-source, warm from the genial earth, and breathing up into the snow drift that is piled over and around its outlet. It turns the obstacle into its own form and character, and as it makes its way increases its stream. And should it be arrested in its course by a chilling season, it suffers delay, not loss, and waits only for a change in the wind to awaken and again roll onwards. [*F*, 65][9]

This current is the same "life ebullient stream which," Coleridge claims near the conclusion of *The Friend*, "breaks through every momentary embankment, again, indeed, and evermore to embank itself, but within no banks to stagnate or be imprisoned" (*F*, 519).[10] Like the staircase which ascends from its ground, the stream is progressive: it flows steadily onward from its source. Like the staircase, which elegantly spirals upward to a point symmetrically correspondent with but substantially higher than its beginning, the stream eventually completes a circuit: it starts from the fountain of truth and proceeds through space toward an eventual renewal in the restorative waters of its source.

But the analogy of the stream has greater claim than the staircase to be the master metaphor of *The Friend* because, unlike the artifact, it represents movement as temporal process; moreover, that process involves tension and conflict: the tension of the current itself, which advances by contrary forces, and the conflict of that progressive current with the banks which retard its advance. As the stream bonds together in a life-ebullient circuit the natal source (the fountain, roots of opinions) with the terminus of a rejuvenated adult understanding of the child's

---

[9]Truth may be a continuous fountain, but authors are not so inexhaustible. Coleridge writes to his brother George in 1809 that "the Friend will be the outlet of my whole *reservoir* as well as of the living Fountain—till it shall be dried up" (*CL* III, 239).

[10]The eternally circulant stream is a favorite metaphor of Coleridge's (for a discussion of its antecedents and correspondes see Beer, *Coleridge's Poetic Intelligence* [New York: Barnes & Noble, 1977], chap. 3), but this particular image, which comes near the end of *The Friend*, echoes a similar one, directed to Coleridge, near the end of the 1805 *Prelude* (XIII, 193-205).

forgotten intuitions, so does the stream bring together in its current the pulse of polar energies popularly considered as antithetical. The stream is the preferred emblem of Coleridge's favorite proverb "Extremes Meet" (*F*, 110), on which *The Friend* as a whole is an extended gloss. As an emblem, the stream both illustrates the proverb and authorizes its premise that "THERE IS, strictly speaking, NO PROPER OPPOSITION BUT BETWEEN THE TWO POLAR FORCES OF ONE AND THE SAME POWER" (*F*, 94) by situating it within an intellectual analogy based on natural correspondence. Finally, the stream has its equivalent to the landing-place in the eddy, the spot where the current pauses, whether in a streamy vacation or a sublime suspension.[11]

Yet to state that extremes do meet and to furnish an emblem of their progressive interaction is not to demonstrate how they meet. Nor is the mere assertion of the delightful communication of instruction and amusement in one's own life proof that such a communication can be achieved in others, let alone the instrument required to effect it. There remain problems similar to those of the prophet of the maddening rain: how to communicate one's own experience of the truth in intelligible prose; how to endow that communication with more authority than the periodical appearance of a small eminence on a stamped sheet. The Friend's situation is even more complicated than the oracle's, however, because his message, difficult in its own right, must compete with the clamorous pleas for attention of every vain posturer who has somehow learned to manipulate a pen and gained access to a printing press. Such competition is la-

---

[11]The eddy is both a part of and apart from the stream. Its valorization depends on the perspective one takes upon it, from within or without. In "The Story of Maria Eleonora Schoning," the Friend, celebrating the musicality of his heroine's voice, comments, "If you had listened to it in one of those brief sabbaths of the soul, when the activity and discursiveness of the thoughts are suspended, and the mind quietly *eddies* round, instead of flowing outward . . . in such a mood you might have half-fancied, half-felt, that her voice had a separate being of its own" (p. 343). In this passage from the *Notebooks*, on the other hand, Coleridge looks at the eddy from the standpoint of the stream: "Our mortal existence a stoppage in the blood of Life—a brief eddy in the everflowing Ocean of pure Activity, from wind or concourse of currents" (*CN* II, 3151). On Coleridgean eddies see Beer, pp. 41-69, and Edward Kessler, *Coleridge's Metaphors of Being* (Princeton: Princeton University Press, 1979), pp. 15-37.

mentable but not daunting, however, for one accepts at the out-set that the life that would be grounded on principle is a life of struggle: "That which doth not *withstand*, hath *itself* no standing place. To *fill* a station is to exclude or repel others,—and this is not less the definition of moral, than of material, *solidity*. We *live* by continued acts of defence, that involve a sort of offensive warfare. But a man's principles, on which he grounds his Hope and his Faith, are the life of his life" (*F,* 97).

If appropriate to moral living, that less than amicable simile is even more pertinent to moral writing, which will be scrutinized by the publicists of personality for any pretext to challenge the authority of the moral essayist. Acting on his own counsel, the Friend defends his standing place by going on the offensive and anticipating those charges of presumption and arrogance which he expects will be leveled against him because, as he says, "I have spoken in my own person," and dared "to dissent from the opinions of great authorities, and, in my following numbers perhaps, from the general opinion concerning the true value of certain authorities deemed great" (*F,* 27). To stand is to with-stand. To establish his own authority the Friend will dissent from supposed authorities such as Priestley, Warburton, and Hobbes and perhaps thereby offend the general opinion; to defend against the reaction his aggression will arouse he antici-pates the criticism before the act—such are the prosaics of defer-ral. Evidence of the arrogance of his antagonists is the eclipse of their authority, which is in turn evidence of the Friend's enlight-ened freedom from arrogance—*ergo,* presumptive evidence of the Friend's authority. As defense is turned into offense and withstanding into standing, so is dilatory self-reflection turned into what seems to be an advance. An eddying reflection on one's own possible presumption or arrogance becomes a con-centering on one's own place in which one discovers authority.

What begins to emerge early in *The Friend* is a form of opposi-tion fundamentally allegorical and completely distinct from the amiable dialectic crystallized by the aphorism "Extremes meet." The Friend defers a direct advance toward first principles in order to expel permanently all foreign disquisitions that would contaminate or displace his home truths. Various versions of the foreign, the vicious, the artificial, and the shallow are considered as alternatives to the truth; collectively they make up a cluster of antitheses that negatively affirm the positive integrity of truth, and implicitly confirm the Friend as its champion: to be a friend to truth one must be an enemy to falsehood. This allegorization can be observed in the Friend's approach to the first problem under the topic of The Communication of Truth: whether it is ever inexpedient to tell the truth, and if so, whether it be wisdom to tincture truth with falsehood. He approaches the question with a moral absolutism empowered by the allegorical rhetoric of scripture:

> Truth is self-restoration: for that which is the correlative of Truth, the existence of absolute Life, is the only object which can attract toward it the whole depth and mass of his fluctuating Being, and alone can unite Calmness with Elevation. But it must be Truth without alloy and unsophisticated. It is by the agency of indistinct conceptions, as the counterfeits of the Ideal and Transcendent, that evil and vanity exercise their tyranny on the feelings of man. The Powers of Darkness are politic if not wise; but surely nothing can be more irrational in the pretended children of Light, than to enlist themselves under the banners of Truth, and yet rest their hopes on an alliance with Delusion. [*F*, 36-37]

Maintaining the absolute distinction between truth and false-hood, as absolute as that between good and evil, depends on preventing truth from being alloyed, sophisticated, or counter-feited by evil. One difference then between truth and falsehood is the perspective on the difference between them; that is, from the perspective of truth its distinction from falsehood is an onto-logical one,[12] whereas from the perspective of falsehood or evil the difference is merely ideological. It is not in the nature of evil to *be* evil; it is the (un)nature of evil not to *be* anything; instead what constitutes evil, darkness, delusion, is that it is completely politic, willing to ally with anything to any end. Hence the Friend condemns the Jesuitical category of "PIOUS FRAUDS" because it is "among the numerous artifices, by which austere truths are to be softened down into palatable falsehoods, and Virtue and Vice, like the atoms of Epicurus, to receive that

---

[12]"Truth is the correlative of Being" (*BL* I, 94).

insensible *clinamen* which is to make them meet each other half way" (*F*, 37). "Sophisticating," "alloying," "counterfeiting," "softening"—all are metaphors for the slight, almost imperceptible, swerve that brings together in a politic rapprochement extremes that should not meet but keep a constant metaphysical distance. Fortunately, the real character of the sophisticating expression "pious frauds" can be determined easily, the clinamen retraced; like arrogance and presumption it bears distinguishing marks: the marks of Catholicism, an alien, mystery-mongering, and fraudulent religion, which has been repelled in the past and whose delusions will be rejected by all men who understand that "no real greatness can long co-exist with deceit. The whole faculties of man must be exerted in order to noble energies [*sic*]; and he who is not earnestly sincere, lives in but half his being, self-mutilated, self-paralyzed" (*F*, 41).

The judgment would seem to be decisive in favor of truth absolute and entire, given the proper motives on the part of the speaker; but the curious redundancy employed by the Friend to characterize those motives, "earnestly sincere," acts with the force of a qualification, and one wonders if it is the idea of mutilation that draws the Friend into a digressive meditation on the dangers not only of books "in which the morality of intentional falsehood is asserted," but of other books whose so-called truths are themselves impious:

> The suspicion of methodism must be expected by every man of rank and fortune, who carries his examination respecting the books which are to lie on his breakfast-table, farther then to their freedom from gross verbal indecencies, and broad avowals of atheism in *the title-page.* For the existence of an intelligent first cause may be ridiculed in the notes of one poem, or placed doubtfully as one or two possible hypotheses, in the very opening of another poem, and both be considered as works of safe promiscuous reading "virginibus puerisque." [*F*, 41-42]

There is a swerve of logic here: the assertion of the morality of intentional falsehood becomes the equivalent of the assertion of the absence of an intelligent first cause. That equivalence *could*

[200]

be furnished with a philosophical rationale—ultimately, deceit is atheistic—but this swerve eludes rationalization: the extremes of pious fraud and impious hypothesis are imagined to conjugate somehow within the covers of a book where heresy masking as honest surmise clings to the margins. What seems to be "safe promiscuous reading" may conceal a point that can penetrate virgins and disable young men.

This surprising and subversive alliance of hypothetical truths with subversive falsehoods calls for a refinement of the model of the communication of truth, which must begin with a distinction between mere verbal truth and veracity: "By *verbal* truth we mean no more than the correspondence of a given fact to given words. In *moral* truth, we involve likewise the intention of the speaker, that his words should correspond to his thoughts in the sense in which he expects them to be understood by others" (*F*, 42-43). The Friend goes on to urge that "veracity, therefore, not mere accuracy; to convey truth, not merely to say it; is the point of duty in dispute; and the only difficulty in the mind of an honest man arises from the doubt, whether more than *veracity* (i.e., the truth and nothing but the truth) is not demanded of him by the law of the conscience; whether it does not exact *simplicity*; that is, the truth only, and the whole truth" (*F*, 43). The addition of simplicity as a criterion completes a change in the model of communication: no longer is communication conceived of as the direct translation of an intuited truth into language; rather the emphasis falls on the *conveyance* of truth and, accordingly, the earnest sincerity of the moral speaker.

To flesh out the distinction between saying and conveying the Friend introduces the crucial difference between a right and an adequate notion of the truth.[13] "The conscience, or effective reason," he claims, "commands the design of conveying an *adequate* notion of the thing spoken of, when this is practicable: but at all events a *right* notion or none at all" (*F*, 43). Although

[13]A Platonic distinction. Before Socrates begins the investigation of justice in *The Republic*, he advises Cephalus, "Suppose, for example, a friend who had lent us a weapon were to go mad and then ask for it back, surely anyone would say we ought not to return it. It would not be 'right' to do so; nor yet to tell the truth without reserve to a madman" (I. 331).

the Friend gives some attention to the unusual circumstances when the right notion may be communicated though it be adequate, he is fascinated by the other side of the possibility, the various instances when the communication of a right notion may be both inadequate and immoral, especially in those books that may slip past the ˙immethodist father, books where the pious fraud swerves from being a falsehood expediently substituted for the truth toward the truth becoming itself a variety of falsehood. As he has associated the pious fraud proper with the alien deceitfulness of the Papists, so here he connects this new variety of fraud with the lapsed Catholicism and dangerous *sottise* of the Encyclopaedists. Acting on a shallow and fanciful notion of benevolence, the Encyclopaedists cleanly stripped the simple rustic of his superstitions and exacted from him only, the Friend sardonically notes, "the price of abandoning his faith in Providence and in the continued existence of his fellow-creatures after their death." Bushels of sophisticating slogans, "the teeth of the old serpent," were first "planted by the Cadmuses of French Literature, under Louis XV [and then] produced a plenteous crop of Philosophers and Truth-trumpeters of this kind, in the reign of his Successor." By casting their serpent seeds promiscuously about, these reckless truth-sowers "diffused their notions so widely, that the very ladies and hair-dressers of Paris became fluent *Encyclopaedists*: and the sole price which their scholars paid for these treasures of new information, was to believe Christianity an imposture" (*F,* 46). The Friend calls these French writers "hurrying enlighteners," and finds their shameful haste to be characteristic of the "imposters of all professions," who are driven by "the desire of arriving at the end without the effort of thought and will, which are the appointed means" (*F,* 56). The consequence of this hurry and diffusion is that instead of communicating the durable, steadying truth, the enlighteners merely incite the rapid exchange of one superstition for another—the superstition of truth-telling itself. Having gotten rid of God and king they end by worshipping a tyrannical idol: "Folly and vice have their appropriate religions, as well as virtue and true knowledge: and some way or other fools will dance round the golden calf, and wicked men beat their timbrels and kettledrums

To Moloch, horrid king, besmeared with blood
Of human sacrifice and parent's tears."[14]

Excess breeds excess.

Breeds excess: for as the Friend admits, his fascination with these hurrying enlighteners has propelled *him* faster than he intended; he has been carried willy-nilly beyond the deliberate analysis he had planned in a heady slide toward the vision of the horrid king besmeared with the blood of children. A curious mimesis is at work here; like the Encyclopaedists the rightness of the Friend's criticism has outdistanced the adequateness of its conveyance: "My feelings have led me on, and in my illustration I had almost lost from my view the subject to be illustrated" (*F*, 47). This is a turning point in *The Friend*. The writer is a critic who shares neither the Encyclopaedists' notions of truth nor their idea of the communication of truth, yet he is caught up in a surge of rhetoric that diverts him from his subject and rushes him to the same conclusion as his opponents, to Milton's Moloch, the false and bloody monarch.[15] We shall inquire into this mime-

---

[14]*F*, 47. The links between diffusion of knowledge, eradication of superstition and an inevitable regicide are displayed by Burke with cutting irony: "The age has not yet the compleat benefit of that diffusion of knowledge that has undermined superstition and error; and the king of France wants another object or two, to consign to oblivion, in consideration of all the good which is to arise from his own sufferings, and the patriotic crimes of an enlightened age" (*Reflections*, p. 166).

[15]The application of imagery associated with blood sacrifice and monstrous gods to the direct and indirect consequences of French Enlightenment philosophy is a regular practice of Coleridge's. In part the lurid imagery is intended to restore a proper—indeed, a sacred—sense of scandal at the physiocrats' transgression of the distinction between persons and things, as in this 1818 letter to William Mudford: "The very term, and that a most appropriate one, by which the French Psilosophers (Royalist or Republican, alike Despotists) designated thus their darling Science, namely, *Physiocratic*, implies the utter contempt of all that distinguishes or rather that forms the chasm, the *diversity* in *kind* between man & beast. It is a science which begins with *abstractions* in order to exclude whatever is not subject to a technical calculation: in the face of all experience, it assumes these as the *whole* of human nature—and then on an impossible Hypothesis builds up the most inhuman edifice, a Temple of Tescalipoca" (*CL* III, 856). In *The Statesman's Manual* Coleridge calls Jacobinism a "*monstrum hybridum,* made up in part of despotism, and in part of abstract reason misapplied to objects that belong entirely to experience and understanding" (*LS*, 63-64; in a note on page 63 the editor refers to other examples in Coleridge of the hybrid

sis, an instance of what René Girard has called mimetic desire.[16] First, however, I want to examine both the grounds upon which the Friend accuses the *philosophes* of error and the criteria by which he distinguishes himself as a truth-teller—which means examining in more detail the import of the Friend's distinction between a right and an adequate notion.

Although the Friend would like to adhere to a moral absolutism that makes the speaker responsible only to his own honest intentions, the fact that truth must be communicated qualifies his autonomy. The absolute model of communicating the truth would correspond to the ideal model of the will that we have examined earlier: truth, completely free and undetermined, would pass without distortion from its inner source in the god-like faculty of the reason to the external, phenomenal world of understanding and sense. Yet this process is even more overtly problematic in the case of truth than it is for the will, as inner truth must be communicated through the medium of language—in the Friend's case through the published text. Once the criterion of the adequate is raised it becomes clear that it is very difficult to give a completely adequate notion of the will or of truth in writing; one seems to be moving from one region (the dictates of an invisible reason uttered to the mind in an interior cavern) to another, entirely different topography (the communicating of reason's dictates to the understandings of the assembled multitude by the visible figure on a small eminence or by the visible marks on a blank page). Communication implies translation, which, in turn, bears on the continuity of the

---

monster image). The title "Moloch" is associated in *The Statesman's Manual* with Napoleon and Nimrod, whom Coleridge cites as examples of "COMMANDING GENIUS," "mighty Hunters of Mankind," and "Molocks of human nature" (*LS*, 66). Cf. also *Essays on His Times*, ed. David Erdman, *Collected Works*, 3 (Princeton: Princeton University Press, 1978), 234.

[16]According to René Girard, a mimetic desire is the competition that springs from the "double bind" placed on a disciple by a master who simultaneously enjoins "'Imitate me!'" and "'Don't imitate me!'": "Whenever the disciple borrows from his model what he believes to be the 'true' object, he tries to possess that truth by desiring precisely what this model desires. Whenever he sees himself closest to the supreme goal, he comes into violent conflict with a rival. By a mental shortcut that is both eminently logical and self-defeating, he convinces himself that the violence itself is the most distinctive attribute of this supreme goal!" *Violence and the Sacred* (Baltimore: The Johns Hopkins University Press, 1977), pp. 147, 148.

metaphysical with the physical. Were it possible, the translation of truth directly into the language of the tribe would disclose a right notion, but that notion could very well be dangerous once the word leaves the pen of the prophet-writer. It is dangerous because: (1) the truth may be instantaneously and completely misunderstood; (2) it may be instantaneously and completely understood but nonetheless *inadequately* understood. The former possibility is less grave because it is potentially reversible. Inadequate understanding is both more dangerous and more likely. Indeed, translated into words too completely and too rapidly the truth *must* be inadequately communicated simply because the presumption behind the communication is that the truth *can* be fully translated into words. The visible is taken for the invisible; God has been transformed into an idol. This exchange communicates a vandalized truth: absolute truth becomes the truth *soi disant*, translation traducement, with the consequent loss of the vital sense of something in reserve waiting to be uttered or acted, which is the metaphysical and moral gravity necessary to all right and adequate notions of the truth. God, the will, and the truth represent what is not exhausted in their communication.

The hurried, inadequate communication of the truth is, as we have seen, the vice of the Enlightenment, the *French* Enlightenment, whose ideology and whose very style incur the Friend's unremitting hostility. Early in his campaign he proclaims his "aversion to the epigrammatic unconnected periods of the fashionable *Anglo-gallican* taste" and explains his refusal to "cast [his] sentences in the French moulds" by dramatizing a scene of reading:

> It cannot but be injurious to the human mind never to be called into effort: the habit of receiving pleasure without any exertion of thought, by the excitement of curiosity and sensibility, may be justly ranked among the worst effects of habitual novel reading. It is true that these short and unconnected sentences are easily and instantly understood: but it is equally true, that wanting all the cement of thought as well as of style, all the connections, and (if you will forgive so trivial a metaphor) all the *hooks-and-eyes* of the memory, they are as easily forgotten: or rather, it is scarcely possible that they should be remembered.—Nor is it less true, that those who

confine their reading to such books dwarf their own faculties, and finally reduce their understandings to a deplorable imbecility: the fact you mention, and which I shall hereafter make use of, is a fair instance and a striking illustration. Like idle morning visitors, the brisk and breathless periods hurry in and hurry off in quick and profitless succession; each indeed for the moments of its stay prevents the pain of vacancy, while it indulges the love of sloth; but all together they leave the mistress of the house (the soul I mean) flat and exhausted, incapable of attending to her own concerns, and unfitted for the conversation of more rational guests. [*F*, 20-21]

Fit only for the asthmatic, the French style, "in which the merest commonplace acquires a momentary poignancy, a petty titillating sting, from affected point and wilful antithesis" (*F*, 26) is ruinous for the healthy, who, by exposing themselves to such "short and unconnected sentences" in the solitary habit of novel reading, will "dwarf their own faculties" to an eventual stage of "imbecility." In a metaphor where vehicle and tenor are so confused that they need to be sorted out in a parenthesis, the Friend imagines a woman alone at home in the morning being subjected to the titillating sting of "idle morning visitors," moving in "brisk and breathless periods," momentarily preventing the pain of vacancy, but finally leaving the woman "flat and exhausted." That is metaphor become fantasy—a fantasy of masturbation: solitary habits; involuntary visitations; breathless, hurrying thoughts; sudden exhaustion; and the superstitious fear of an imbecility which is the mental version of the sudden loss of power that that Friend has already represented as self-mutilation. As novel reading is motivated by nothing but curiosity, the simple desire to get from one word to the next, so the French style is imagined as a linguistic machine, one marvelous, ineluctable circuit where affect is meaninglessly transferred from word to word in random succession. The machine obeys an erotic dynamics of rapid and total exchange, which ends in an efflux that leaves the system (the mind) flat and exhausted, "incapable of attending to its own concerns, and unfitted for the conversation of more rational guests." This apparently irresistible circuit of energy depletes the soul and unmans (or unwomans) the reader.

As the characterization of the French style attracts the language of masturbation, so does it delineate a recognizably associationist system in which affect circulates wholly mechanically. Words lack any proper syntactic or semantic connections; mindless of the proprieties, the machine functions without any cooperation on the part of the higher faculty of the imagination, which has within the system's linear circuit of crackling exchanges no haven from which to organize the dispersion of energy. And since energy never fills a word longer than the time it takes to articulate its restless auto-affective passage toward its termination, reason has no place in which to assume a supervisory position from which in order to inform and direct the machine's blind discourse. As it is restless, masturbatory, and associationist, so is the French style nightmarishly egalitarian: it lacks any topography of height or depth, any distinction between words besides quantitative consecution—a democratic difference just sufficient to allow the thrust of affect from one ghostly point to the next.

Only by understanding the negative investment that the Friend makes in the French style can we make sense of his scorn for the *philosophes* who employed that breathless, epigrammatic style. Only then can we appreciate the importance of his own investment in the alternative, moral style, "the stately march and difficult evolutions, which characterize the eloquence of Hooker, Bacon, Milton, and Jeremy Taylor" (*F*, 20),[17] the great English prose writers of the seventeenth century. Stately rather than titillating, marching rather than running, difficult rather than facile, evolving rather than exhausting, periodic rather than pointed, intentional rather than willful, manly rather than feminine, robust rather than asthmatic, English rather than French—the seventeenth-century style that the Friend adopts (or that has imperceptibly adopted him) requires both attention and thought. The seventeenth-century periodic style has, the

---

[17]The Friend's odd lumping together of Hooker and Bacon, leaders, respectively, of the Ciceronian and anti-Ciceronian movements in the late sixteenth and early seventeenth centuries (cf. George Williamson, *The Senecan Amble* [1951; rpt., Chicago: University of Chicago Press, 1966], p. 186) is not evidence of confusion but the consequence of a discrimination between two Baconian styles, as is clear in his remark to Thomas Poole on the prose of "Lord Bacon, whose style mine more nearly resembles than any other, in his greatest works, [but who] thought Seneca a better model for his essays" (*CL* III, 234).

Friend claims, "intrinsic excellence," not despite its laboriousness and obscurity, but *because* of those apparent liabilities.[18] In the beginning of the fictive letter that he uses to introduce the discussion of his style, the Friend characterizes the progress of his moral essay by means of the metaphor of a journey "through countries of various prospect," and forecasts a "slow and laborious ascent" (*F*, 19). Though stated here as a likely inconvenience, the Friend gradually turns the handicap of obscurity into a virtue. Superficially he does so by means of an argument that reduces to the moralism that nothing worth getting has ever been gotten without a good deal of effort. Not far removed from that *topos* is the humanist commonplace that the exertion in the pursuit of a good is essential to the good. But there is a deeper reason, one that bears directly on the Friend's conception both of truth itself and of truth's connection to language, a reason that emerges at the end of the essay "Virtue and Knowledge," where the Friend prescribes,

> the habituation of the intellect to clear, distinct, and adequate conceptions concerning all things *that are the possible objects of clear conception,* and thus to *reserve* the deep feelings which belong, as by a natural right to those obscure ideas that are necessary to the moral perfection of the human being, notwithstanding, yea, even in consequence, of their obscurity—to *reserve* these feelings, I repeat, for objects, which their very sublimity renders indefinite, no less than their indefiniteness renders them sublime: namely, to the Ideas of Being, Form, Life, the Reason, the Law of Conscience, Freedom, Immortality, God! [*F*, 106, emphasis added]

[18]The absence of difficulty in even a native style is reason for disapproval. For Coleridge the best English style of the eighteenth century is represented by the manner that Addison employed in his periodical, *The Spectator*—a style which has been urged on Coleridge as a model by his friend Thomas Poole and which he admires but rejects as inappropriate to his aims: "Consider," he urges Poole, "the very different Objects of the Friend & of the Spectator: & above all, do not forget, that these are AWEFUL TIMES!—that the love of Reading, as a refined pleasure weaning the mind from grosser enjoyments, which it was one of the Spectator's chief Objects to awaken, has by that work, & those that followed . . . but still more, by Newspapers, Magazines, and Novels, been carried to excess: and the Spectator itself has innocently contributed to the general taste for unconnected writing" (*CL* III, 281). Though not precisely Anglo-Gallican, *The Spectator* has formed readers vulnerable to French influence. One must go back beyond the eighteenth century to find a truly solid, bookish style.

This is a passage where the mimesis of style and subject is as neat as one could wish: obscure language perfectly reflecting a justification of obscure language as a reflection of intrinsically obscure ideas. It is in its mastery of that mimesis that the "intrinsic excellence" of the seventeenth-century style inheres. The key word above is the repeated "reserve." The obscure style has an intrinsic excellence because it properly reserves the deep feelings appropriate to deep truths. Its reserve represents an interiority of the language which is the only place where anything *intrinsic* could be lodged. To be adequate to the highest truth requires one to resist the leveling tendency of discourse by postponing the simplification, even the clarity, that would turn the object of reason into just another counter for the understanding. A studied deferral of meaning is, then, the proper criterion of a virtuous style. Sublimely indefinite ideas (the only ideas of final interest to the Friend) can be adequately communicated only by the obscure, periodic style, because only it does not fully divulge any meaning but always withholds some meaning, reserves a place meant for Being, Form, Life . . . God.

The obscure style conveys truth because its virtue is not merely a manner of syntax or diction but a matter of habituation. The labor of reading a periodic style accustoms the reader to deferral—whether it be the deferral of a sentence, a paragraph, a thought, or an argument. Attention is necessary to follow the syntax, to bring home the Latinisms; thought profits from attention's lead by accepting that it must delve for what it would discover. Eventually the weight of the prose, no longer a burden, becomes as familiar as gravity. Once habituated to deferral, the reader learns not to anticipate the arrival of that which has been periodically postponed but to expect and relish continued deferral. The obscure style tranquilizes the reader's desire and nurtures his imagination.

Great stylists though they were, those British moralists whom the Friend takes as his models have, however, been dead for over a century by the time he essays his own moral communication. Though their style may be for the ages, it may not be for the magazines. The Friend admits that difficult periods are "notwithstanding their intrinsic excellence still less suited to a periodical essay" and reflects, "I have in some measure injured my style, in respect to its facility and popularity, from having almost confined my reading of late years, to the works of the Ancients and those of the elder Writers in the modern languages" (*F*, 20). Although the sense of an archaic novelty, of idle and ephemeral interest, which is accidentally attached to the periodic style, may actually be evidence of a historical decline and implicitly a rebuke to the moderns, and though it may not bear at all on the permanent and intrinsic excellence of the style, such a sense does taint that style's appearance—taint it by giving it an *appearance*, by making it look cosmetic. The Friend admits the "fault" in his insensible imitation of the elder style (*F*, 20) and promises sensibly to modify his style to accommodate it to his forum and his readers' circumstances but insists that he will never go so far as to adopt "this self-sufficient, self-satisfied *plain good common-sense sort* of writing, this prudent saleable popular style of composition" (*F*, 24). Hence, despite his promise to do his best to make "all allowable sacrifices" to the taste of his contemporaries, the Friend's style will remain, despite slight adjustments essentially the same. It *must*, and for two reasons, one structural and the other moral. Because the Friend has divided all of composition in terms of only two mutually exclusive possibilities—the good, difficult, periodic, and British style versus the bad, popular, pointed, and French style—he has restricted his standing place to the domain of the periodic. The Friend supplies the moral reason in this address to his readers: "The primary facts essential to the intelligibility of my principles I can prove to others only as far as I can prevail on them to retire *into themselves* and make their own minds the objects of their stedfast attention" (*F*, 21)—a return upon oneself promoted only by the difficult style, which renders intelligibility as the effect of obscurity.

The avowal of a deliberately obscure style is striking and apparently peculiar to Coleridge. According to George Williamson, the one prose style consistently associated with obscurity during the Renaissance is the Tacitean, which is an "extreme development" of the "curt Senecan style" that is itself "marked by the cultivation of brevity, staccato form, and point."[19] Identi-

---

[19]Williamson, *Senecan Amble*, p. 188.

fied by its truncation of syntactic ligatures and its "strong lines," the Tacitean is a style of extreme brevity and aphoristic impaction, its obscurity the corollary of a search for the most forcible form of expression. Insisting on its development from the curt style and differing from Morris Croll, Williamson refuses to grant independent formal status to the Tacitean or obscure style; indeed, he argues that the distinction between obscurity and perspicuity is not "a trustworthy guide to the ideas or affinities of styles, since perspicuity is the constant of language as a vehicle of communication."[20] The Friend's stylistic ideal, which holds obscurity as the correspondent of matter and philosophy, could hardly be more remote from the Tacitean, which has all the features of the French *stile coupé* and which indulges obscurity as a species of wit and an instrument of policy.[21] The final cause of the Friend's cultivation of obscurity is his elevation of the standard of an ultimate intelligibility above that of an immediate perspicuity. The Friend proposes a style designed to direct the interpretation a reader will make of it as language rather than to assist an auditor to understand it as speech; for the Friend style is a matter of hermeneutics rather than rhetoric. Viewed from this perspective, the Friend's notion of an obscure style, though still distinctive, can be referred to a tradition different from the "Senecan Amble."

The most influential expositor of the virtues attendant on the obscure style is Augustine, "the Cicero and Ciceronian of patristic Latin."[22] Though himself a writer of elegantly perspicuous schematic prose, when Augustine turns to the formulation of a

---

[20]Ibid., p. 191.

[21]Coleridge's expressive combinations of seventeenth-century models would seem to be described by the characteristics that Morris W. Croll identifies as "baroque": "Expressiveness rather than formal beauty was the pretension of the new movement, as it is of every movement that calls itself modern. It disdained complacency, suavity, copiousness, emptiness, ease, and in avoiding these qualities sometimes obtained effects of contortion or obscurity, which it was not always willing to regard as faults. It preferred the forms that express the energy and labor of minds seeking the truth, . . . to the forms that express a contented sense of the enjoyment and possession of it." *Attic and Baroque Prose Style*, ed. J. Max Patrick, Robert O. Evans, and John Wallace (Princeton: Princeton University Press, 1969), pp. 208-9. But because Croll's impressions do seem to apply to "every movement that calls itself modern," there seems no more profit in calling Coleridge's style *baroque* than in calling it *romantic*.

[22]Ibid., p. 96.

model of biblical interpretation in *On Christian Doctrine*, he constructs a sophisticated justification for the obscurity of the Scriptures. For Augustine, unlike the Friend, the obscurity of a style is wholly attributable to the effect of figurative language; and when he explains the spiritual benefit that figurative obscurity confers on the pious and assiduous reader of Scripture, Augustine accounts for it in terms of a theory of allegory which the Friend would find insupportable. According to Augustine, "no one doubts that things are perceived more readily through similitudes and that what is sought with difficulty is discovered with more pleasure."[23] Because of its obscurity figurative language challenges the reader, arouses him from a spiritless indifference, and, in its solution, produces a spiritual pleasure. In his study *Allegory*, Angus Fletcher includes Augustine's justification of difficulty under the rubric of "Thematic Effects of Allegory," and comments that for Augustine the "very obscurity is a source of pleasure, especially to the extent that the actual process of deciphering the exegetical content of a passage would be painfully arduous and uncertain."[24] Arduous, certainly, but uncertain only within an area sharply circumscribed within a space of infinite assurance. The pleasure that is for Augustine proper to interpreting difficult passages is the pleasure not of a spiritual quest but of a spiritual exercise, of seeking and reaching a solution that is foreordained. Because Augustinian allegorical interpretation is a decipherment, pleasure can always be confidently expected to follow and cancel all pain; unlike the modern Hartley, the medieval Augustine is certain of the true key. Indeed it is the prior, assured possession of the key that dictates the difference between literal and figurative language: "Therefore in the consideration of figurative expressions a rule such as this will serve, that what is read should be subjected to diligent scrutiny until an interpretation contributing to the reign of charity is produced. If this result appears literally in the text, the expression being considered is not figurative."[25] There is, then, no

[23]St. Augustine, *On Christian Doctrine*, trans. D. W. Robertson (Indianapolis: Bobbs-Merrill, 1958), p. 38.
[24]Angus Fletcher, *Allegory: The Theory of a Symbolic Mode* (1964; rpt., Ithaca, N.Y.: Cornell University Press, 1970), pp. 234-35.
[25]St. Augustine, *On Christian Doctrine*, p. 93.

essential difference between the figurative and the literal; and even the discursive difference is negligible because "Hardly anything may be found in these obscure places which is not found plainly said elsewhere."[26]

Augustine's model is much more like Hartley's than it is like the Friend's, even to the assertion of an associationist explanation for the formation of figures.[27] The Friend would object to the former's model much as Coleridge did to the latter's: the concept of figurative language is reductionist to the extent that figures are considered as merely ornamental; given the availability of the key and the overcoming of a superficial difficulty, the process of interpretation becomes the trot, trot, trot of association—a mechanism suspiciously akin to the breathless hurrying he deplores in the French. Moreover, the structuralist presuppositions shared by Augustine and Hartley make the figurative language of the Bible essentially unnecessary, and, therefore, introduce a caprice into Scripture which portends as first cause a calculating but willful character wholly incongruous with the Friend's authorized version of the deity. The Friend would never advocate the *opening* of the biblical text; he is repelled by the suggestion of a penetrant intelligence on the part of the interpreter and fearful of the implication that an initial opening will lead to a final closing in the exhaustion of meaning. When Coleridge writes specifically about biblical language as he does in *The Statesman's Manual,* he describes it in terms of a symbolism that discloses its spiritual meaning to the faithful reader without any trace of willfulness on the part of author or reader.[28] The word that Coleridge uses for the property of language that permits this congenial accord between the extremes of divine author and mortal reader is "translucence," which is, crucially, neither the transparency of the French's "plain good commonsense sort of writing" nor the opacity of hard allegory (or of pious frauds)—two sides of the same worthless coin, two phases of the same mechanical circuit: open, shut, open, shut. The

[26]Ibid., p. 38.
[27]"When a figurative locution appears, the words of which it is composed will be seen to be derived from similar things or related to such things by some association" (Ibid., p. 99).
[28]*LS,* 30.

metaphor of translucence, itself resistant to reduction, supposes not only that essential truth is communicated by biblical figures but also that that communication involves a withholding of the essential; the minimal resistance of translucence guarantees a divinity in reserve.

A nearer precedent for the Friend's valorization of obscurity comes from the tradition of the sublime. In his *Philosophical Inquiry into the Origin of Our Ideas of the Sublime and Beautiful,* Edmund Burke writes, "But let it be considered that hardly any thing can strike the mind with its greatness, which does not make some sort of approach towards infinity; which nothing can do whilst we are able to perceive its bounds; but to see an object distinctly, and to perceive its bounds, is one and the same thing. A clear idea," Burke concludes, "is therefore another name for a little idea." To illustrate, Burke chooses a passage from the Book of Job (4: 13-17) wherein the "sublimity is principally due to the terrible uncertainty of the thing described."[29] For Thomas Weiskel, who quotes this passage in his book *The Romantic Sublime,* Burke's comments epitomize the dynamics and the implicit teleology of the negative or reader's sublime, in which what is "indistinct is phenomenologically in-finite, and this leads to an hypostasized infinitude."[30] The uncertainty of the thing described is certainly terrible to the mind that cannot comprehend it, but only to the lower, notional powers of the mind. The mind, as Burke implied and as Kant later sought to prove, has another and a nobler power, reason, which is not chastened by obscurity but instead dialectically returns upon itself in the recognition of its own transcendent infinitude, the sole interior correspondent for the phenomenologically infinite. In the Kantian sophistication of Burke's model, "the real motive or cause of the sublime is not efficient but teleological; we are ultimately referred not to the failure of empirical imagination but to reason's project in requiring this failure. The cause of the sublime is," according to Weiskel's summary, "the *aggrandizement of reason at the expense*

---

[29]Edmund Burke, *A Philosophical Enquiry into the Origin of Our Ideas of the Sublime and Beautiful,* ed. J. T. Boulton (Notre Dame, Ind.: University of Notre Dame Press, 1968), p. 63.

[30]Thomas Weiskel, *The Romantic Sublime* (Baltimore: The Johns Hopkins University Press, 1976), pp. 78-79.

*of reality and the imaginative apprehension of reality.*"[31] Were we to substitute "understanding" for "empirical imagination," we would be close to the Coleridgean symbol, which bears within it the discourse of humiliation and power that Weiskel identifies in Kant. Indeed, a superb example of "translucence" is the passage from Psalm 104 which Weiskel identifies as "Hegel's chief instance of the negative sublime," where "'the Lord is addressed as He who coverest [Himself] with light as with a garment; who stretchest out the heavens like a curtain.'"[32] In the sublime moment of the Coleridgean symbol Reason identifies with the awful majesty of the veiled divinity.[33]

The lineaments of the negative sublime are also apparent in the Friend's discussion of the obscure style, as when he announces his hope that the difficulty of his prose will prevail on his readers "to retire *into themselves* and make their own minds the objects of their stedfast attention"—a return upon oneself structurally homologous and thematically correspondent to the turn in the Kantian dynamical sublime. Yet a distinction must be made between the sublime moment and Coleridge's ideal of a *continuously* sublime style. Weiskel, following Kant, describes the sublime as a singular, complex, self-contained experience in the text or in the world read as text. But when the Friend adapts this model according to the requirements of a moral prose style, he both domesticates the obscurity that is the first stage of the negative sublime and disseminates the blockage that is its second, catalytic stage.[34] Blockage occurs at every point of the Friend's prose—or, more precisely, blockage occurs throughout a prose that never fully comes to a point. The Friend's style is meant to be continuously obscure and the reader's understanding is meant to be continuously blocked, thereby continuously provok-

---

[31]Ibid., p. 41.

[32]Ibid., p. 77.

[33]See "Christmas out of Doors," the Friend's set-piece in the sublime, in which the description of the onset of winter on the Lake of Ratzeburg builds to a vision of transfigured ice-islands (*F*, 367). I analyze this passage and discuss the concept of translucence as it pertains to the Coleridgean concept of the symbol in my essay "The Symbol's Errant Allegory," *ELH*, 45, no. 4 (Winter 1978), 640-59.

[34]See Neil Hertz, "The Notion of Blockage in the Literature of the Sublime," in *Psychoanalysis and the Question of the Text: Selected Papers from the English Institute, 1976-77*, ed. Geoffrey H. Hartman (Baltimore: The Johns Hopkins University Press, 1978), pp. 62-86.

ing the turn inward toward a transcendent entity continuously withheld. Its overriding concern for continuity is the criterion of the Friend's style as it is of the Friend's metaphysics, psychology, and political philosophy. Unlike either Augustine's theory of difficult ornament, which presumes a discontinuity between figure and meaning, or Kant's theory of the dynamical sublime, which presumes both the isolation of the sublime moment within a text and the discontinuous transcendence of the text, the Friend's prose is meant to be the continuous reflective discourse of reason, a truly sublime style. If the structure of the Kantian sublime, whether in aesthetic theory or in poetic practice, conforms to an "ethos of alienation,"[35] the Friend desires to find the sublime expression of his principles in an ethos of continuity, a prosaics of the obscure.[36]

The difference between the Kantian model and the Friend's can be engaged by admitting the difficulty of distinguishing the reader from the writer within the prosaics of the sublime style. The negative sublime is a reader's sublime because it may be said to begin with the reader's sense of blockage; the identification between reader and author or authority may be the final cause of that blockage, but the end recognition owes its force to a prior separation. The Friend writes, defends, and prescribes a style which imitates in its eddying involutions the similar inward turning of both writer and reader. One may presume that the self-reflection of writer precedes the reflexive style and that the self-retirement of the reader is its consequence, but the pretext of continuity makes it theoretically and even practically difficult to discriminate reader from Friend (the writer who is always reading himself, reflecting on his own language) and either from the style. The Friend justifies the way he writes by identifying the effects his style is meant to produce, effects which are in turn ideally legitimated by the metaphysical final cause that informs all moral acts; but, and crucially, the Friend demonstrates that one of the "effects" his style is capable of producing is the hypopoesis of the very authority which is supposedly its final

[35]Weiskel, *The Romantic Sublime*, pp. 34 ff.
[36]Raimonda Modiano makes the case for Coleridge's success in maintaining a desired continuity within the sublime in the essay "Coleridge and the Sublime," *Wordsworth Circle*, 9, no. 1 (Winter 1978), 110-21.

cause. The moral and metaphysical burden borne by the Friend's obscure prose is that in the sublime style sublimity becomes a style, a tool at hand for anyone deft enough to put it to use and fabricate a divinity, whether or not there subsists the proper ground to sustain Him. The sublime style is one step farther down the line than the negative sublime: the subreption or cheat of appearance is no longer disclosed in a momentous dialectical reaction; the cheat is dispersed throughout the prose until dialectic itself seems suspicious, cagily rhetorical. What we read in the Friend is the intrinsically excellent *verging* on the completely sufficient style. The book that was to have been the occasion for the Word, consecrated by God so to consecrate the reader, works just as well with God and readers lapsed into charming formalities; the book turns and returns like a blessed machine of language.

One way to think about this machine is to figure it, as the Friend does in the analogic web of his essays, as a marvelous economy, which unceasingly generates wealth without natural resource or manual labor. Replacing labor is the inward turn of style and reader, an investment in self which, the Friend promises in Essay II, will produce an "intellectual profit." Self-investment, reserving a place for the ego, is the essential capitalization without which a profit could not be returned. French style and philosophy is called "profitless" because it does not capitalize but puts everything into play, all or nothing, on every flippant flourish of the pen. The Friend's model for such diseconomic recklessness is the infectious "Mother-vice" of the lottery (*F*, 60), in which the pathetic player hangs expectantly on the chance which lets him down time after time as it comes up blank after blank. True economy has nothing to do with chance; it begins with the premeditated dislodging of dumb matter from its fixed position in the earth, which is not *natura,* no mother, until she first delivers her offspring to the first economist. To have an economy, matter, posited in the earth, must be re-posited by man; to have a rational economy, that matter must be de-posited by a banker, put down, that is, in some strongly held, central place as a capital reserve, the principal that will produce the continuing, calculable interest on which one may draw and by which one may live. Economy has nothing to do with chance and everything to do with logic, for to deposit is, in the Greek, to make an *hypothec,* which corresponds to the logical action of making an hypothesis: the fact, (gold, the good) is put down (as principal, as principle) so that money or ethics may be produced.[37] Matter, the brute thesis of earth, becomes wealth, the sound hypothesis of economy, which is in turn both generator and nexus of all the transactions of men, considered as social agents. The Friend presumes this binding power of wealth—tieing each to all and all to each—in the hypothesized economy of his essay on taxes and taxation. There he contends that the common complaint that the war with Bonaparte has made taxes on the British cruelly exorbitant is shortsighted because critics only cry up the amount that is taken away by taxes. The true economist, however, is aware that whether "a System of Taxation is injurious or beneficial on the whole, is to be known, not by the amount of the sum taken from each individual, but by that which remains behind" (*F,* 230); and by that standard the British are better off than the citizens of any other nation in the world.

But when the Friend turns to consider Britain's singularly successful resistance to the threat of Bonaparte, who "professes to entertain no hope of purchasing the destruction of Great Britain at a less price than that of the barbarism of all Europe" (*E,* 232), he sophisticates his economics further to allow for a standard that will distinguish the British economy qualitatively as well as quantitatively from that of every other nation, to identify a fiscal system that is a standing place beyond calculation, the inner life of the British state:

> To what then do we owe our strength and our immunity? . . . .
> What has rendered Great Britain, from the Orkneys to the Rocks of Scilly, indeed and with more than metaphorical propriety a BODY POLITIC, our Roads, Rivers, and Canals being so truly the veins, arteries, and nerves, of the state; that every pulse in the metropolis produces a correspondent pulsation in the remotest village on its extreme shores! What made the stoppage of the national Bank the conversation of a day without causing one

---

[37]I owe the statement of this correspondence to Marc Shell's *Economy of Literature* (Baltimore: The Johns Hopkins University Press, 1978), pp. 45-46.

irregular throb, or the stagnation of the commercial current in the minutest vessel? I answer without hesitation, that the cause and mother principle of this unexampled confidence, of this *system* of credit, which is as much stronger than mere positive possessions, as the soul of man is than his body, or as the force of a mighty mass in free motion, than the pressure of its separate component parts would be in a state of rest—the main cause of this, I say, has been our NATIONAL DEBT. [*F*, 232-33]

The national debt is not, as is commonly supposed, a liability but a strength, indeed, *the* strength, the cause of the system of credit that is the soul of the state, the matrix that gives life to the metaphor of the body politic. The national debt "has wedded in indissoluble union all the interests of the state" (*F*, 233) because as the debt is shared by all, all have a common interest in the indefinite deferral of its payment. "Whose possible interest could it be," the Friend asks, "either to demand the Principal, or to refuse his share toward the means of paying the interest?" (*F*, 235). Debtors all, all Englishmen derive their interest in the state from the interest they pay on the debt that is the heart of the state, the principal blessing of the machine. The national debt— always owed, never to be redeemed—is a national reserve shared by all Englishmen who are part of the system; it is the invisible source of each man's wealth, the not quite natural resource of the commonwealth.

The economy of the English style reflects the economy of the English state: the truth that is reserved by difficult periods is a debt owed to expression, which renders "with more than metaphorical propriety" a body of the book. Although the two economies are congruent, the symmetry would be cold comfort to the Friend, who carefully restricts his approval of the debt to its fiscal consequences; indeed, he promises a future essay in which he will boldly develop "the injurious effects" the national debt has had "on the Literature, the Morals, and religious Principles" (*F*, 233). Lacking such a title, we can nevertheless guess the injurious effects of the debt by noting the damage it does to the Friend's own moral essay. The sophistication of the Friend's economic model is made possible by a substitution of the hypo- poetical for the hypothetical; in the economy of the national debt, not only the position of the reserve is imagined (as when the hypothesis of gold is *de*posited) but the fact is also invented (there is no gold). The injury of the debt is to represent a system that generates interest despite the fact that it lacks any principal except the differential between borrower and lender, that lacks any principle besides continuance of its complex circulations, and that reinscribes the "owe" in "ownership" for all to read. The injury is the analogy that can be made between this system and the Friend's moral style, his professed attempt to communicate the truth. Is a style of reserve truly a moral act? The essay that would develop the injurious effects of the system of the national debt on literature, morals, and religious principles will not be written because it *is* being written as *The Friend*.

National economies, the Friend has shown, can run without gold; all they require is a substantial debt and the circulation of pieces of paper with a few scratches of ink on them in order to achieve a prosperous self-sufficiency floating on surplus value. "Whose interest could it be either to demand the Principal, or to refuse his share toward the means of paying interest?" The interest only of "men desperate from guilt or debt, or mad with the blackest ambition" (*F*, 235). Moral essays can be floated without truth or God; all that is required to produce the surplus of value is some paper, a pen, and a suitably reserved style. But there will always be the desperate man, the perverse member of the body of the book, who will act against all rational interest and call in his debt even if his return be the blank articulation of empty air.

II

The Friend would hardly stand behind such a venture, any more than he would endorse the unbecoming analogy of the living truth with the abstraction of the national debt. Here he chastens zeal by invoking truth's natural metaphor:

> Observe, how graciously Nature instructs her human children. She cannot give us the knowledge derived from sight without occasioning us at first to mistake images of reflection for substances. But the very consequences of the delusion lead inevitably to its detection; and out of the ashes of error rises a new flower of knowledge. We

not only see, but are enabled to discover by what means we see. . . .
In a similar train of thought, though more fancifully, I might have
elucidated the preceding condition, and have referred our hurrying enlighteners and revolutionary amputators to the gentleness
of Nature, in the oak and the beech, the dry foliage of which she
pushes off only by the propulsion of the new buds, that supply its
place. My friends! a cloathing even of withered leaves is better than
bareness.[38] [*F*, 47-48]

It is the discourse of the simile to liken the communication of
truth to the universality and continuity of natural process. It is
the rhetoric of the figure to contrast the benefits of the natural
progress of truth in which the new seasonably and gently
"pushes off" the old with the effects caused by those unnatural,
indiscriminate men who ruthlessly chop heads from kings. The
simile encourages the hope that absolute truth will eventually be
communicated despite obstructions, that good intentions will
eventually be translated into good words and finally good
deeds—at the same time it marks as unnatural all that discredits
that hope. The metaphor of nature introduces an antithetical
logic which has the rhetorical virtue of *not* being dialectical: the
symbolic stream in which extremes meet is a *natural* stream from
which the unnatural is allegorically excluded. If the natural excludes the unnatural, the unnatural antithetically confirms the
positive and permanent existence of the natural, which it may
threaten but which it can never fully corrupt. Such is metaphysics.

And politics. In order to confirm the absoluteness of truth
and protect its life-ebullient continuity from disruption the
Friend develops his fortunate simile into a resonant allegory that
insulates truth's communication geographically, historically, and
ideologically. The insular patch of ground on which truth naturally grows is Protestant England, where "as the inheritors of so
ample an estate of might and right, an estate so strongly fenced,
so richly planted, by the sinewy arms and dauntless hearts of our
forefathers, we of all others have good cause to trust in the

[38]The best example of how one first mistakes images of reflection for substances appears in Coleridge's experiment with his son, the mirror, and the
mountain. See above, Chapter 2.

truth." The strong fence insures that what should be outside is separated from what should be inside and that the unnatural is segregated from the natural. Because the estate has been so protected and "so richly planted" little labor remains for the caretakers of truth but mild husbandry:

> From the great æras of national illumination we date the commencement of our national advantages. The tangle of delusions, which stifled and distorted the growing tree, have been torn away; the parasite weeds, that fed on its very roots, have been plucked up with a salutary violence. To us there remain only quiet duties, the constant care, the gradual improvement, the cautious unhazardous labors of the industrious though contented gardener—to prune, to engraft, and one by one to remove from its leaves and fresh shoots the slug and the caterpillar. [F, 68]

Safe from the vandals who would strip from the tree the few yellow leaves that shake against the cold, the English estate contains only natural pests, easily removed. Latter-day English authors do not so much write as gently cultivate.[39] England, for the Friend, is a moral refuge, the guarantor of the right and adequate communication of truth, one term in a triple correspondence of island-garden-moral truth. The mutual implication of principle and politics is such, however, that it is unsettlingly difficult to tell which term is to be the criterion of the other, as difficult as it is in close quarters to distinguish amity from conspiracy. Moreover, the concord of allegory represents an uneasy peace: the middle term of this alliance, the garden, has its own ambivalent logic. The Friend's garden is the English version of the biblical paradise. (Nearby he alternatively calls truth "a pillar of fire" [F, 68] and England "the inisled Ararat, on which the Ark of the Hope of Europe and of Civilization rested" [F, 69].)[40] And the

[39]There is also an echo of Burke in Coleridge's image of England as an estate planted and entailed by dauntless forefathers. "We wished at the period of the Revolution, and do now wish," he writes, "to desire all we possess as an inheritance *from our forefathers*. Upon that body and stock of inheritance we have taken care not to inoculate cyon alien to the nature of the original plant" (*Reflections*, 117).

[40]On paradise in Coleridge see Max F. Schulz, "Coleridge and the Enchantments of Earthly Paradise," in *Reading Coleridge: Approaches and Applications*, ed. Walter B. Crawford (Ithaca, N.Y.: Cornell University Press, 1979), pp. 116-59.

English version of the biblical paradise is Milton's Eden. The Friend blandly congratulates his fellow citizens on their good fortune of having inherited the rich plantation and the quiet duties ordained by their demi-divine forefathers, one among whom was Milton, whose *Areopagitica* set authoritative standards for the communication of truth.[41] Yet this Miltonic emparadising establishes a symbolic space with an allegorical project; it tropes the advent of a predator more vicious than slugs and caterpillars, and it imagines both temptation and fall—a temptation from the alien within, a fall that is brought about by the complicity of the inexplicably desperate gardener himself.

A sense of desperation emerges during the Friend's reflection on the so-called "quiet duties" of moral husbandry in the English garden. He has already established the principle that each man is responsible solely to his own conscience regarding the communication of truth and has adopted as his own the heroic words with which Luther defied the consequences of possible scandal and offense: "'Talk not to me of scandal and offence. Need breaks through stonewalls, and recks not of scandal. It is my duty to spare weak consciences as far as it may be done without hazard of my soul.'" (*F*, 63). But though the communication of truth is obliged only to obey the law of conscience and to refrain from hazarding the soul, in Essays X and XI the Friend argues that the *publication* of truth, which involves other hazards, is a matter for the law of the state because the "law of men's actions is one, if they be respected only as men; and another, when they are considered as parts of a body politic" (*F*, 71). The Friend affirms that "Words are moral acts and words deliberately made public the law considers in the same light as any other cognizable overt act" (*F*, 77). Journalists must be considered as members of the body politic—and rarely the conscience. There are weeds among them, publicists of error and even treason, whose immoral acts would lay waste the garden were we not provided with the libel law, "fence and bulwark of

[41]"We have abundant reason then to infer, that the Law of England has done well and concluded wisely in proceeding on the principle so clearly worded by Milton: that a book should be as freely admitted into the world as any other birth; and if it prove a monster, who desires but that it may justly be burnt or sunk into the sea?" (*F*, 77).

[223]

public decency and public opinion" (*F*, 82), which enables the government to segregate and control poisonous plants. Executing that law is a quiet duty, perhaps, but to imagine its neglect is to conjure disquieting, even dreadful, consequences:

> Were we to contemplate the evils of a rank and unweeded press only in its effect on the manners of a people, and on the general tone of thought and conversation, the greater the love, which we bore to literature and to all the means and instruments of human improvement, the greater would be the earnestness with which we should solicit the interference of law: the more anxiously should we wish for some Ithuriel spear, that might remove from the ear of the public, and expose in their own fiendish shape those reptiles, which *inspiring venom and forging illusions as they list,*
>
> > thence raise,
> > At least distempered discontented thoughts,
> > Vain hopes, vain aims, inordinate desires.
> > PARADISE LOST   [*F*, 82]

The idea of an uncontrolled press stimulates a dreamlike process of associative conversion: what had been weeds or at worst slugs turn into reptiles; the gentle gardener's spade becomes Ithuriel's spear, and out of a discussion of *Areopagitica* issues the talismanic invocation of *Paradise Lost*. All that separates this fabulous shifting nightmare from actuality is the fragile logic of the "Were": "Were we to contemplate . . . the more anxiously should we wish." The membrane of the subjunctive acts like the "fence and bulwark" of the libel laws, preventing the invasion of evil thoughts and preempting the necessity of righteous vengeance. The bulwark of the law is faulted with dangerous seams, however; the libel laws are on the books, yet both their force and their existence (both the spirit and the letter of the law) depend on the mind's ability to imagine a libelous, unweeded press. But what can be imagined to be written can be contemplated *as* written; to imagine bulwarks is to contemplate their breach. The subjunctive is similarly permeable, for it articulates the margin of actuality and fantasy; it is the flap between logic and rhetoric, here fluttering in the (asthmatic or inspired?) breeze of the imagination. A passage in the subjunctive: to imagine, to contemplate, to wish, to have. To imagine an enemy, to contemplate its violence, to wish for a weapon, to have both enemy and weapon. To wish for a fabulous spear is the desperate forging of a point, the concentration of one's defenses against an alien who has already breached the walls. As the insensible clinamen of the subjunctive brings together the fantastic and the actual, so does desperate rhetoric slide from period to point. This sentence, the last of Essay XI, is a good example of the Friend's periodic style: the "were" marshals a double premise which advances logically under the benign criterion of "the greater the love," which in turn issues in a consequence decorously parallel and similarly proleptic, "the greater would be"; the colon deliberately accents the logical extension of consequences and anticipates an increase of magnitude: "the more anxiously." The need to bring this periodic increase to a satisfactory close is sharpened by the desire to bring the essay to a strong conclusion. As if it were the "anxiously" rather than its periodic rhythms which has been superintending the stately march of the sentence, the rhetorical force is nervously supplemented by italics, an artificial means of reinforcing the natural development of the syntax: "*inspiring venom and forging illusions as they list.*" The emphasis drastically alters the syntactical rhythm: though it temporally retards the march toward closure by freighting each word with a supplementary anxiety, it excites a novel affect only marginally related to the sense and structure of the prose, an affect which deflects the sentence from the rounded close which it has prepared and rushes it to a sudden end that is charged with a renewed intensity. This terminus, the quotation from Milton, brings the period syntactically, typographically, and theologically to a point. As hypothesis becomes anxiety, so the wish becomes act, and the sentence is forged into a spear in the heat produced by rhetorical friction. The Friend's illusion of reptiles has, despite the bulwark of libel and the membrane of the subjunctive, introduced "distempered, discontented thoughts." The sentence concludes with the desperate inscription of a magical weapon that would expose (*has exposed*) the duplicitous seams in writing—the writing of laws, the writing of sentences—which permit the insidious access of the glibly vicious alien. The sentence and essay end with "inordinate desires."[42]

This is the third time in his reflections on the morality of writing that the Friend has quoted from *Paradise Lost*. On the first occasion he compared his program to the Miltonic mission "which justifies the ways of God to Man" (*F*, 13). Later, during his denunciation of French style, he invoked the awful Moloch. By conscripting Milton, sovereign seventeenth-century authority, into battle against both the breezy French and the libelous Francophiles in the British press, the Friend both reasserts and judges their ideological kinship. A return to the question of French style and its relation to Moloch may suggest the way Milton's "'inordinate desires'" tie together light-headed *philosophes* not only with reptilian pamphleteers, but also with the desperate Friend.

The Encyclopaedists' crusade against superstition began with right though partial notions of truth: there are no such things as ghosts, and one should be skeptical of self-interested witnesses (*F*, 46). The Friend is not explicit about what full truth these notions are part of, but his argument suggests that for him it would apply to a philosophical demonstration of the truth of Christianity's belief in an invisible deity and a reinforcement of its proscription of all forms of idolatry. Whether or not the Encyclopaedists subscribed to any version of Christian truth, their enslavement to a light, rapid, and pointed style prevented them from adequately communicating whatever moral truth was meant to follow their preliminary instruction in skepticism. To understand the mechanism of this enslavement, the dialectical

---

[42]"Observation of animal behavior shows that regularly, when an animal is embarked on some recognizable pattern of behavior but meets in the course of it with an insuperable obstacle, it will betake itself to energetic, but quite unrelated, activity of some wild kind, such as standing on its head. This phenomenon is called 'displacement behavior' and is well identifiable. If now, in the light of this, we look back at ordinary human life, we see that displacement behavior bulks quite large in it: yet we have apparently no word, or at least no clear and simple word, for it. If, when thwarted, we stand on our heads or wiggle our toes, then we are not exactly *just* standing on our heads, don't you know in the ordinary way, yet is there any convenient adverbial expression we can insert to do the trick? 'In desperation'?" J. L. Austin, "A Plea for Excuses," in *Philosophical Papers*, 2d ed., ed. J. O. Urmson and G. J. Warnock (Oxford: Oxford University Press, 1970), pp. 203-4.

consequence of a capricious liberty, it will be helpful to concep-
tualize the communicative model that, I think, the Friend has in
mind. For the Friend the ideal communication would conform
to a vertical axis of signification exemplified by the symbolism of
the Bible and the natural world, wherein God is the Author in
possession of some spiritual truth (the truth that ultimately *is*
God), which he projects downward onto the translucent screen
of language, where it is viewed from the other side by a reader
who is deeply affected by his authentic perception of the incar-
nate, worded truth. Both authorial projection and readerly vision are decorously deliberate, and they combine in an epipha-
nic moment of meaning in which all action is suspended. What
happens with the chattering French philosophers, however, is
that before the truth to be signified can be wholly instituted by
the signifier in a right and adequate sign, the pointed style propels the signified on to another signifier and thence to another,
surpassing the power of the author to fill any signifier with
truth. The originally intended truth slips out of a direct one-to-
one correspondence with the signifier and is dragged along by
the signifying machine. Thus the intended truth is attenuated
until there is virtually nothing left but the agitations of the empty air. A similar attenuation occurs on the other side of the
vertical axis of author-words-reader, for the rapidity of the style
prevents the reader from properly centering his affect in a single expression. The affect that was to be vertically directed is, like
the signified of which it is the reflection and should be the
completion, slipped hurriedly along the signifying chain. Truth
may be attenuated, but affect, though dislocated, is preserved;
indeed, if changed, affect is somewhat magnified by the asynde-
tic friction of the style. Now, however, rather than the affect
being directed toward the pathetically strained, almost unrecog-
nizable truth, it is displaced to the sheer velocity of the signifying
chain, regardless of the lack of any informing signified. To fill
out the Friend's example of skepticism toward ghosts: it is as if
an author wrote, "There are no ghosts"; but instead of fully
explaining why and even risking, as he ought, obscurity to do so
(as Coleridge himself does in his marvelous exegesis of Luther's
legendary encounter with the devil [see Essay II of the First
Landing Place]), he went rapidly on: "There are no goblins,

there are no unicorns, there are no nobles, there is no nobility, there are no kings by divine right, there is no divine right." What would eventually be communicated by a rhetoric more skillful than my own are first, the loss of any sense of reasoning, second, the superior wisdom of the incantation "there is no" to any particular expression of skepticism, and finally, an exaltation in the feel and the power of movement alone. This power is revolutionary because it overturns the relationship between thought and word, and it is amputatory because it ends in cutting off thought, the signified, from any relation to the word. The necessary implication of the chain of "there is no's" is "there is no God"—a phrase which need not be spoken because it is the affective consequence of the chain itself, which has the destructive potential of the whirlwind. In a populace rhetorical velocity foments political fanaticism: the frenzy of language figures as revolutionary terror, which amputates the society from its source in the king and mankind from its source in God as language has been sundered from its source in the truth. It is this process of mechanical language turning into the machinery of the guillotine and not a specific ideology to which the Friend objects in the Encyclopaedists' pointed style.[43]

Yet even this devouring rhetoric cannot go on indefinitely; eventually even the affect of the reader or populace is attenuated beyond bounds and approaches the natural limit of confusion and exhaustion. Eventually the "mechanical agitation of empty air" stalls, and in order to be saved from complete chaotic collapse the reader demands a meaning. In a sublime moment the whirlwind seems to speak. That sibylline voice is taken by the stunned multitude for the voice of a God and worshipped. The ironic cycle is completed: for a somewhat superstitious but pious notion of the Christian God, the skeptic has willy-nilly substituted a bloody Moloch to which not only the populace but he himself sacrifices. The nature of this sacrifice is indicated in Milton's image of "blood and parent's tears." In a literally preposterous situation, parents grieve for the death of children they have sacrificed to the bloodthirsty demands of a god they them-

---

[43]This fear of rhetorical excess is based on experience. See the 1803 letter to the Beaumonts (*CL* II, 1000-1001; quoted above).

selves have created by projection. They sacrifice the natural and rightful representatives of their chaste affection to a bloody delusion which is the grim consequence of their most unnatural and inordinate desires.

If we examine the metalogical association the Friend makes among the representative, sacrifice, and a certain style, we can, I think, get closer to an understanding of the kind of hazard the Friend contemplates in his own writing. In Essay III he manages the transition from an apology for his own style to a general ethics of style by introducing a telling simile: "An author's pen, like children's legs, improves by exercise." In its most immediate sense the simile merely excuses the Friend's slow progress toward his subject, but, more resonantly, it states a connection between author and pen that supplements the conventional phallic associations by figuring a benign genealogy moving from a paternity in the mind of the author to the child whose legs are like a pen. Whereas a moral style of writing furnishes healthful exercise for the child's legs, the French style, whirring like a buzz saw, cuts those legs off, sacrificing child and pen to idolatrous machine of language. And the natural parent, the author, weeps at the loss of *his* natural representative to the unnatural father who is the projection of his unnatural and inordinate desires. We have already seen the Friend's use of "self-mutilation" to describe the harmful effects of writing in a certain literary style; his use of other terms such as "self-contradiction," "softening," and "alloying" to describe the effects of that style all confirm a fear of a kind of writing that is castrating, that "will break up and scatter before it all robustness and manly vigor of intellect, all masculine fortitude of virtue" (*F*, 24). The criticism of others is an anxiety for himself: though he is willing, he says, "to make all allowable sacrifices, to render my manner more attractive and my matter more generally interesting" (*F*, 21), he hopes that his readers "might yet find a pleasure in supporting the FRIEND during its *infancy*" (*F*, 22; emphasis added)—to support it by patience and funds rather than to murder it by withdrawing attention or by demanding a style that moves beyond "allowable sacrifice" to self-mutilation in a text "besmeared with blood / Of human sacrifice and parent's tears."

The evidence of oedipal anxiety is strong. The Friend imagines the rapidity of a certain kind of writing as a powerful amputatory weapon which lops off all symbols of the Father's original authority: the signified, the king, truth. The inevitable punishment for this parricidal violence is castration, here a murdering of the child's child—a punishment that seems to come from the outside but which is actually the guilty transgressor's self-mutilation. According to the Friend's script the writer is mutilated by a desire whose articulate trajectory inordinates the antithesis between inside and outside essential to meaning. What should be outside—the signifier, the sound, the script— fabricates its own inside in the rhythms of excited speech or in the spacings of pointed prose; it simulates the original force of meaning by mixing the actual and the fantasized in the fantasmatic. The soul is hazarded in these black marks on this white page: dim, uncanny presages of the death of the Father. For the undermining of the kingdom of Truth, the grotesque rule of Moloch is the writer's proper reward.

If the Friend's allegorization of styles can be explained by oedipal anxiety, we already know what the inordinate desire is for: the penetration of the mother. Locating that penetrative desire in *The Friend* requires the only interpretive step thus far that assumes a repressed quotient in the proposed communicative model. The Friend would have it that danger is limited to a particular style of writing that first turns into a weapon against the true Father (the sovereign Truth) and inevitably results in the vicious reign of the grotesque surrogate father by which one is mutilated. That account is the authorized version of the oedipal struggle in which the rebellious son gets what he deserves. It is the authorized version because it is the account that allows the Friend to *be* an author by guiltlessly accommodating himself to the wise authority of his predecessors. It is the father's version because it explains what happens to sons, to bad stylists and good stylists, to the French Cain and the English Abel, according to a justice that rigorously excludes the place of the mother. The authorized version expatiates on "inordinate" and represses "desire." Desire may not be in the story of the style, but it is in the Friend's text. The Miltonic image tells us that it is the child who is sacrificed to Moloch—understandably, because, as we know from other stories, it is the child who offends against the Father.

That child in this text is associated with the writer's pen, the device that simultaneously acts out and records an inordinate desire for the mother—not, however, by adopting a particular style, but *by merely touching* the blank of white paper at all. The pen, we need remember, is not exactly the child or the child's phallus but the child's legs, which do not, can never puncture the page across which they walk. The writer's transgression for which he fears to be punished is a transcription; his penetration is a pen-iteration, a going over of a piece of paper which is maternal but not the mother by a pen which is phallic but not the phallus. Because the pen has *not* the "bodily vigor and strong Grasp of Touch," the pen is a rigid eunuch "in all degrees even to the full ensheathement and the both at once." No writing will penetrate the mother. But all pen-iteration of the page feels like desiring the mother—an inordinate desire not because it has an incestuous object but because all objects are simulacra, because the pen transcribes the mutually *dissimulant* junction of love and lust, real and symbolic, parent and child, inside and outside, black and white, without even ordaining an object that would bring this desirous transcription to a climax.[44] Although we may agree that oedipal anxiety betrays a repressed desire for the mother, the Friend's deployment of the fable of Moloch suggests that the whole oedipal network, which observes the order of a fable, is a second level sublimation of an inordinate desire (always *of* rather than *for* the mother: preposition propped on genitive) that is both the mark and the *habit* of writing, an irreducible "Desire of a Desire" that makes even an undramatic moral essay in a guarded style the hazard of one's soul.[45]

The Friend has turned to the authority of Milton for an image to depict the folly of a kind of writing that tries to rid itself of what it can only repress. The Puritan's fierce verse arises in the

[44]In arguing that desire precedes its object I am in general agreement with René Girard's conception of mimetic desire (*Violence and the Sacred*, pp. 145-49), although I would urge that the Friend's desirous writing lacks the structure of reciprocity and symmetry which dramatizes mimesis for Girard (pp. 158-59 and *passim*).

[45]"Is not *Habit* the Desire of a Desire?—As Desire to Fruition, may not the faint, to the consciousness *erased*, Pencil-mark *memorials* or relicts of Desire be to Desire itself in its full prominence?" (*CN* I, 1421). The *Notebooks*, with all their jottings, reflections, erasures and cryptograms, are the "site" where Coleridge indulges his habit.

Friend's text as the harsh judgment of that repression. Milton later returns when the Friend is drawn into an anxious contemplation of the enemy already within. The metonymic transformation of the Friend's pen into first the gardener's tool and then Ithuriel's spear is both a defense against that contemplated threat of the snake and a defense against the uncontemplated threat that constantly inscribes itself within the garden, within the book: his own pen. The spear, unlike a child's legs, is solid iron and cannot be severed. Moreover, Ithuriel's spear has divine and Miltonic warrant: it is at once an extension of the warrior angel and of the Godhead, a device which approaches the mother at the service of the Father and which will leave no marks. The Friend intends to use the spear to remove the snake from its post at the ear of Mother Eve where it sows the subliminal into her sleeping mind: alien impulses that grow as if in native soil, queer notions that, were she to contemplate them, would spring forth as sinful acts. Ithuriel's magical spear is a pen that does not write, a phallus that does not slash. Gently it would touch the membrane of Eve's ear where insinuates the serpent, and gently it would remove the impenetrant snake—leaving no mark to trouble Eve's innocent slumber, to streak her immaculate dawn. Such is the wish of the Friend for friendship. He does not raise Milton as vain hope for the Father or as distempered thought of Moloch; he makes wish of Milton to forge his own fabulous point.

III

*Socrates.* One might almost say . . . that the type you mention—the genuine as opposed to the sham philosopher—is not much easier to recognize than is a god. These men, as they travel from one city to the next, surveying from on high the life below, appear (such is human ignorance) in every sort of guise. Some look on them as of no consequence, others as beyond all praise; now they are taken for statesmen, now for mere sophists; and sometimes they give the impression of being just plain crazy.—*The Sophist*

The last climb in the Friend's long journey "through countries of various prospect," the last turn in *The Friend* before its spiral staircase reaches the final landing place, begins with a scenario for a recognition scene. "What is that," the Friend asks, "which first strikes us, and strikes us at once, in a man of education? And which, among educated men, so instantly distinguishes the man of superior mind, that (as was observed with eminent propriety of the late Edmund Burke) 'we cannot stand under the same arch-way during a shower of rain, *without finding him out?*" The Friend dismisses as distinguishing marks "the weight or novelty of his remarks," "any unusual interest of facts communicated by him," as well as "any peculiarity in his words and phrases" (*F,* 448). He concludes that there "remains but one other point of distinction possible; and this must be, and in fact is, the true cause of the impression made on us. It is the unpremeditated and evidently habitual *arrangement* of his words, grounded on the habit of foreseeing, in each integral part, or (more plainly) in every sentence, the whole that he then intends to communicate. However irregular and desultory his talk, there is *method* in the fragments" (*F,* 449).

"The whole that he then *intends* to communicate"—nothing is said regarding the complete communication of that whole, for method refers to the process of communicating the truth, not to the truth as communicated. Intention's proper discourse, method is the projective logic that relates an original purpose to its ultimate end. The *virtue* of thought, method exhibits "the first merit, that which admits neither substitute nor equivalent, [which] is, that *every thing is in its place*" (*F,* 449). Hard upon the heels of metaphysics comes method; after the ontological assurance of places and things comes the first merit of properly matching one with the other. There is no substitute nor equivalent for method because method is the principle by which substitutes and equivalents are legitimately made; it ordains what to admit and what to exclude both by establishing the proper line of succession and by delimiting the paradigm for substitutions. Because it puts everything in its place, method assures itself of first place.

Abstractly considered, method would appear to be one of many arts of discourse, an important skill, certainly, laborious to acquire and difficult to practice, perhaps; but generally accessible to the willing student. The Friend, however, does not consider method abstractly; he discovers it in the man, for whom it is not the acquisition of a course of study but the product of a genial development.[46] "METHOD," according to the Friend, "becomes natural to the mind which has been accustomed to contemplate not *things* only, or for their own sake alone, but likewise and chiefly the *relations* of things, either their relations to each other, or to the observer, or to the state and apprehension of the hearers" (*F*, 451). The natural representative of an internal discipline, method is the external development and disposition of relations contemplated within. What becomes natural to the man of superior mind is to be able to traverse a network of relations (between himself and things, things themselves, things and his hearers) that is the discourse by which he is recognized and in which he comes to recognize himself—not only the occasionally fragmentary self that appears but the whole self that he then intends to communicate.

By taking, at last, its place of privilege in *The Friend*, method satisfies three persistent and crucial needs of the essayist. First, it supplies him with a concept that both operates discursively and is a prior condition of discourse. Second, because it is substantive without being substantial, method occupies a place or vantage ground that does not displace and that therefore cannot be displaced. Third, the discovery of method furnishes a teleological justification for the eccentric windings of the Friend's irregular construction and desultory style. Out of the digressive windings has emerged method, a principle that places digression within a context of purposive relations. Aimlessness happens upon its aim. The discovery of method is recognizing method in the fragments of the argument, which, regarded retrospectively, seem arranged with remarkable foresight both to bring the book to this striking point and to reveal its streamy eddying as the natural expression of a superior mind. Though the man of superior mind be abroad somewhere in the anonymous city, perhaps huddled under an arch-way where he takes refuge from a drenching rain, his genius concealed, as soon as he speaks he is found out, for he is always at home in his discourse

[46]The strongest case for the centrality of "The Essays on Method" in Coleridge's criticism is made by J. R. de J. Jackson in his *Method and Imagination in Coleridge's Criticism* (Cambridge, Mass.: Harvard University Press, 1969).

as nowhere else. By finding out this naturally methodical man, the traveling inquirer has put the mysterious stranger in his proper place, exercising, offhandedly as it were, the first merit and the mark of a superior mind. In Coleridge the scenario for recognition is always a scene of self-recognition: examining the distinguishing marks of a superior mind, the Friend discovers method; discovering method, the Friend recognizes his own genius.[47]

Method may distinguish the superior mind, but it does not constitute that mind. The Friend insists on "the necessity of a mental Initiative to all Method" (*F*, 469), "the leading Thought" (*F*, 455) and "master-light" (*F*, 468), without which any arrangement is merely artificial. To exemplify such "artificial arrangement" the Friend invokes the vast classificatory system of Linnaean botany, which, when examined, reduces to "the mere verbal definition" of sex, a technical convenience that has been abstracted from "the central idea of vegetation itself" (*F*, 468, 467). Currently, botany is "little more than an enormous nomenclature; a huge catalogue, *bien arrangè*, yearly and monthly augmented, in various editions, each with its own scheme of technical memory and its own conveniences of reference!"[48] Lacking an initiative of its own, Linnaean botany could only conceive of vegetables without vegetation, with the ironic consequence that the science of growing plants has become the most lifeless and mechanical of all contemporary systems, "a mass enlarging by endless appositions, but without a nerve that oscillates, or a pulse that throbs, in sign of *growth* or inward sympathy." The book of nature has become the "dictionary" of the Encyclopaedists (*F*, 469).

Against such "blind and guideless industry" the Friend counterposes the work of the "philosophic seer" whose vision is armed by "the knowledge of LAW [in which] alone dwell Power and Prophecy, decisive Experiment, and, lastly, a scientific

[47]A self-recognition that may not be as others see one. Cf. Coleridge's scene of the arch-way (borrowed from Samuel Johnson) with Thomas De Quincey's famous account of meeting the gazing, perplexed Coleridge under a gateway in Bridgewater (*Recollections of the Lake Poets,* ed. David Wright [London: Penguin, 1970], pp. 43-44).

[48]Note that in the shift to the French, rare in Coleridge, the Frenching of "well arranged" makes it a synonym for the English "artificially arranged."

method" (*F*, 470). Such philosophical scientists can be found among the English chemists, whose luminous example excites comparison with Shakespeare and quotation from Milton:

> If in SHAKESPEARE we find nature idealized into poetry, through the creative power of a profound yet observant meditation, so through the meditative observation of a DAVY, a WOOLASTON, or a HATCHETT;
>
> > By some connatural force
> > Powerful at greatest distance to unite
> > With secret amity things of like kind,
>
> we find poetry, as it were, substantiated and realized in nature. . . .
>
> > > > [*F*, 471]

The forebears of these chemists include Plato, Bacon, and particularly Kepler, who "seemed born to prove that true genius can overpower all obstacles. If he gives an account of his modes of proceeding, and of the views under which they first occurred to his mind, how unostentiously and *in transitu*, as it were, does he introduce himself to our notice: and yet never fails to present the living germ out of which the genuine method, as the inner form of science springs up!" (*F*, 485).

The organic metaphor is, of course, no accident; nor is it arbitrary, for the method we acknowledge in the work of man corresponds to the organization which it is our instinct to find in nature, and in "a self-conscious and thence reflecting being, no instinct can exist, without engendering the belief of an object corresponding to it. . . . Least of all can this mysterious predisposition exist without evolving a belief that the productive power, which is in nature as nature, is essentially one . . . with the intelligence, which is in the human mind above nature" (*F*, 497-98). Correspondents reflect a transcendent unity and imply with an unignorable force that the law of nature as of science is in "act and substance" finally spiritual: "It is the idea of the common centre, of the universal law, by which all power manifests itself in opposite yet interdependent forces . . . that enlightening inquiry, multiplying experiment, and at once inspiring humility, perseverance will lead him to comprehend gradually and progressively the relation of each to the other, of each to all, and of all to each" (*F*, 511). Such is the "mid-channel" of the stream of truth, the method of method, which has "its bed, its banks, and its line of progression" (*F*, 512). And though nothing of certainty can be said about the connection between the knowing of the mind and the being of Nature, the coincidence between the method of science and the general, beneficent teleology of nature prepares the mind to accept the conclusion that this method must derive its initiative from a genius who is united with but different from his effects and continuous in his changes, from the divine author whose existence is predicated in the very statement of its possibility, and who manifests himself as the master-light of all conception:

> The truths, which it manifests are such as it alone can manifest, and in all truth it manifests itself. By what name then canst thou call a truth so manifested? Is it not REVELATION? Ask thyself whether thou canst attach to that latter word any consistent meaning not included in the idea of the former. And the manifesting power, the source and the correlative of the idea thus manifested—is it not GOD? Either thou knowest it to be GOD, or thou hast called an idol by that awful name! [*F*, 515-16]

"The self-unravelling clue" (*F*, 511) of method unwinds both the phenomenal world and the products of mind to reveal at the end of the line and the end of *The Friend*'s ascent the one true principle which is both end and beginning:

> Yea (saith an enlightened physician), there is but one principle, which alone reconciles the man with himself, with others and with the world; which regulates all relations, tempers all passions, and gives power to overcome or support all suffering; and which is not to be shaken by aught earthly, for it belongs not to the earth— namely, the principle of religion, the living and substantial faith, "which passeth all *understanding*," as the cloud-piercing rock which overhangs the strong-hold of which it had been the quarry and remains the foundation." [*F*, 523-24]

It is as if the Friend's windings, his qualifications, his doubts, his investment in a difficult style have finally paid off; as if all those years of attentively reading the Ancients, all that effort at understanding the advances of contemporary science, all that anonymous labor at journalism had been united by some connatural force powerful at greatest distance; as if the Friend seemed born to prove that true genius can overpower all obstacles. If is as if philosophy had finally found that discourse of which it was in danger of being robbed[49] and the genuinely moral intention of the Friend had fully engaged the intuitive reason at the triumphant completion of an arduous ascent. It is as if amidst the digressions, fragments, epigraphs, plagiarisms, and metaphors method had been active all along, unostentatiously and *in transitu,* as it were, communicating the true principle, which is finally encountered with a gentle shock of recognition. The principle discovered, the discovery seems only natural; and it is as if where "the nurture and evolution of humanity is the final aim, there will soon be seen a general tendency toward, an earnest seeking after, some ground common to the world and to man, therein to find the one principle of permanence and identity, the rock of strength and refuge, to which the soul may cling amid the fleeting surge-like objects of the senses" (*F,* 508).

The rock, "the cloud-piercing rock"—a foundation, a strength, a refuge is the common ground of both *The Friend* and the *Biographia,* one to which the writer has often clung, whether it was the stone that savours any soup, the "inisled Ararat, on which the Ark of the Hope of Europe and Civilization rested," or the "merest rock" of Malta (*F,* 271), which anchored the justice of Britain's war and Britain's government. In each instance the sensible bulk situated in soup, flood, or sea could only take its place by displacing the waters around it. The re-inscription of that rock here, as the principle to which method purposes, makes visible method's substance and recalls the economy that the Friend has already enunciated and observed and to which, it seems, even method is subject: to stand is to withstand; to defend is to attack. In order to learn how that economy already governs method from the first, it is necessary to try to forget that

[49]"*Stranger.* Deprived of discourse, we should be deprived of philosophy. That would be the most disastrous result; but in addition, we have here and now to agree as to the nature of discourse, and had we been robbed of its very existence, we should obviously not be able to discourse any further" (Plato, *The Sophist,* trans. John Warrington [1969; rpt., New York: Dutton, 1961], p. 260).

## The Method of *The Friend*

*The Friend* has reached its conclusion and return. We know that "a penny on the waters pays interest when the flood turns";[50] and we observe that the Friend's method has bred a profit; but we need to inquire at what concealed cost?

> *Socrates.* If my soul happened to be golden, Callicles, don't you think I should be overjoyed to find a stone to test the metal, the best stone possible, which, when I applied to it, if it agreed that my soul had been well cared for, then I would know that I was in a satisfactory state and never needed another touchstone?
>
> —*Gorgias*

Though proposed as a discursive movement that naturally integrates differences within a progressive continuity, method, like the garden of England, is only natural because it is opposed to unnatural and hostile artifice. The Friend exposes the alien artificer in his essay "On the Origin and Progress of the Sect of Sophists in Greece," which prefaces the section on method.[51] Unlike the title "philosopher," which originally identified a true "lover of wisdom," "sophist" signified "one who professes the power of making others wise, a wholesale and retail *dealer* in wisdom—a wisdom-monger. . . . In this and not in their abuse of the arts of reasoning, have Plato and Aristotle placed the *essential* of the sophistic character" (*F*, 436). Further aspects of that character appear in further echoes of Plato and his disciple Aristotle, rivals allied in their steadfast contempt for the sophist. For the former he was "one who hires himself out or puts himself up at auction"; for the latter his generic character was the "baseness of

[50]I. O. Snopes in William Faulkner, *The Hamlet* (1940; rpt., 3d.; New York: Vintage Books, 1956), p. 65.

[51]As the editor notes, much of the Friend's account of the origin and progress of the Sophists has been taken without attribution from Wilhelm Gottlieb Tenneman's *Geschicte der Philosophie* (Leipzig: 1798-1819). It is the equivocal fulfillment of a project that Coleridge set for himself in 1803: "I do not think, that as yet the whole of the *crime*, the cause, nature & consequences of *Sophistry* has been developed. Try it dear Coleridge!" (*CN* I, 1511). For a recent evenhanded account of both the sophists and the various ways their origin and progress have been interpreted, see W. K. C. Guthrie, *A History of Greek Philosophy* (Cambridge: Cambridge University Press, 1969), 3: 3-319.

motives joined with the impudence and delusive nature of the pretense." Just less important than this "pretense of selling wisdom and eloquence" in distinguishing the sophists was their "itinerancy," their ceaseless traversal of Greece from the provincial towns and villages to Athens, "their great emporium and place of rendezvous" (*F*, 437).

Each spot on the sophist's route was merely an opportunity for him to make use of his impressive rhetorical techniques: place as sophistical pretext, itinerary as sophistical iteration. "Some of these," according to the Friend, "applied the lessons of their art in their own persons, and traded for gain and gainful influence in the character of demagogues and public orators; but the greater number offered themselves as instructors, in the art of persuasion and temporary impression, to as many as would come up to the high prices, at which they rated their services" (*F*, 438). Though repugnant, the direct acquisition of power through rhetorical suasion was not the worst practice of the sophists. Nor was the dissemination abroad of the art of acquisition their greatest evil. The Friend returns to Plato to reiterate that the sophist's most essential and most vicious characteristic was that in "the baseness of his motives" the sophist *sold* his talent for money, as if the communication of knowledge were a commercial transaction:

> *Hireling hunters of the young and rich,* they offered to the vanity of youth and the ambition of wealth a substitute for that authority, which by the institutions of Solon had been attached to high birth and property, or rather to the moral discipline, the habits, attainments and directing motives, on which the great legislator had calculated (not indeed as necessary or constant accompaniments, but yet) as the regular and ordinary results of comparative opulence and renowned ancestry. [*E*, 438-39]

Using rhetoric to make the worse cause appear the better or to raise a demagogue in the guise of a statesman are, doubtless, vicious practices, but at least in each case vice implies virtue, and the rhetorician conveys by his very immorality the antithesis between good and evil. That inversion can be eventually exposed and the proper relations restored by the authoritative application of true method. But the base motives of the sophist are fundamentally more subversive than that, for the sophist is not motivated by ambition for power and prestige, but by money, which is for him *the* base motive, one which can be substituted for all others, into which all others can be successfully transformed.

The viciousness of sophistical substitution can be gauged in the disruptions it caused in the calculations of Solon, who had methodically devised a state in which the criteria of authority were high birth and property, natural signs of a nobility that it was presumably the interest of those with authority to maintain; it was beyond Solon's method to conceive of anything more that a citizen could want than property, position, and the authority that accompanied them. But in their willingness to accept a sophistical, delusive substitute for their inheritance, the Athenian youths upset calculations based on either reason or prudence. They were ambitious for wealth, but to have sacrificed property and position to that ambition was to have perversely relinquished the sensible ends in order to indulge in the blind means. Sophistical exchange seems to abstract wealth from its source in value into pure motive: what one does not have, what one can desire—the provocative difference that makes things move, space themselves into positions for an as yet unconfigured dance. In opting for the sophist, Athenian youths chose unnaturally, of course, but the uncanny unanimity of their deviance would seem somehow to have naturalized the unnatural. The dynamics of that bizarre substitution ferment in the very metaphor with which Plato snags the sophists, "hireling hunters of the young and rich"—a trope that in turning its trick on the sophists presumes its own scandal: that the young would sacrifice all that belongs to them in order to hire their hunters.

According to the Friend, the appearance of the sophists in Athens came at a time, during the aftermath of the Persian War, when the "light and sensitive Athenians" were caught up in "the giddiness of sudden aggrandizement" (*F*, 438) and were dangerously susceptible to sophistical advances. We recognize symptoms of the French disease, already infecting the English, in this description of an Athens ripe for corruption: "The restless spirit of republican ambition, engendered by their success in a just war, and by the romantic character of that success, had already formed a close alliance with luxury in its early and most vigorous state, when it acts as an appetite to enkindle, and before it has exhausted and dulled the vital energies by the habit of enjoyment" (*F*, 439). The French, light-headed and susceptible, succumbed to just such vicious habits of enjoyment and have since paid the price. One would hope that, left to themselves, the level-headed English, anchored by the gravity of their ancient institutions and their weighty traditions, could resist the rare dizziness that follows upon ambition's sudden success. The sophists represent the futility of that hope; his meditation on sophistic power displays the Friend's seasoned awareness that men, as moral agents, are never left to themselves. To contemplate the possibility of the sophists is to have already admitted them within the walls: "But this corruption was now to be introduced into the *citadel* of the moral being, and to be openly defended by the very arms and its instruments, which had been given for the purpose of preventing or chastising its approach" (*F*, 439). The weightiness of institutions and traditions is little protection against a "*sleight-of-word* juggler" (*F*, 437) who does not defy gravity but teases it into playing his own game. The sophist owes his success to his wizardly ability to turn aggression into the appearance of defense, a withstanding that gives him a kind of standing equivalent to the principles he has supplanted.

When the Friend examines the means by which the sophists accomplished their sensational turnabout, he attributes it to their strategy of sensualizing the understanding. Like their modern type the hirelings of the British press, the sophists' arguments may not have been true or reasonable or even persuasive in themselves, "yet the principles so attacked were brought into doubt by the mere frequency of hearing *all* things doubted, and the most sacred of all now openly denied, and now insulted by sneer and ridicule" (*F*, 439). Such a character may be reprehensible, but at least it is comprehensible. Perhaps too comprehensible to trap the evasive sophist. The Friend, at least, goes on to erase the dramatic criteria of doubt, denial, and sneer in a remarkable paragraph where it becomes clear it is no particular weapon, such as the "there is no" of the physiocrats, that morally incapacitates the sophist's victim, indeed, no weapon at all; rather it is the "mere frequence" of languaging principles that sensualizes the mind and encourages the substitution of idols for ideas:

> Religion, in its widest sense, signifies the act and habit of reverencing THE INVISIBLE, as the highest both in ourselves and in nature. To this the senses and their immediate objects are to be made subservient, the one as its organs, the other as its exponents: and as such therefore, having on their own account no true *value*, because no inherent *worth*. They are a *language*, in short: and taken independently of their representative function, from *words* they become mere empty *sounds*, and differ from *noise* only by exciting expectations which they cannot gratify—fit ingredients of the idolatrous *charm*, the potent Abracadabra, of a sophisticated race, who had sacrificed the religion of faith to the superstition of the senses, a race of animals, in whom the presence of reason is manifested solely by the absence of instinct. [*F*, 440]

The sophistication of the race is accomplished by abstracting words from their true source in the invisible and manufacturing a language of empty sounds that can be hypnotically jingled like idolatrous charms for the superstitious. Though acidly contemptuous, the Friend's acknowledgment of the special, almost magical charm of sophistic rhetoric complicates the antithetical framework which he had initially conscripted the sophist to support. Above soars the vital word, plumed by the eternal bounty of the invisible; below lies the chaos of brute noise. Sophistic rhetoric, though obviously consigned to somewhere in the nether regions of the linguistic model, has no clear place of its own; it differs from noise, according to the Friend, in so far as it excites expectations it cannot gratify; that is, it differs from noise by differing noise into sound, the empty but all too plausible facsimile of the true communication of the word. The Friend does try to contain the charming mechanics of sophistry by recuperating it within the antithetical economy of the sacrifice— something gained, something lost—but that desperate grab comes up emptyhanded: if gratification be rigorously excluded as a possible result of sophistical rhetoric, there can be no imputation of gain in the practice of the sophist, who, therefore, will never have anything on hand to be lost or sacrificed. One might charge that the sophist seeks power, if it were not that such a claim forfeits its moral force in the absence of any teleology (such as that, for example, which legitimates the reason's aggrandizement in the dialectics of the negative sublime) in which to fit that drive and by which one could gauge success or failure; the sophist's power, if power it is, cannot be conceived apart from the indefinite excitation of which it is both cause and effect. Sophistry exhibits neither a desire for power nor a power over desire but the power *of* desire.

As synonym for sophistical rhetoric and sophistic sound the Friend offers "language," and one way of placing the sophist is to describe his habitat as that traverse where language is first differentiated, where noise takes on the slightest resistant obscurity which endows it with a significance remarkably like meaning. The charm (excitement and power) of sophistical rhetoric, language before the first word, is the charm of ornament, the primordial gilt that languages base noise into aural aurum:

> To shape, to dye, to paint over, and to mechanize the mind, he [Plato] resigned, as their proper trade, to the sophists, against whom he waged open and unremitting war. For the ancients, as well as the moderns, had their machinery for the extemporaneous mintage of intellects, by means of which, *off-hand,* as it were, the scholar was enabled to *make a figure* on any and all subjects, on any and all occasions. [*F*, 473]

Shaping, dyeing, and painting over are the ornamental arts by which the offhanded sophistic craftsman transfigures the mind into the machine of language. Like the poet whose personifications dramatize a scandalous impropriety, the sophist who makes figures on all subjects (the subjects of a sovereign reason), transgresses the sacred distinction between persons and things; he not only mints the intellects of others, he is "himself" only the figure, the ornamental equivalent of empty sounds, made on his own invisible subject. Moreover, the sophist seems insensible of any trespass and immune to loss; because he performs his legerdemain offhandedly, the sophist extends nothing of his that could be wounded or severed by reason's harsh dictate.

Given that the sophist is capable, at no cost to himself, of minting intellects in feckless mimicry of those powers that are reserved to God alone, and accepting that his rhetoric demoralizes any reasonable attempt to trap him in an antithetical framework that would disarm him and restrain his criminal enterprise, the problem of how to discriminate the counterfeiter's artifice from the genius's method becomes embarrassingly acute and explains the Friend's reaffirmation of the single Platonic criterion of wage-earning: selling wisdom is not so much disdained for being a debasement of wisdom as it is embraced as the sole visible sign by which the sophist can be identified and by which his appeal to otherwise noble and blameless youths can be understood, thereby erasing the scandal of their voluntary victimage. Ambitious for gain, the sophist sells the ability to make money to those who have been secretly afflicted by the same greed. The exchange of a coin signals the avarice that is a clear expression of the sophist's inordinate desire and permits the Platonic philosopher to arrest and indict the unauthorized minter of intellects for violating the sovereign's law. The hard case of the sophist permits the philosopher to test his gold against an antagonist worthy not merely because of his inveterate hostility but because he seems to challenge the grounds of the antagonism itself. The coin is the mark of the greedy counterfeiter. It signifies not only the sophist's essential vice but that there is *an essence to sophistry* which can be retrieved from the labyrinth of evanescent differences, echoes, and reflections and which confirms the essentiality of the philosopher's gold. Yet between the indictment and the verdict falls the defense. It might be argued by the sophist that desire for gold is not true greed (the sacrifice of reason to a base instinct) when gold is conceived of as a token of exchange that will gratify no desire. It might be urged by the sophist that it is impossible to certify the real value of a gold coin once it has become a counter in the sophistical shell game. Or the sophist might mount a cross-examination. How could Plato wage unremitting warfare against an offhanded enemy who did not return the compliment? How was the philosopher's campaign financed? What sound investment paid his wages?

*Stranger.* . . . [W]e must quarter the ground without further delay by dividing the art of Image-making; then if we go down

[245]

into our enclosure and immediately find the Sophist at bay, we must arrest him on a warrant issued by King Reason, report his capture and deliver him to His Majesty. But if he finds cover among the various subdivisions of the imitative art, we must keep up the chase by repeatedly quartering the area in which he lurks until we catch him. It is quite certain that neither he nor any other kind of creature will ever boast of having eluded so close and so comprehensive a process of investigations.

—*The Sophist*

The case of Philosophy versus the Sophist is not merely a historical curiosity for the Friend. The successful prosecution of the sophist is urgent to an Englishman who lives in a culture where, as in the languidly skeptical Athens following the Persian War, traditional values have lost their presumptive authority and where "arguments," as the Friend has commented earlier, "are the sole current coin of intellect." Because there is "no royal mintage for arguments," it is often frustratingly difficult to tell the difference between "the honest man's intellectual coin" and the "light or counterfeit." Despite confusing signs and even willful error, however, the Friend insists that there are criteria that enable the truth seeker to discriminate between the true worth of a superior mind and the sham sense of an imposter; these evidences may be "only *conjectural* marks; yet such," he claims, "as will seldom mislead any man of plain sense, who is both honest and observant" (*F*, 277-78). For the Friend the conjectural mark is the sign of method, the discourse of a superior mind. His supposition of method as the "rock of refuge" presupposes the displacement of the insidious sophist and requires a hermeneutics of conjectural marks which can assure the honest and observant reader that what he recognizes as method is the real thing and not a base simulacrum.

Episode after episode in *The Friend* inclines the writer to a semiotic impasse where duplicitous marks thwart honest observation,[52] yet the Friend never does undertake a hermeneu-

[52]See, for example, the two essays on Luther (*F*, 135-47), the "illustration" from Michael Angelo (*F*, 320), and the essay "The War and International Law" (*F*, 263-75). The latter essay, devoted to an examination of the circumstances surrounding the signing and the breaking of the Treaty of Amiens is the subject of my essay, "Politerotics: Coleridge's Rhetoric of War in *The Friend*," *CLIO* 8 (Spring 1979), pp. 339-63.

tics of conjectural marks. The nature of his problem precludes the enterprise that would resolve it. If we accept E. D. Hirsch's formulation of one of the tenets of a general hermeneutics that "a text cannot be *interpreted* from a perspective different from the original author's,"[53] then *a fortiori* a theory of interpretation cannot be constructed without the validating hypothesis *of* an original author. A hermeneutics of conjectural marks that would validate or even legitimate the honest observer's intuition of an original, methodical author would involve the theorist in the conundrum of a theory of interpretative method which would determine the authenticity of those marks that have been hypothesized as the criteria of both authenticity and method.

Lacking a hermeneutics to authorize an interpretation, when confronted with marks that coerce conjecture the Friend nonetheless goes ahead and reads them anyway. According to Hirsch, the alternative to a true interpretation grounded in the original author is a "self-imaging authorship."[54] The phrase has a superficial aptness for the character of this collection of essays in which all texts produce and reproduce versions of the Friend. But the category of "self-imaging authorship" utterly fails to engage the problematic of the conjectural mark, which puts in question and in play the notions of self, imaging, and authorship that inform Hirsch's hermeneutical cosmology. If not interpretations, the Friend's figurative transactions with various texts *are* readings, readings which *because* of their hermeneutical *askesis*, produce a rhetoric that traduces the ideology and metaphysics, exposes the hypopoesis, of interpretation and authorship. This rhetoric is not a self-imaging of anyone but a transaction between the Friend, the figure of Coleridge, and a sequence of texts, which, regardless of authorship, tell in *The Friend* as figures, not images, of the Friend.

In the *Biographia* the recognition of Wordsworth's genius is followed by an attempt to deduce the imagination that is eventually rescued from foundering by the man of the letter. The "Essays on Method" begin with a recognition scene also, but here the enthusiastic hypothesis of the man of method is not followed by an attempt at rigorous theoretical validation. Instead the

[53]E. D. Hirsch, Jr., *The Aims of Interpretation* (Chicago: University of Chicago Press, 1976), p. 49.
[54]Ibid., p. 49.

Friend substitutes exemplification and commentary for deduction; he deploys characters from Shakespeare as the figures of the presence and absence, range and nuance of method. Whereas the man of the letter appeared in Chapter XIII as interruption, the figures from Shakespeare stage a plot—a plot of illustrations that is also a plot of reading. It is necessary to read that plot to conceive the rhetoric of the Friend's method.

The Friend first cites the conversation between Falstaff and Mrs. Quickley in *Henry IV, Part II*, which he uses to portray the shallow mind whose thought, lacking hooks, eyes, or any principle of progression, is at the mercy of a verbal association that confuses the idea at hand with a flurry of remembered incidents:

> "FALSTAFF: What is the gross sum that I owe thee?
> MRS. QUICKLEY: Marry, if thou wert an honest man, thyself and the money too. Thou didst swear to me upon a parcel-gilt goblet, sitting in my dolphin chamber, at the round-table, by a sea-coal fire, on Wednesday in Whitsun week, when the prince broke thy head for likening his father to a singing-man in Windsor—thou didst swear to me then, as I was washing thy wound, to marry me and make me my lady thy wife. Canst thou deny it? Did not goodwife Keech, the butcher's wife, come in then and call me gossip Quickley?—coming into borrow a mess of vinegar: telling as she had a good dish of prawns—whereby thou didst desire to eat some—whereby I told thee they were ill for a green wound, &c. &c. &c." [F, 450-51]

Mrs. Quickley's speech, the voluble rehash of a sensualized understanding, exemplifies "the absence of Method, which characterizes the uneducated, [and which] is occasioned by an habitual submission of the understanding to mere events and images as such, and independent of any power in the mind to classify or appropriate them" (F, 451). But it is equally significant that in the eddying of this speech, which of all other possible Shakespearean examples (mentioned are the clown in *Measure for Measure* and the Nurse in *Romeo and Juliet*) the Friend chooses to reproduce, Mrs. Quickley tosses up, like foam on the current, the pointed *topos* of the true king—a *topos* central to both *Henry IV* and *The Friend*. Mrs. Quickley recalls a moment when Falstaff was punished by Hal for insulting the king with a crude simile, a presumption which might seem to have been authoritatively answered by the application of an appropriate penalty, except that the recording angel registers the punishment without being impressed by the presumption, thus mooting the authority of Hal's lesson. Mrs. Quickley recalls Hal's punishment of Falstaff for presumptuously dragging the king down to a base level in common tavern conversation as if it were just another incident in the anarchic whirl of her seamy establishment, more fuel for the engine of her tongue—of as much interest or meaning as "the round table, by a sea-coal fire." Not only, then, has the king been abused by Falstaff's reaching simile, the abuse is itself debased by Mrs. Quickley's promiscuous recollection: kings make no special difference in her immethodical mind and in her spindrift world. Tavern life endangers Hal because it attracts him into a democratic carnival of circumstance which would sever him from his natural sovereignty not only by force of habit but also by the gibbering of an idle tongue. If I thus boldly read the theme of endangered sovereignty in Mrs. Quickley's apparently themeless tangle, it is because the Friend habituates his readers to the reading of all language as rhetoric and of all rhetoric as spanning the gap between the common and the singular, the lapse between the joke and the guillotine. What theme Mrs. Quickley has is the Friend's.

As counterexample to Quickley and as illustration of genial method, the Friend chooses the passage from *Hamlet* where the Prince describes to Horatio the events that occurred during his interrupted voyage to England. Although Hamlet's discourse is oceans apart from the landlady's, once again the issue of method attracts the theme of sovereignty:

"HAM. Sir, in my heart there was a kind of fighting
That would not let me sleep: methought I lay
Worse than the mutines in the bilboes. Rashly,
And prais'd be rashness for it—*Let us know,*
*Our indiscretion sometimes serves us well,*
*When our deep plots do fail: and that should teach us,*
*There's a divinity that shapes our ends,*
*Rough-hew them how we will.*

HOR. That is most certain.
HAM. Up from my cabin,
My sea-gown scarf'd about me, in the dark
Grop'd I to find out them; had my desire;
Finger'd their pocket; and, in fine, withdrew
To my own room again: making so bold,
*My fears forgetting manners,* to unseal
Their grand commission; where *I* found, Horatio,
A royal knavery—an exact command,
*Larded with many several sorts of reasons,*
*Importing Denmark's health, and England's too,*
With ho! such bugs and goblins in *my* life,
That on the supervize, no leisure bated,
No, not to stay the grinding of the axe,
My head should be struck off!
HOR. Is't possible?
HAM. Here's the commission.—Read it at more leisure."

Act v. sc. 2 [*F*, 451-52]

The Friend relies on his first set of italics to alert the reader to Hamlet's testimony of a continuity between the methodical shaping of divinity and the rough-hewn ends of man. Coleridge praises Hamlet's narration for the way "the events, with the circumstances of time and place, are all stated with equal compression and rapidity, not one introduced which could have been omitted without injury to the intelligibility of the whole process" (*F*, 452). Nothing added injures but something omitted halts: "If any tendency is discoverable, as far as the mere facts are in question, it is the tendency to omission: and, accordingly, the reader will observe, that the attention of the narrator is called back to one material circumstance, which he was hurrying by, by a direct question *from the friend* to whom the story is communicated, 'HOW WAS THIS SEALED?'" (*F*, 452, italics added). Horatio's query recalls the omission which shatters Hamlet's continuity, the one material circumstance that has the deepest spiritual import. The seal, we know, is the signature of the king, the unequivocal representative of his ruling arm, the certain mark of a sovereign authority beyond conjecture. Although in Denmark the seal has fallen into the hands of the usurper, the sovereign symbolism of the seal is unaffected, for its meaning is subject to neither the vagaries of politics nor the virtues of a particular individual. If the seal were to be debased by the usurper's mounting to power, it would by default absolve him of usurpation by proving that what he has seized had no intrinsic worth, was not the authentic property of the sovereign after all. Hence it is the logic of the seal, which is the logic of sovereignty recognized by both Claudius and Hamlet, that, for the sake of intelligibility, requires the death of the Prince; in the hands of the usurper the seal must mean the decapitation of the true king. That death had been sealed by the time the ship disembarked, and throughout his transit Hamlet was caught in what seems a fatal dilemma: he had the choice of reverence or rebellion, of submitting to the proscription of the seal or breaking it. The logic of the seal dictates that either decision must mean his death, since the sealed message is an order for execution and the unauthorized rupture of the seal is itself punishable by death. Recounting his own adventure, however, Hamlet seems insensible of the dilemma; he rushes past it in the exuberance of his telling as Mrs. Quickley had hurried past Falstaff's punishment. Horatio arrests that exuberance by questioning the errant tendency in Hamlet's otherwise methodical narrative, the single omission that explains its life.

Until Horatio's question Hamlet had been the exemplar of method; but the Friend comments on the following passage, where Hamlet tells how he altered the commission of Claudius in order to command the death of Rosencrantz and Guildenstern, that the Prince is "ever disposed to generalize, and meditative to excess" (*F*, 452). Hamlet, of course, like Coleridge himself, is renowned for his abstruser musings, but I would suggest that Hamlet's meditative excess is objected to here not because it occludes action but because it reveals too much about an action which has the fascination of the breaking of a taboo. To put it even more pointedly, Hamlet's excess is the excess of Hamlet, the man who is left over, first, after the crunch of the dilemma that should have killed him and, second, after the awful question "HOW WAS THIS SEALED?" which should have subdued meditation and silenced speech forever. Unmoved, the Prince answers: "Why, even in that was heaven ordinant." But this time the Friend withholds his applauding italics from an exculpatory piety that flirts with blasphemy by confusing heavenly ordinance with inordinate desires: "I had my father's signet in my purse,/ Which was," the Prince continues, "the model of that Danish seal: folded the writ up in the form of the other;/ Subscribed it; gave't the impression; placed it safely,/ The changeling never known" (*F*, 453). Hamlet's ploy to escape his dilemma has been to produce, as if from nowhere, the model of Claudius' seal, which until then had been the presumptive original. What had been taken to be the original is disclosed by Hamlet to be a copy of a model which, though passed from father to son and symbolic of the unbroken genealogy of authority, has its sole value for Hamlet in that it can duplicate its own replica. By forging with the original Hamlet has not only imitated the mark of his uncle's supposed sovereignty but also mimicked Claudius' usurpation in a finer tone. By the mere self-saving frequency of his repetition of the seal, the desperate Hamlet has certified the so-called usurper's employment of the seal as just another pretext for power or survival, purposes which in both *Hamlet* and *The Friend* come to the same thing. By replicating the seal, in effect substituting the original for itself, the king has turned his signet, the one infallible sign of his sovereignty, into an instrument of forgery with which he or anyone can offhandedly mint the impression of a king. Hamlet does commit regicide and parricide but "only" figuratively: the king and father are not killed *because* they are king and father but *by* conceiving of them as figures, manipulable by the ingenious conjuror who acts from no oedipal instigation but according to motives which combine power and survival in differentials too subtle to stage. By betraying his father's seal as the self-unraveling clue of sovereignty, the putative heir has divulged that not only is there no royal mintage for arguments, there is not even a royal mintage for monarchs.[55] The seals of kind and usurper are identical, each the counterfeit of the other.

[55]Cf. the republican Tom Paine's comments on Pitt's and Fox's debate on the question of the Regency: "Among the curiosities which this contentious debate afforded, was that of making the Great Seal into a King; the affixing of which to an act, was to be royal authority. If, therefore, Royal Authority is a Great Seal, it consequently is in itself nothing." *The Rights of Man*, Part I (1791: rpt., London: Pelican Books, 1969), pp. 152-53.

The marks of no signet satisfy our conjectures into the truth of a character who, like the Friend's Hamlet, lavishes the mind with his essential excess.

Hamlet's insouciance regarding his forgery is matched by his unsettling lack of remorse or even polite regret for the demise of the false friends Guildenstern and Rosencrantz. He makes some attempt to dismiss their fate as the organic consequence of their actions when he claims that "their defeat doth by their insinuation grow," but he concludes by sophisticating their deaths into a necessary byproduct of the machinery of the seal, a mark of its intelligibility: "*Tis dangerous when the baser nature comes / Between the pass and fell incensed points / of Mighty opposites.*" Hamlet drains the blood from the sacrifice of Rosencrantz and Guildenstern by coining a figure that explains their role in terms of an economy that exploits base nature as fuel for the conflict of mighty opposites, which themselves owe all semblance of might and opposition to the seal that sophistically turns base wax into sovereign sign. In his exuberance, Hamlet, the model of method's excess, has substituted for "the divinity that shapes our ends" a trope that paints over death and gives murder a rhetorical gloss.

In Hamlet, then, we see method in "undue preponderance," the proof that "when the prerogative of the mind is stretched into despotism, the discourse may degenerate into the grotesque or the fantastical" (*F,* 455). And in the penultimate passage that the Friend quotes from the play, Hamlet himself comments on the dissolution of the sovereign prerogative into not just despotism but the baser elements from which it had been magically raised. Madly methodical, he "explains" his melancholy disposition by a trope that unravels sovereignty in an entropic regress halted only by a terminus that pointedly jests at conclusions:

> "To what base uses we may return, Horatio! Why may not imagination trace the noble dust of Alexander, till he find it stopping a bung-hole? HOR. It were to consider too curiously to consider so. HAM. No, faith, not a jot; but to follow him thither with modesty enough and likelihood to lead it. As thus: Alexander died, Alexander was buried, Alexander returneth to dust—the dust is earth; of earth we make loam: and why of that loam, whereto he was converted, might they not stop a beer-barrel?

> Imperial Caesar, dead and turn'd to clay,
> Might stop a hole to keep the wind away!"
>
> [F, 455]

In the method of *The Friend* the base use of the signet returns Hamlet to this meditation on baseness, which conceives of the difference between the elemental clay and the imperial monarch as only a matter of turns on a figurative path that the wayward mind at once both tracks and forges. Hamlet's path may seem more controlled than Mrs. Quickley's drift, but he does not offer even the illusive stability of a simile between king and singing-man to which to cling along the way. As for Alexander, as for Caesar, as for all fathers and all singing-men of Windsor, so for Hamlet: he is elemented as they. In the madness of his method he hangs suspended between the mighty points of king and clay, his eddying life sustained only by the improper power of sub-stitution for which he exchanged sovereignty of throne and soul. That power is his seal.

The last quotation from Shakespeare in the chapter is offered as another perversion of method, to show that if "the excess [of thought and imagination] lead to Method misapplied, and to connections of the moment, the absence, or marked deficiency, either precludes Method altogether, both form and substance: or . . . retains the outward form only." But that which is pro-posed as a version of immethod (the empty, outward form of method) is at the same time a comment on the preceding illus-trations; it is Polonius' explanation to Gertrude of her son's madness:

> "My liege and madam! to expostulate
> What majesty should be, what duty is,
> Why day is day, night night, and time is time,
> Were nothing but to waste night, day and time.
> Therefore—since brevity is the soul of wit,
> And tediousness the limbs and outward flourishes,
> I will be brief. Your noble son is mad:
> Mad call I it—for to define true madness,
> What is't, but to be nothing else but mad!
> But let that go.
> QUEEN. More matter with less art.

POL. Madam! I swear, I use no art at all.
That he is mad, tis true: tis true, tis pity:
And pity tis, tis true (a foolish figure!
But farewell it, for I will use no art.)
Mad let us grant him then! and now remains,
That we find out the cause of this effect,
Or rather say the cause of this defect:
For this effect defective comes by cause.
Thus it remains, and the remainder thus
Perpend!"

*Hamlet*, act ii. scene 2 [*F*, 456]

The Queen demands more matter after an address that has, in truth, been all matter, in which the definitions of majesty, duty, day, night, and time have been abandoned as so much dead weight, and whose self-evidential nature is epitomized in the final tautology "True madness" is "to be be nothing else but mad." The matter of factness of madness is the certainty which confirms the matter of all the previous terms in Polonius' catalog, endows them with a place, an implicit tautological gravity of their own that need not be formulated. The queen insists that her councilor make more sense, however, and at her command Polonius demonstrates the art of significance by methodically differentiating the base tautology as a chiasmus which is its best commentary: "That he is mad, tis true: tis true, tis pity:/And pity tis, tis true. . . ." Polonius has promised to use no art, and, indeed, the tautegorical chiasmus[56]—identity doubled and spaced; a base nature between points which are, at least on the face of the page, opposed—is the merest art, tautology's own "progressive transition" (*F*, 457) toward significance, the outward form by which significance is foolishly figured as a vagrant on the boundary of meaning. If art, the chiasmus is the almost artless art by which the dead weight of tautology is minted into the charm of tautegory, given the cymbalic jingle of sense. The art is in the matter, the matter in the art as the king is in the earth, the earth in the king. The friendly councilor has watched

[56]A Coleridgean coinage: "*tau*tegorical (i.e. expressing the *same* subject but with a difference) in contra-distinction from metaphors and similitudes, that are always *alle*gorical." *Aids to Reflection* (London: 1825), p. 199.

his charge closely and has reproduced well the method of his madness.

Polonius' chiasmus, with its baroque redoubling, may be, as he says, "a foolish figure," but the same figure is employed with deeper seriousness and deployed with greater effect in the address of William Sedgwick to the Parliament's Army, a speech which the Friend gives place of precedence at the head of the final section of his essays, rescuing it "from oblivion, both for the honor of our forefathers, and in proof of the intense difference between the republicans of that period, and the democrats, or rather demagogues of the present" (*F,* 411). Sedgwick's speech to his comrades was a futile attempt to dissuade them from their intent to execute the defeated and imprisoned Charles. He argues that regicide under such and indeed any circumstances is a kind of suicide, for on the sanctity of the monarch depends the religious fidelity of the people, which is in turn the soul of both state and individual, and the only sure foundation of the parliamentary cause. Sedgwick's defense of the king, in which the argument to withhold the ax for the sake of a greater truth is inseparable from a style of stately reserve, is the organic expression of the values that the seventeenth century symbolizes for the Friend; its vital seed is a chiasmus:

> He that doth and can suffer shall have my heart: you had it while you suffered. But now your severe punishment of him for his abuses in government, and your own usurpations, will not only win the hearts of the people to the oppressed suffering king, but provoke them to rage against you, as having robbed them of the interest which they had in his royalty. For the king is in the people, and the people in the king. The king's being is not solitary, but as he is in union with his people, who are his strength in which he lives; and the people's being is not naked, but an interest in the greatness and wisdom of the king who is their honor which lives in them. And though you will disjoin yourselves from kings, God will not, neither will I. God is king of kings, kings' and princes' God, as well as people's, theirs as well as ours, and theirs eminently (as the speech enforces, God of Israel, that is, Israel's God above all other nations; and so king of kings), by a near and especial kindred and communion. Kingliness agrees with all Christians, who are indeed Christians. [*F,* 413]

"The king is in the people, the people in the king" represents the richly ceremonious interchange of a diversified yet united nation. By bringing king and people together in the chiasmus Sedgwick affirms their union while maintaining their difference; the repetition and inversion of terms is a transitive movement carried out within a horizon of identity that disarms extremes of their antithetical point. In this commonwealth the head of the king is the capital which produces all interest, makes possible all economy. In this nation the king may not abuse his prerogative by ruling according to fiat; nor may the people confuse *vox populi* with *vox dei*. The chiasmus states that king and people are each essentially inside the other; the chiasmus formulates an existential distribution of powers and grants a delimited place to each outside the other. Each term in Sedgwick's chiasmus is the soul of the other's body.

Yet merely to state the figurative principle of Sedgwick's address is to ignore the pathos of its expression. At one and the same time Sedgwick claims to state a truth that is independent of the imagination of men and yet yields to the imagination's restless desire for a sensible figure to represent the manifest self-evident truth. Thus, although he warns of a danger to come, he contemplates it as a catastrophe completed; for the chiasmus figures to the imagination what is no longer fully present to the reason: to imagine the dissolution of the symbol is to represent it within an allegory that presupposes the breach of its monolithic integrity. The death of the king—Charles, any king, all kings—depends not on scaffold, guillotine, or gibbet, awaits not the sinister stratagems of desperate men, but lies in the conception of sovereignty as subject to the actions and arguments of men in the discourse of history—a conception that does not murder but memorializes. Like the old man in the fable of the maddening rain, Sedgwick tries to communicate a truth in order to prevent a catastrophe, and like that pathetic prophet his utterance is the conjectural mark of the catastrophe it would forestall: his chiasmus at once figures the true, timeless link between people and the king and tropes truth into history; his figure, like Hamlet's signet, is at once both model and excess. When we look back at the seventeenth century, we find a speaker minting the gold that will float an insolvent sovereign, trying to give currency to that which has lost its value. When we hearken to his words, we hear not an authoritative voice but an echo of the Friend's own accents, inflections, and intonations.

For the amicable chiasmus is the figure of method. The chiasmus expresses the transitive integration of opposites by impressing it on the page: "And this is METHOD, itself a distinct science, the immediate offspring of philosophy, and the link or *mordant* by which philosophy becomes scientific and the sciences philosophical" (*F*, 463). The discovery of method corresponds to the religious strength of a "true *efficient* conviction of moral truth," which is, in discursive terms, "the implication of doctrine in the miracle and of miracle in the doctrine, which is the bridge of communication between the senses and the soul" (*F*, 431). In its limitless fecundity method connects Shakespeare and Plato, "the philosophic poet to the poetic philosopher" (*F*, 472), identifies the continuity between the deductive Plato and the inductive Bacon, "the Athenian Verulam and the British Plato" (*F*, 488), and synthesizes poetry and science, as when we find the correspondent to the "observant meditation" of Shakespeare which produces "nature idealized into poetry" in the "meditative observation" of the British chemists by which "poetry, [is] as it were, substantiated and realized in nature" (*F*, 471). The "self-unravelling clue" of method will lead the investigator to comprehend "gradually and progressively the relation of each to the other, or each to all, and of all to each" (*F*, 511). Link, mordant, bridge, infinitesimal elementary body, solution of continuity—method morally communicates between soul and sense, reason and understanding, God and world, king and subject, author and book. Partaking of both poles, distinct from either, method is both the crossing plank from one side of the stream to the other and the eddy where circulates the proprieties of intention and act: *a* in *b*, *b* in *a*. Translucent, provisional, faultlessly deferential to the truth it serves—method follows the track of the chiasmus.

To appreciate the especial productive power of method it is necessary to recover the vitality of both metaphor and verbal in the Friend's description of it as "the immediate offspring of philosophy." Not the child who has been born, delivered, and deposited in a strange world, method is always springing off from philosophy's solitary, profound, and spontaneous initiative. Not a child who is either fathered by or who fathers the' man, method bursts directly from the fertilizing source, a genius fully fledged before it suffers the meditations toward which it bravely projects. Did not Plato, after all, spring forth fully armed from the forehead of Socrates?

> *Call.* What a slave driver you are, Socrates! If you'll take my advice, you'll let this argument alone, or else do your talking to someone else.
> *Socr.* Yet who else is willing? Let's not have our conversation go by the board.
> *Call.* Why can't you finish it yourself? Talk to yourself and give yourself answers!
> *Socr.* So that the words of Epicharmus may be filled:
> Where two men spoke before
> I alone am to be equal to the task, though single-handed!
> —*Gorgias*

If we hesitate to give full assent to the fabulous Platonic genealogy, it is only because of the telling absence of Plato in those texts that bear his name. Plato's dialogues are the method by which he engages the world, the way in which the original voice of philosophy is made audible to the uninitiated without the intercession of prophet or sage and without the intervention of translator, commentator, or disciple. Although Plato does not appear, the dialogue which springs forth from Socrates is nevertheless the *figure* of Plato, himself unseen, the figure of him who has exchanged his birthright in order to write philosophy and thereby give it a universal currency. Plato has exchanged his own position in order to enhance Socrates' prestige and philosophy's value, but he has, in truth, sacrificed nothing, because sacrifice cannot occur under the dispensation of philosophy, where offsprings are immediate, where the son is not the father's representative—a sign both diminished and dangerous because of its distance from the original—but an expression of the father, his own externalization. Sacrifice cannot occur under a dispensation in which genealogy eludes the scenario of the family romance: there is no romance without the descendental representation that provokes affect; there is no family without the mother. By writing the dialogues, Plato at once ascribes all of genealogy to Socrates whose immediate offspring they are and removes himself from the line of filiation—unrepresented, he is no representative, no son who must sacrifice inordinate desires, who both wishes and fears the knife. The Platonic way up depends on the Socratic way down: truth retains its pristine unity and force throughout its philosophical passage because Plato has dexterously removed philosophy from the bloody stage of Oedipus and furnished as if by heavenly ordinance what the Friend has been seeking throughout his essays, a model for writing without desire.

To communicate morally philosophy must generate itself without generations. Thus for the drama Plato substituted the dialogue, for representation dialectic, for the desire and violence of the family romance he substituted an amicable exchange. The dialogues are a place of exchange between the voiceless Socrates and the characterless Plato, an intercourse not motivated by desire but regulated by amity, which breaks no bones, threatens no God, no father, no self. HOW WAS THIS SEALED?

The figure of Plato is introduced only in transition, as it were, in the gradual and continuous progression of the dialogues, which are at every point themselves the chiasmic link between the soundless voice of Socrates and Plato's absent presence. The two antithetical points of silent speech and withheld presence mirror each other by means of the reflective link of a quicksilver writing that limns likeness as the gently ironic play of identity with space and time. Socrates' muteness is the mirror image of Plato's withholding of himself from among the characters of the dialogue, exploiting invisibility, as do the sophists, for the power that it holds,[57] but, unlike the sophists, forging for that invisibility an uncanny legibility through writing, so that "Plato" can exercise power solely by his signature, without quite becoming a character. The sophists—Hippias, Gorgias, Protagoras—not the writer, are dispatched as the men of letters in the Platonic dialogues.[58]

[57]Shell analyzes the relation of invisibility to political and economic power in his *Economy of Literature*, pp. 30-36.

[58]For a discussion of the Platonic dispatch of the sophists, of writing, and of the *pharmakon*, see Derrida, "La Pharmacie de Platon" in *La Dissemination* (Paris: Seuil, 1972), pp. 71-197.

We imagine the itinerant sophists condemned to pass like night from land to land, hungry for a fee, dependent on the reputation that precedes them and the letters of introduction which they bear, peddling their virtuosity from one town to the next, whereas Plato unostentatiously introduces himself in transition, while all the time residing in one place—in the dialogues which are both his proper figure and the eternal property of philosophy. It is in the interest of philosophy to fear the sophist, to raise the specter of "open and unremitting war," and to mark its own allies with the hypnotic brilliance of a glittering eye,[59] for the light of that eye obscures the powerful mechanics of method, and that vision of a bloody defensive struggle justifies centuries of inkshed. But the sophists, if sophists there were, have been bought out long ago. Their wares could not compete with the power of Plato's method to both comprehend and exclude them. For though the sophists may have had the ability "to shape, to dye, to paint over, and to mechanize the mind," even "to make a figure on any and all subjects," Plato's method enabled him to resign such dealings to them "as their proper trade," to resign, that is, to the sophists what belong to them and them alone, thereby endowing their very impropriety with a philosophical propriety. If the danger of the sophists is that they exchange knowledge for money, money which "appears as a *disruptive* power for the individual and for the social bonds" because it "changes fidelity into infidelity, love into hate, hate into love, virtue into vice, vice into virtue, servant into master, stupidity into intelligence and intelligence into stupidity,"[60] philosophy appears as the power to make a figure of the sophists; the power, that is, to identify their inversions, to contain their disrup-

---

[59]The Ancient Mariner, of course, "hath his will" by means of the force of his "glittering eye" (lines 13-16): so, finally, does the patient Stranger in *The Sophist*, whose wandering inquiry into absolutely reliable criteria of sophistry is supervised by the authoritative eye, emblem of the divine genealogy which he upholds and claims to represent. Responding to a question about the origin of natural life, Theaitetos says, "Owing perhaps to my youth, I often move from one opinion to the other; but here and now, looking into your eyes and believing you to hold that the things in question are of divine origin, I too am convinced" (*The Sophist*, 221). The vacillation of Theaitetos, of sophistry and philosophy, is restrained by the master's eye. Cf. Coleridge's experiments with double touch (Chapter 2).

[60]Karl Marx, "Money," in *Early Writings*, trans. and ed. T. B. Bottomore (New York: McGraw-Hill, 1964), p. 193.

tion, even to confer an instructive value on their subversion by means of the superior virtue of method's friendly chiasmus.

Plato could buy out the sophists and even make them slave for him because his method is the money of the mind,[61] a fund more fecund than Nature herself, minted from the basest nature of all, black marks on a white page. If there were a royal mintage for arguments, it would be indistinguishable from Plato's; and he who runs the mint can afford to scoff at those who work for hire. Thus Plato does not lose anything by exchanging his inherited wealth and position for the writing of Socrates' speech, because in so doing he removes his self and philosophy from an economy of loss and gain: Socrates' method is the method of Plato. The history of philosophy, as we have been told, is a series of footnotes to Plato, which is to say, no history at all. What passes for history is the interest generated by Plato's initial reserve, truth's notional debt: once the blessed machine is set in motion, all play with the counters supplied; all profit from keeping the game going because it's the only game in town.

It is surely the only game in *The Friend,* where method is that "connatural force, / Powerful at greatest distance to unite / With secret amity things of like kind." When the robust style and the home truths of *Paradise Lost,* make their last appearance in the prose of the nineteenth-century moral essayist (*F*, 471), they emerge not as challenge, prohibition, or warning, not even as legacy, but as one more likening in a green and pleasant island of likeness. As if by a connatural force working across a great distance, Milton's method—like Plato's, like Shakespeare's, like Kepler's, like Bacon's, like Sedgwick's—has become the Friend's own: the Friend is in the method, the method in the Friend. Extremes meet in the chiasmus: it is the "charm" (*F*, 449) which can communicate moral principles while preserving the sovereign principal because it substitutes for family romance an amicable exchange.[62] Yet that substitution by which principle's

[61]Shell uses the phrase "money of the mind" to describe Plato's fear of what may be the true economy of Socratic thought. I suspect that what fear is evident (Shell gives no clearcut examples) is merely the canny pretense of a lack of financial sophistication.

[62]Cf. Walter Pater's characterization of Coleridge's work as "the production of one who made way ever by a charm." In "Coleridge," *Appreciations* (London: Macmillan, 1898), p. 68.

# The Method of *The Friend*

matter is shaped into artful discourse chastens and subdues the sovereign it serves as well as the sophist it suppresses. As in Sedgwick's speech before the court of history, as in Hamlet's secret replication of the royal seal, so in the Friend's essays, the figure which methodizes the king moots sovereignty. As Socrates mirrors Plato in the dialogues, so all versions of the king— God and genius, prince and usurper—when subjected to the quicksilver medium of the chiasmus, mirror the motile Friend, figure to figure, preface to preface.

The Friend's surprising and strenuous efforts to work up the sophists into a credible, traumatic threat to the living body of thought describe an anxiety *for* the sophist, the other who must be without for the self to be within, the wily counterfeiter who would by his fraud validate the Platonic signature, the opponent whom one can withstand and thereby confirm one's standing. True philosophy may be "Truth without alloy and unsophisticated," but Plato and the Friend show that philosophy must be sophisticated in order to prove its value as gold. Subjected to method, the supposed sophist, like his Platonic adversary, never appears in his own right. "We found no such order. The men indeed and the name we found. . . . It is nothing more or less than a practical pun" (*F*, 273) that would turn those poor fellows Protagoras and Thrasymachus into the supposed febrile hunters of the young, whom they are supposed to represent. Plato, and the Friend after him, puns the sophists into something like life in order to paint over his chrematistics into the appearance of an economy of loss and gain.[63] The philosopher values the sophists for the continuing interest they can generate. As the figure of Bonaparte, "genuine offspring of the old serpent," drives the marvelous economy of the British state, so does Callicles, "Napoleon of old" (*F*, 443), fuel the blessed machine of philosophy. We come only as close to the face of the hypothetical sophists as we come to the face of the hireling, itinerant, periodical writer who is the Friend and whose amity, unconstrained by the awful deco-

---

[63]Shell, following Aristotle, distinguishes between chrematistics and true economy. "The tyrant," he explains, "is defined as a chrematistical profit-making ruler interested only in selfish ends. On the other hand, the statesman is defined as an economist who dispenses or disposes but does not make a profit" (pp. 91-92). Cf. Aristotle, *Politics*, 1257b.

[263]

rum imposed by the oedipal tragedy, "by its own moods interprets, everywhere / Echo or mirror seeking of itself, / And makes a toy of Thought." The flow of amity "turns the obstacle into its own form and character and as it makes its way increases its stream"; no more than England or truth or an enchanted spot within a waste of sands does any island of likeness in that stream afford a firm place to stand. The secret ministry of method carries on its getting and spending—political, philosophical, and erotic—unhelped by any awful sovereign, unhindered by any rebellious subject.

Secret ministry, secret amity—the force that unites all within an island of likeness partakes of the same essential and functional obscurity that the Friend has attributed to the difficult style, a powerful obscurity, whether it be the impressive congestion of perpending periods, or the chiasmus that paints over matter into art and philosophy into discourse, or, to shave it further, whether it be the merest resistance that is brute nature's profession of significance. To reduce my argument drastically would be to ask the pointed question, "Is not *The Friend,* then, the Friend alone?" Yet to reduce a text, to reduce a reading of a text, is not so easy as that; to follow the "self-unravelling clue" is not, is precisely never, to undo. To state that *The Friend* is the Friend alone is not to summon the humanist's cherished nightmare of solipsism. To note that *The Friend* is the Friend merely figures Coleridge's blessed machine of language; for the blessedness, insofar as it can be tracked down, subsists in that mechanical addition of the italics that mark the Friend with an eminence, however marginal, that he alone could never have, that grant him a title, a prerogative, and a discourse. From base letters the secret ministry of the compositor makes book of the Friend, turns identity into amity, figure into author.

To conceive of language or text as a blessed machine whose transitive action, articulated by baffles, mirrors, and other rare devices, are elaborations of an ever obscure force, both moots the opposition between free will and determinism that is the pretext of the Coleridgean text and disarms the antithesis of originality and plagiarism which is its murderous offspring. Yet the questions remain: Did philosophy write/plagiarize Coleridge or did Coleridge write/plagiarize philosophy? To whom do these books belong? As an answer I would like, if I could, to take my stand on the hypopoetical ground of the chiasmus, sanctioned by the "Essays on Method," and emblem of the Coleridgean text: Coleridge is in the book, the book in Coleridge. That answer, however, methodical as it is, merely reproduces the anxiety about origins, about property and propriety, that worries forth the question. A rhetorical answer cannot resolve a query that betrays a fundamental anxiety about rhetoric. Probably there is no answer that would wholly quiet that anxiety by reserving it from the eddies of matter and art. Yet to the question of possession a more precise reply can be formed, anxiety assigned a local habitation (if not a name) where it can at least be addressed in its ceaseless transit. In Chapter 4, I tried to make something of Coleridge's rhetorical shift from "Wordsworthian genius" to "Wordsworth's genius"; I would here like to make as much of the difference between the loose statement that the chiasmus is the Friend's figure and the more precise formulation that the chiasmus is the figure of the Friend. That "of," which slips between preposition and genitive, between allegorical representation and symbolic extension, is the liminal address of anxiety, the margin of desire in the Friend's text, in Coleridge's text—for if the Friend realizes his genius in the method of the chiasmus, Coleridge realizes his genius in the Friend, who is the figure of Coleridge. Not a detached representative, the Friend is not one of those eggs which the imprudent ostrich buried in the sand to be hatched, grown, and eventually to furnish, with fatal impropriety, the feathers for the quivers of his enemies. Not a continuous extension, however pure was the Friend in his secret conception, once he has been delivered to language, Coleridge must make his way in the machinery of the text, subject to signs and motions not his own property. Coleridge moots plagiarism because he moots authority; he finds himself in the Friend at the hazard of his soul. Though he would be the pilgrim who finally runs things to the fountainhead of truth, the oracle of absolute principle, Coleridge reads as the circulation of an unfathered desire. He is his own figure, raised and restrained by his writing: "the still rising Desire still baffling the bitter Experience, the bitter Experience still following the gratified Desire" (*CN* I, 1456).

IV

"I have repeatedly said," writes Coleridge in a notebook entry (*CN* I, 1725), "that I could have made a volume, if only I had noted it down, as they occurred to my Recollection or Observations, the instances of the Proverb, Extremes Meet / ." Despite Coleridge's regret, that volume is not lost: *The Friend* is one episode in a volume of writings which variously elaborates that congenial proverb. The work did not, however, turn out as anticipated, for instead of a catalog of instances piously circumscribed, *booked*, by an aphoristic monitor, Coleridge left a hazardous rhetoric motivated, though scarcely contained, by the resounding chiasmus.[64] Yet in its fashion Coleridge's diversion is true to its marginal origin, for the first instance cited under the caption "EXTREMES MEET" is a chiasmus from *Paradise Lost* II, 594-95: "The parching Air / Burns frore, and Cold performs the Effect of Fire." Proverb and figure are connatural force from their initial, relatively necessary juxtaposition. The perdurable power of that affiliation, once forged, receives a thoroughly Coleridgean commentary in the lines in Milton that follow, like a guilty consequence, Coleridge's self-unraveling clue:

> Thither by harpy-footed Furies hal'd,
> At certain revolutions all the damn'd
> Are brought: and feel by turns the bitter change
> Of fierce extremes, extremes by change more fierce. . . .
> 
> [*Paradise Lost*, II, 596-99]

It is tempting to place the figure of Coleridge on the background of Milton's infernal wilderness of ice, to see Milton's hell

---

[64]"*Aphorism*, determinate position, . . . to bound or limit; whence our horizon.—In order to get the full sense of a word, we should first present to our minds the visual image that forms its primary meaning. Draw lines of different colours round the different counties of England, and then cut out each separately, as in the common play-maps that children take to pieces and put together—so that each district can be contemplated apart from the rest, as a whole in itself. This twofold act is circumscribing, and detaching, when it is exerted by the mind on subjects of reflection and reason, is to aphorize, and the result an aphorism." Coleridge, *Aids to Reflection*, ed. Henry Nelson Coleridge (London: William Pickering, 1843), I, 16 n.

as the punishment suffered by Coleridge's prosy error. Certainly the metaphysical depths to which Coleridge alludes in the *Biographia* are but one *topos* of the hell through which the damaged archangel forlornly wanders in all his writing, pathetically described in the "Conclusion" of his literary life as "the state of reprobate spirits . . . , [a] dreadful dream in which there is no sense of reality, not even of the pangs they are enduring" (*BL* II, 208). In such a streamy state of influence without hope, prose without poetry, grief without pang, pain *is* mere interruption.

Such at least is the interpretation that a Miltonic deity, grasping at mountains, would put on Coleridge's lot. He would bury Coleridge by assigning the initiative for the chiasmic turn upon turn in the Coleridgean "palpable obscure" to the sin of a belated self-consciousness. Yet to join Milton's party and impute to Coleridge a frigid satanism, though a triumph of divine method, would be a failure of ordinary reading, for S. T. C. is conducted to this text not by Miltonic harpies but by the legs of his pen; the chiasmic initiative occurs in the legible juxtaposition of proverb with quotation, text with illustration. Rhetoric may be hell, but Hell is rhetoric. Myself am rhetoric. It is not possible to ascertain whether Coleridge is conscious or unconscious of the rhetoric in which he finds himself, because consciousness in the prose is consciousness of the chiasmus, which "prior to all direction" figures "one power with its two inherent indestructible yet counteracting forces, and the results or generations to which their inter-penetration gives existence" (*BL* I, 197-98), tropes "the primary forces from which the conditions of all possible directions are derivative and deducible" (*BL* I, 197). The conciousness of the chiasmus is the hypopoesis that invests gaps with power, gives life to a lapsed link, and prevents the repetition of the figure from sinking into tedious redundancy. Coleridgean hypopoesis is both the interruption of imagination's gratified desire and the pretext of fancy's eccentric play.

To condemn Coleridge either to a voluble delerium or to Milton's Hell would merely betray a critical anxiety for intelligible causes and final judgments. As Coleridge diverts the dreadful dream of shapeless fears into inky tears which he disseminates among friends, so does he rewrite hell as rhetoric. Milton's infernal machine of the mind succeeds to Coleridge's blessed machine of language, a difference that is marked for conjecture if not for interpretation by the unimaginable touch of the pen:

> I will at least make the attempt to explain to myself the Origin of moral Evil from the *streamy* Nature of Association, which Thinking = Reason, curbs & rudders/how this comes to be so difficult/Do not the bad Passions in Dreams throw light & shew of proof upon this Hypothesis?—Explain those bad Passions: & I shall gain Light, I am sure—A Clue! A Clue!—an Hecatomb a la Pythagoras if it unlabyrinths me.—Dec. 28, 1803—Beautiful luminous Shadow of my pencil point following it from the Candle—rather going before it & illuminating the word, I am writing. 11 °clock/—But take in the blessedness of Innocent Children, the blessedness sweet Sleep, &c &c &c: are these or are they not contradictions to the evil from *streamy* association?—I hope not: all is to be thought *over* and *into*—but what is the height, & ideal of mere association?—Delirium. —But how far is this state produced by Pain & Denaturalization? And what are these?—In short, as far as I can see any thing in this Total Mist, Vice is imperfect yet existing Volition, giving diseased Currents of association, because it yields on all sides & *yet* is—So think of Madness:—O if I live! Grasmere, Dec. 29, 1803.

The anxious meditation on interruption is divided into two inversely related comments from two consecutive days. Interrupting the search for the clue to sanity and the thought of madness is an eddying sentence that belongs to neither day, neither passion: "Beautiful luminous Shadow of my pencil following it from the Candle—rather going before it & illuminating the word, I am writing." Awaiting Light, fearing Darkness, Coleridge transcribes a luminous shadow. The fierce extremes of observation and invention, before and after, darkness and illumination, rudder and stream, reality and delirium are tranquilized by the gentlest of styles. Neither truth nor addition, neither text nor commentary—Coleridge simply inscribes the difference that a shadowy glow makes on the lustrous blackness of the words he is inscribing. Is the last phrase merely a restrictive clause, or does the pause transfigure it into a reflexive summary? So much—and so little—depends on the interruption of a comma. Following Coleridge, however, we need not strain at the difference. For a moment at least, the endless struggle between hurrying enlightener and guilty shadower has vanished within the prosaic activity, "I am writing."

# Index

Abrams, M. H., 84n, 132n, 195n
Addison, Joseph, 100, 208n
"Aeolian Harp," 83
*Aids to Reflection,* 116n, 255n, 266n
Alexander, 118, 253, 254; and Clytus,
    175-177, 182, 185
Allegory, 22-23, 198-200, 212-213,
    221, 230, 255n, 257, 265
Amiens, Treaty of, 246n
Ammerbach, Vitus, 98
Analogy, 38-41, 44-45, 46, 54, 56-
    57, 75-76n, 87-89, 124, 141, 168,
    197, 220. *See also* Mutual indefinite
    implication
Anonymous reviewers, 137, 162, 164,
    170, 182-183, 191-192n
Aphorism, 20, 188-189, 266
Appleyard, J. A., 73-74, 75-76n, 84n
Aquinas, Thomas, 98
Aristotle, 75, 77, 96n, 97-98, 143-
    144, 239, 263n. *See also* Associa-
    tion of ideas
Association of ideas, 166-169, 206-
    207, 213, 224, 268; Aristotelian,
    74-75, 97-98, 106-107, 115;
    Coleridge's confutation of, 17-20,
    76-95, 96-117; Coleridge's espousal
    of, 58-76; Hartley's doctrine of,17-
    20, 33-57; Kantian criticism of,
    33-34, 77, 83-85; streaminess of,
    90-93, 147, 268. *See also* Hartley,
    David
Augustine, St., 118, 211-213, 216
Austin, J. L., 226n
Authoritative voice, 46-49, 56-57, 94,
    187, 189, 257
Authority, 15, 18, 20, 24-25, 131,
    139-140, 147, 163, 165, 168, 177-
178, 183-185, 189-192, 195,
    197-198, 216-217, 226, 231, 240-
    241, 246, 249-251, 265

Bacon, Francis, 74, 207, 236, 258, 262
Bate, W. J., 34n, 59n, 137n
Beer, John, 86n, 197n
Benjamin, Walter, 26
Berkeley, Bishop George, 75-76n, 86
Bialostosky, Don, 141n
Bible: authority of, 24-25, 47-49, 67-
    68, 76n, 112; criticism of, 23-
    25, 50, 211-214
*Biographia Literaria,* 16, 18, 20-
    21, 74, 82, 96-117, 118-185, 247,
    267; ANCIENT of days passage
    in, 124-125; as autobiography,
    118-120; Coleridge's stated intent
    in, 122; Conclusion to, 178-181,
    187; deduction of imagination in,
    167-174; as essay in discipline,
    183-184; as exculpation, 161-185;
    *Genius loci,* 185; as narrative,
    178-182; origins celebrated in,
    122-137; property and propriety
    of poet in, 137-161; real *poetic*
    character in, 122-137, 145-152,
    176; slogan for, 161; subject
    of, 121; unity of, 121-137. *See
    especially* Alexander; Association of
    ideas; Genius; Hartley, David; Man
    of letters; Machinery; Marginal
    method; Plagiarism; Wordsworth,
    William
Blake, William, 23, 25-26, 185
Bloom, Harold, 181, 184
Bower, George Spencer, 34n
Brett, G. S., 34n

[271]

# Index

# Index

# Index

Infinitesimal elementary body, 39-40, 171, 258
Interruption, 55-56, 78-79, 87, 90-94, 117, 137, 147, 164, 171-173, 175, 267-268
Ithuriel's spear, 224-226, 232

Jackson, J. R. de J., 234n
Jacobi, Friedrich, 105

Kallich, Martin, 34n
Kant, Immanuel, 19, 25, 33-34, 77, 83, 85, 103, 112, 113, 214-216
Kepler, Johannes, 74, 97, 99, 236, 262
Kessler, Edward, 197n

Lamb, Charles, 118, 175
*Lay Sermons*, 108n, 123, 127, 203-204n, 213
Leavis, F. R. 116n
"Lectures on Revealed Religion," 29, 65n, 66n, 67-68, 72, 75n, 113-114, 191n
Leibniz, G. W., 98
Linnaean botany, 235
Lipking, Laurence, 105n
Locke, John, 35, 43, 58, 59-60, 74-75, 77, 84n
Lockridge, Laurence, 76n
Lovejoy, A. O., 79n
Luther, Martin, 25, 223, 227, 246n

Maass, J. G. E., 74n, 98-102, 104, 106, 113, 116n
Machinery/mechanics, 17, 23, 27, 53, 56, 62-63, 87, 90, 95, 112, 135, 137, 147, 158, 163, 164n, 167, 177-178, 182-185, 206-207, 213, 217, 219, 228, 243-244, 253, 261-268; critical machine, 183-185
Mackintosh, James, 97-104, 116n, 191n
Mallette, Richard, 121n
Man of letters, 24, 161-177, 260
Mann, Peter, 67
Marginal method, 25, 96-117
Marsh, Robert, 34n, 37n, 75n
Marx, Karl, 261n
McFarland, Thomas, 53n, 76n, 98-99, 105, 137n, 149n
McKillop, Alan, 143n

Melancthon, Philip, 97
Merleau-Ponty, Maurice, 33, 86n
Metaphor, 42, 88, 92, 107-108, 109, 113-114, 133-134, 142-143, 145-146, 195-197, 220-221; *See also* Chiasmus; Hypopoesis; Rhetoric; Symbol
Meteyard, Eliza, 85n, 87n
Method: *See* "Essays on Method"; Marginal method
Michaelangelo, 246n
Milton, John, 25, 73, 125, 128-129, 132n, 136, 169, 203, 207, 223n, 223-232, 236, 262, 266-268
Modiano, Raimonda, 216n
Moloch, 203, 226-231. *See also* Mutilation; Sacrifice
Mutilation, 139, 147, 200-201, 206, 221, 228, 229-232, 244. *See also* Penetration; Regicide; Sacrifice
Mutual indefinite implication, 41, 44, 52, 122. *See also* Analogy; Extremes meet

National debt, 219-220
Newton, Isaac, 41, 74-75, 97, 99

Oberg, Barbara Bowen, 34n
Oedipal anxiety, 26, 176, 229-232, 252, 259-260, 263-264
*On the Constitution of Church and State*, 139n
Ong, Walter J., 34n
Origin of evil, 90-94, 268. *See also* Paradisal state
Orsini, G. N. G., 75n, 77n

Paine, Tom, 58, 252n
Paradisal state, 52-54, 91n, 133-137, 188-190, 195, 221-225, 232, 264. *See also* Origin of evil
Parker, Reeve, 131n
Parrish, Stephen Maxfield, 141n
Pater, Walter, 262n
Penetration, 200-201, 213, 230-232, 267. *See also* Double touch; Mutilation; Sacrifice; Oedipal anxiety
Persecution, 66, 161-164, 189-192
Petrarch, 187
*Philosophical Lectures*, 96n
Pious fraud, 199-202

# Index

# Index

*Coleridge's Blessed Machine
of Language*

Designed by Richard E. Rosenbaum.
Composed by Eastern Graphics
in 10 point Baskerville, 2 points leaded,
with display lines in Baskerville.
Printed offset by Thomson/Shore, Inc. on
Warren's Number 66 Antique Offset, 50 pound basis.
Bound by John H. Dekker & Sons, Inc.
in Holliston book cloth
and stamped in Kurz-Hastings foil.

*Library of Congress Cataloging in Publication Data*

Christensen, Jerome, 1948-
  Coleridge's blessed machine of language.

  Includes bibliographical references and index.
    1. Coleridge, Samuel Taylor, 1772-1834—Prose. 2. Coleridge, Samuel Taylor,
1772-1834—Criticism and interpretation. 3. Hartley, David, 1705-1757. I. Title.
PR4487.P67C5       828'.708        81-66644
ISBN 0-8014-1405-9                 AACR2